ROBERT M. HADDAD

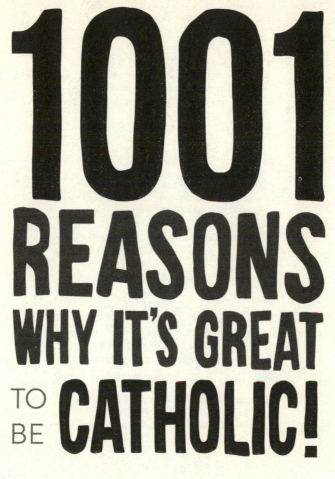

1001
REASONS
WHY IT'S GREAT
TO BE CATHOLIC!

DynamicCatholic.com
Be Bold. Be Catholic.®

1001 REASONS
WHY IT'S GREAT TO BE CATHOLIC!

Printed in the United States of America. [3]

ISBN: 978-1-942611-06-6

In accordance with the Code Cannon Law,
I hereby grant the Imprimatur ("Permission to Publish")
for *1001 Reasons Why It's Great to be Catholic.*

+Most Reverend Peter A. Comensoli
Apostolic Administrator
Archdiocese of Sydney
Sydney, Australia
August 28, 2014

The Imprimatur ("Permission to Publish") is a declaration that a book
is considered to be free of doctrinal or moral error. It is not implied that
those who have granted the Imprimatur agree with the contents,
opinions, or statements expressed.

Cover Design by Jenny Miller

For more information on bulk copies of this title or other books
and CDs available through the Dynamic Catholic Book Program,
please visit www.DynamicCatholic.com or call 859-980-7900.

The Dynamic Catholic Institute
5081 Olympic Blvd • Erlanger • Kentucky • 41018
Phone: 1–859–980–7900
Email: info@DynamicCatholic.com

Contents

Other Works by the Author

A Seat at the Supper

Introduction to Early Church History

Introduction to the Greatest Fathers of the Church

The Apostles' Creed

Law and Life

The Case for Christianity – St. Justin Martyr's
Arguments for Religious Liberty and Judicial Justice

The Family and Human Life

Defend the Faith!

Answering the Anti-Catholic Challenge

Christ our Light and Life

Gratia Series

Initiate!

Introduction

The Catholic Church is the most maligned institution in the world today. No day goes by without some form of public attack being levelled against her, especially in the mainstream media. Some of these attacks are justified, many of them are not. Of course, none of this is any surprise to Catholics who take their faith seriously, nor is it anything new; it's been going on for over 2,000 years. Christ himself warned us to expect this when he said, *"If they have called the master of the house Beelzebul, how much more will they malign those of his household"* (Matt. 10:25).

Catholics are accustomed to having their church and faith attacked. For many centuries the 'attack' came from Jews who rejected Christ as the Messiah, Moslems who denied the Trinity and the divinity of Christ, and Protestants who 'protested' again a myriad of Catholic teachings. In more recent centuries, atheists and secularists have ramped up their own attacks, seeking to marginalize the influence of the Catholic Church in society and erase God from the public sphere. Secularism continues to advance with ever increasing strides, aided and abetted by media and entertainment industries pushing ever more aggressively their anti-God agenda.

Unfortunately, sometimes we Catholics are our own worst enemies, providing plenty of fodder for external opponents to point their fingers at. 'Sins committed in the name of truth', as Pope St John Paul II once put it, have too often blotted our history. More recently, the scandal of child sexual abuse has destroyed innumerable innocent lives, brought much of the Church into disrepute, and demoralized good and faithful Catholics everywhere. Meanwhile, many other Catholics in positions of power and authority have failed in their obligations to live, teach and pass on the Catholic faith authentically, causing countless others to permanently turn their backs on the Church.

These recent scandals have provided further ammunition to the Church's opponents to perpetuate new anti-Catholic 'black myths', while never acknowledging the enormous good the Catholic Church has done over the centuries or her many apologies for her failings. At the same time, these same critics seem to be strangely silent when it comes to the 'sins' of others, especially those committed by anti-Catholic movements and regimes from the 18-21st centuries. This silence is deafening!

However, it is not all doom and gloom. Good things are happening and signs of hope are appearing in many places throughout the Church. While scandal and corruption will always remain a problem, Catholics need not be silent about the good things. This leads us to the purpose of this book — to tell people about the great things, in fact, 1001 great things about being Catholic!

Why 1001 great things? Years ago I saw a news report about the growth of Pentecostalism in Latin America. One firey pastor had at the back of his church a pamphlet entitled, *"Twenty-five reasons why you are no longer Catholic."* I became upset when I saw this and wanted to produce my own response. Naturally, I wanted this response to be both comprehensive and overwhelming — hence the thought of collecting and publishing 1001 reasons why it's great to be Catholic! More than most, non-Catholics should find this book of great interest.

This book does not want to hide the bad things that have happened in the Catholic Church; rather, it simply wants to proclaim to the world what are the many great things about her. In the age of the 'new evangelization' we should no longer simply cower under the relentless attacks against our church and faith but be willing and able to stand confidently and proclaim loudly why it's great to be Catholic. It's not about triumphalism, it's about truth, and it's always a great time to proclaim the truth!

Robert M. Haddad
29 August, 2014
The Passion of John the Baptist

Chapter 1
Great Church!

Preliminary

The Catholic Church has for over 2,000 years attracted either the love or hatred of countless millions of people. To her enemies, she is an obscure sect, a den of iniquity and corruption, an impediment to any real relationship with Christ, the "whore of Babylon" (Rev. 17:9), or the purveyor of superstition and ignorance. These same enemies would be glad to see the end of the Catholic Church, hoping to poach all her members, cause her to be outlawed and forcibly repressed, or watch her slowly wither and die.

However, to those who know and love her, the Catholic Church is something altogether different. Scripture makes it clear that Christ founded a church which would be his "Body", his "bride", "the Israel of God." It would be a visible and spiritual community built on the "rock" of St Peter who would govern it with the power of the "keys" as Christ's 'Prime Minister'. The other Apostles would also have power to "bind and loose" in union with St Peter and their respective successors would provide central and united government over the millennia under the protection of the Holy Spirit. It would be a church with a triple hierarchical structure of bishop, presbyter and deacon, would evidence this structure over its entire history, would spread its branches across the entire world to encompass all peoples, would require obedience from all her members, and would comfortably embrace diversity within unity. The protection of the Holy Spirit would enable this church to be the "pillar and bulwark of truth", to withstand the "powers of death", and ensure her survival until the end of the world.

Only the Catholic Church has the necessary 2,000+ year history to prove an historic link with Christ and qualify as the church founded by him. Only the Catholic Church can show it has all the qualities and attributes mentioned above. Only the Catholic Church can, therefore, be the recipient and beneficiary of Christ's promises and protection. Only those who belong to the Catholic Church, therefore, can comfortably say they belong to the one true Church of God, the one true ark of salvation.

1

Reasons

1. The Catholic Church is the only church that can show that it is over 2,000 years old and hence the only church that can establish that it was founded by Christ himself. St Paul refers to this same Church when he says, *"to him be glory in the church and in Christ Jesus to all generations, forever and ever"* (Eph. 3:21).

2. The Catholic Church is not only a 'Bible-believing' church but also the Church of the Bible.

3. Being over 2,000 years old, the Catholic Church is the only organized society that has outlasted all other empires, kingdoms and nations since the times of the Roman Empire.

4. The Catholic Church is the only church that can show it began as the *"mustard seed"* in the time of Christ and grew into that tree in which all *"the birds of the air come and make nests in its branches"* (Matt. 13:31).

5. Only the Catholic Church can show that it is simultaneously one, holy, catholic and apostolic, that is, one in government and doctrine, possesses all of Christ's holy teachings, is universal in her membership, and can trace her history back to Christ and the Apostles.

6. Being the church founded by Christ, the Catholic Church qualifies to be the one bride of Christ: *"I betrothed you to Christ to present you as a pure bride to her one husband"* (2 Cor. 11:2).

7. Being the church founded by Christ, the Catholic Church is the 'body of Christ', with Christ as its head: *"Christ is the head of the church, his body"* (Eph. 5:23).

8. Being the church founded by Christ, the Catholic Church is also the new *"Israel of God"* (Gal. 6:16).

9. Being the church founded by Christ, the Catholic Church is a divine institution with a universal name, not a human institution bearing the

name of its human founder.

10. Being the church founded by Christ, the Catholic Church possesses a hierarchical authority to govern it (Luke 6:13; Matt. 18:17-18), has the power to sanctify the faithful (John 15:16) and to forgive sins (John 20:23), as well as the authority to teach (Matt. 28:20) and to baptize (Matt. 28:19). So empowered, the Catholic Church continues Christ's mission (John 20:21) until the end of the world (Matt. 28:20).

11. Being the church of Christ, the Catholic Church is as Christ intended it to be, namely a visible *and* spiritual institution: *"A city set on a hill cannot be hid"* (Matt. 5:14).

12. Being the church founded by Christ, the Catholic Church has the triple hierarchical structure of authority apparent in the New Testament, namely, bishops, presbyters (priests) and deacons (1 Tim. 3:1, 8; 5:17).

13. Being the church founded by Christ, the Catholic Church's leaders possess a divine, not human, authority: *"Obey your leaders and submit to them; for they are keeping watch over your souls, as men who will have to give account"* (Heb. 13:17).

14. Being the church founded by Christ, the Catholic Church is both God's church and the pillar of truth: *"... if I am delayed, you may know how one ought to behave in the household of God, which is the church of the living God, the pillar and bulwark of the truth"* (1 Tim. 3:15).

15. Being the church founded by Christ, the Catholic Church enjoys the promise of the Holy Spirit's continuous protection and source of its infallible teaching authority: *"And I will pray the Father, and he will give you another Counselor, to be with you for ever, even the Spirit of truth ... for he dwells with you, and will be in you ... the Counselor, the Holy Spirit, whom the Father will send in my name, he will teach you all things, and bring to your remembrance all that I have said to you"* (John 14:16-17, 26).

16. Being the church founded by Christ, the Catholic Church is founded on the rock that is St Peter: *"And I tell you, you are Peter, and on this rock I will*

build my church" (Matt. 16:18).

17. Being the church founded by Christ, the Catholic Church has the power to bind and loose in Christ's name: *"I will give you the keys of the kingdom of Heaven, and whatever you bind on earth shall be bound in Heaven, and whatever you loose on earth shall be loosed in Heaven"* (Matt. 16:19).

18. Where there was a king and chamberlain in the days of the 'old Israel' (Is. 22:22), the Catholic Church as the 'new Israel' likewise has a king and chief minister, namely Christ and the Popes as successors to St Peter.

19. Those who listen to the Catholic Church as the historic and biblical church of Christ enjoy union with Christ and all other faithful followers: *"... if he refuses to listen even to the church, let him be to you as a Gentile and a tax collector"* (Matt. 18:17).

20. To hear and obey the Pope and bishops as successors to St Peter and the Apostles is to hear and obey Christ: *"He who hears you hears me, and he who rejects you rejects me"* (Luke 10:16).

21. To receive and obey the Pope and bishops as successors to St Peter and the Apostles is to receive and obey both Christ and the Father: *"Truly, truly, I say to you, he who receives any one whom I send receives me; and he who receives me receives him who sent me"* (John 13:20).

22. The authority given by Christ to St Peter and the Apostles did not die with them but was passed on via the laying on of hands (Acts 1:20; Acts 13:2; 1 Tim. 4:14; Tit. 5-10). This is known as 'Apostolic succession.' The Popes and bishops of the Catholic Church can show that they are the successors to St Peter and the Apostles through a continuous chain of successive ordinations over the centuries.

23. Apostolic succession within the Catholic Church was the criterion used in early Christianity to determine authentic Apostolic Tradition and hence authentic Christian truth: cf. St Irenaeus of Lyons, *Against Heresies* 3, 4, 1 (c. 180).

24. The Catholic Church's model of stable and monarchical bishops is identical to the model of church governance evident in the writings of early Church Fathers such as St Ignatius of Antioch, who at the beginning of the 2nd century wrote: "Let no one do anything of concern to the Church without the bishop. Let that be considered a valid Eucharist which is celebrated by the bishop, or by one whom he appoints. Wherever the bishop appears, let the people be there ... Nor is it permitted without the bishop either to baptize or to celebrate the agape; but whatever he approve, this too is pleasing to God, so that whatever is done will be secure and valid" (*Letter to the Smyrnaeans* 8, 1, c. 110).

25. Possessing stable and monarchical bishops, the Catholic Church has a system of local church government that brings order and certainty in administration and doctrine: *"This is why I left you in Crete, that you might amend what was defective, and appoint elders in every town as I directed you"* (Tit. 1:5).

26. Like many of the Apostles and St Paul (1 Cor. 7:8), Catholic bishops are not married, making them free to serve God and his people without reserve or restriction.

27. The Catholic Church's unity of government is assisted by having a comprehensive canon law that covers all aspects of the Church's life and the life of her members.

28. Possessing a centralized teaching authority of Pope and bishops guided by the Holy Spirit, the Catholic Church maintains Christianity as a divinely revealed religion rather than a collection of private individual opinions.

29. Possessing a centralized teaching authority of Pope and bishops the Catholic Church is united in government, doctrine and sacraments in line with the words of St Paul, *"one Lord, one faith, one baptism"* (Eph. 4:5).

30. Since the Catholic Church is united in government and doctrine its faithful members cannot be *"tossed to and fro and carried about with every wind of doctrine"* (Eph. 4:14).

31. Since the Catholic Church is united in government and doctrine its faithful members cannot be misled by the *"ignorant and unstable"* who *"twist"* the Scriptures *"to their own destruction"* (2 Pet. 3:16).

32. Since the Catholic Church is united in government and doctrine it will never be laid waste or fall as per the following warning: *"... Every kingdom divided against itself is laid waste, and house falls upon house"* (Luke 11:17).

33. As the church of Christ, the Catholic Church has his promise of victory over the powers of Hell: *"... the powers of death shall not prevail against it"* (Matt. 16:18).

34. The Catholic Church has managed to survive all heresies, schisms, internal and external threats and attacks over the past twenty centuries, and is guaranteed to continue to do so until the end of the world: *"... and lo, I am with you always, to the close of the age"* (Matt. 28:20).

35. Throughout its history, the Catholic Church has travelled through repeated cycles of growth, stagnation, decay and decline, only to recover to emerge ever stronger and glorious.

36. Though always regrettable, the existence of unfaithful members in the Catholic Church conforms her to Christ's images of the wheat and the weeds (Matt. 13:24-30), the good and the bad fish (Matt. 13:47-52), and the sheep and the goats (Matt. 25:31-46).

37. Only the Catholic Church has heeded Christ's command to *"make disciples of all nations, baptizing them in the name of the Father and of the Son and of the Holy Spirit"* (Matt. 28:19).

38. Being an international church, the Catholic Church is not a national church subject to the whims of any secular government or ruler.

39. Being an international church, the Catholic Church is not a racially based church. It has members from every race, language and culture, making it a truly universal church.

6

40. Being neither a nationalistic nor ethnocentric church, the Catholic Church possesses a universal vision, reflecting God's concern for the whole of humanity.

41. Being a visible and corporate international society, the Catholic Church avoids the radical individualism that is contrary to the vision in the Scriptures (1 Cor. 25-26).

42. Though the Catholic Church is one in government, faith and sacraments there is great diversity within her unity. The many and different Oriental (Eastern) Churches in communion with the See of Peter are highly esteemed for their venerable antiquity and the Apostolic Traditions they possess from the Fathers.

43. The Catholic Church is broad enough to hold together apparent contradictions in balance: the treasures of the Vatican and the poverty of the Franciscans; the silence of the Benedictine monastery and the enthusiasm of charismatics; the sublimity of Gregorian chant and the exuberance of drums; vernacular liturgies and the perennial Latin Mass; violins and guitars; the great university tradition and the plethora of parochial schools; the home Rosary prayer group and massive World Youth Day gatherings.

Chapter 2
Great Popes!

Preliminary

For centuries much has been written and said about the Popes of the Catholic Church. A lot of the commentary has been about the more sordid details of the Papacy, specifically corrupt Popes who bribed their way into office, lived luxurious lives, practised nepotism, begat illegitimate children, kept concubines, murdered rivals, or even waged wars, etc. Others attack the Papacy more fundamentally, condemning it as a usurped office and the Pope as the *"man of sin"* (2 Thes. 2:3) or *"Antichrist"* (1 John 1 & 2).

Undoubtedly, a number of Popes were guilty of terrible scandals and in the process brought disgrace to themselves and their office (six out of two hundred and sixty-six to be exact). However, those who rejoice in pointing out Papal failings tend to ignore the vast majority of Popes who over the past 2,000 years were faithful to Christ and the Church.

Collectively, the great Popes of the Catholic Church have contributed enormously to the betterment of humanity and the world. It is impossible to list all their great achievements but the following are some of the most outstanding: they condemned heresies; approved conciliar definitions and decrees; encouraged missionary endeavors; repressed pagan practices; promoted monasticism, piety and learning; promoted the study of Scripture; composed great writings; assisted victims of plague; saved Rome from destruction; opposed the threat of militant Islam; freed slaves; supported charities; sponsored the arts; defended marriage; established universities and seminaries; reformed the calendar; reformed the liturgy; attacked simony and concubinage; excommunicated corrupt clergy; deposed unfaithful rulers; negotiated peace between warring states; opposed violent political revolutions; and decried the modern errors and horrors of rationalism, liberalism, freemasonry, Nazism, Communism and racism, to name a few.

Above all, however, the great Popes were men of outstanding fidelity and holiness, even to the point of martyrdom. It is the purpose of this chapter to highlight and remember some of these great men.

8

Reasons

44. The Papacy as an institution ensures that the Church has only one legitimate visible leader on earth, avoiding the fragmentary tendency prevalent in other churches and denominations that makes even local ministers de facto 'popes.'

45. St Hegesippus (Fragments in Eusebius, *History of the Church*, Bk 4, ch. 22) and St Irenaeus of Lyons (*Against Heresies* 3, 3, 3) provide identical lists of all the bishops of Rome from St Peter until the mid and late 2nd century respectively.

46. The first thirty-five bishops of Rome, or Popes, from St Peter (+67) to St Julius (+352) are recognized as saints for their outstanding lives of holiness and service, including many martyrs and confessors during the centuries of imperial Roman persecution.

47. The first Pope was St Peter, who arrived in Rome in AD 42, worked among its people for most of the next twenty-five years, and suffered martyrdom during the persecution of Nero c. 67. He was buried on Vatican Hill, the site where the basilica of St Peter's in Rome now stands.

48. St Clement of Rome was the fourth Pope (88-97) and is known to history due to being asked by the church in Corinth to resolve a dispute between the clergy and the baptized members. St Clement's intervention is embodied in his famous *First Letter to the Corinthians* which is still extant. St Clement died a glorious death after being exiled by the Emperor Trajan to the copper mines of the Crimea. He was thrown into the sea with a heavy stone tied to his neck.

49. St Callistus I was Pope from 217-222. During his short reign he bore the caustic attacks from rebel intellectuals and puritanical extremists for confirming the availability of confession and absolution for all post-baptismal mortal sins and also for recognizing the validity of marriages before God contracted by Christian women of higher rank with Christian men of social inferiority. In so doing, he laid the foundation for the noble teachings that the availability of the sacraments is always independent of

social status and the authority of the State. On 14 October, 222, St Callistus was rewarded with the martyr's crown, being set upon by a raging mob and thrown to his death from a height.

50. St Pontian was Pope from 230-235. Under the persecuting Emperor Maximinus Thrax he was arrested and exiled to the salt mines of Sardinia. As a result, he resigned the pontificate to allow a successor to be elected as soon as possible. Also sent to the salt mines was the anti-Pope, St Hippolytus, who on encountering St Pontian's humility, renounced his claim to the pontificate and died in full communion with the Church.

51. St Fabian was Pope from 236-250. During his pontificate the schism with the followers of St Hippolytus was healed, the church in Rome was divided into seven deaconates, the Catacombs were developed for the burial of Christians, and seven missionary bishops were sent to Gaul. With the advent of Decius as Emperor, all Christians were ordered to offer incense to images of Roman deities. St Fabian was one who refused, being subsequently imprisoned and dying in custody in January, 250.

52. St Cornelius was Pope from 251-253. During his pontificate he was opposed by the hard-line anti-Pope Novatian and his followers who refused to re-admit serious sinners and apostates back into the Church without re-baptism. The 'Novatianists' were condemned by a synod of sixty bishops convoked by St Cornelius, which also declared that serious sinners could be re-admitted to communion after doing penance. Under the Emperor Gallus, persecution was resumed and St Cornelius was arrested and exiled to Centumcellae (Civitavecchia) where he died, perhaps from beheading, in June, 253.

53. St Stephen I was Pope from 254-257. During his pontificate he defied opposition to advocate a lenient policy towards lapsed Christians who sought reconciliation with the Church and insisted on the validity of baptism administered by heretics. St Stephen was arrested and beheaded on 2 August, 257, during the reign of the Emperor Valerian.

54. St Sixtus II was Pope from 257-258. During his brief pontificate the controversy over the validity of heretical baptism that split the North

African and some Eastern churches from full communion with Rome was resolved. Under the Emperor Valerian Christians were forbidden to gather. It was while celebrating Mass in the Catacombs on 6 August, 258, with his six deacons that St Sixtus was arrested by Roman soldiers and summarily beheaded. All six deacons suffered the same fate with a seventh, St Lawrence, being cooked alive three days later. It is this St Sixtus who is mentioned in the canon of the Roman Mass.

55. St Sylvester I was Pope from 314-335. During his long reign a strong relationship was forged with the Emperor Constantine, with the latter commissioning the construction of the great churches of St John Lateran, Santa Croce, and St Peter's Basilica. St Sylvester sent two legates, Vitus and Vincentius, to represent him at the first Council of Nicea in 325, and he later approved the Council's determinations against the Arian heresy.

56. St Damasus was Pope from 366-384. He was strong and vigorous, particularly pro-active against the prevalent heresies of his day, namely Luciferianism, Arianism, Macedonianism and Donatism. Pope Damasus also commissioned St Jerome to translate the Bible into Latin (the so-called 'Vulgate' version) and introduced Latin into the liturgy (both measures aimed at meeting the spiritual needs of the Latin-speaking western Christians). Pope Damasus also asserted the primatial claims of the See of Rome against the growing influence of Constantinople.

57. St Siricius was Pope from 384-399. He was elected unanimously and was very conscious of his universal jurisdiction over the Church. His decrees, distributed widely to other bishops throughout the Church, dealt with the condemnation of Jovinianism and Priscillianism, the election of worthy candidates as bishops and priests, and the enforcement of discipline, particularly clerical celibacy. St Siricius also upheld the perpetual virginity of Mary against Bishop Bonosus of Sardica and settled the 'Melitian Schism' that plagued the church in Antioch.

58. St Innocent I was Pope from 401-417. He reinforced the pre-eminent authority of the Bishop of Rome, writing to and receiving appeals from bishops across the wider Church, including St John Chrysostom. In 416, St Innocent condemned the Pelagian heresy, affirming the decision of the

bishops of North Africa. He also took or encouraged measures against the Novatians, Manicheans, Montanists, and Priscillianists. In addition, St Innocent participated in an unsuccessful embassy to prevent the barbarian Goths from sacking Rome, which occurred in 410.

59. St Celestine was Pope from 422-432. In his zeal for orthodoxy, he condemned the Pelagians, removed all public churches in the city of Rome from the Novatians, and affirmed the Council of Ephesus against the Nestorian denial of the title 'Mother of God'. St Celestine also upbraided the bishops of Gaul for their lax attitude towards heretical novelties. In 431, he sent Bishop Palladius on mission to Ireland, and a year later commissioned the great St Patrick to continue the same work.

60. St Leo the Great was Pope from 440-461. He was the first Pope to be called "the Great." St Leo is best known for confronting Attila the Hun in 452 and persuading him not to attack Rome. Theologically, St Leo is most remembered for issuing the so-called 'Tome of Leo', a document that guided the fathers of the Council of Chalcedon in 451 to reject Monophysitism in favor of the doctrine of the hypostatic union, namely, that Christ possesses two distinct natures – divine and human – united in one divine person "with neither confusion nor division."

61. St Gelasius I was Pope from 492-496. He was the last Pope of African origin. During his short pontificate he vigorously asserted the primacy of the Bishop of Rome over the entire Church, continued the struggle against Monophysitism in the East, and repressed the last remnants of Roman pagan purification rituals, replacing them with the celebration of the purification of the Virgin Mary (Candlemas) on 2 February.

62. St Silverius reigned as Pope for less than a year, from 536 to 537. According to Liberatus of Carthage, he was a victim of Vigilius, a "greedy and treacherous pro-Monophysite", who schemed with the Byzantine Empress Theodora to advance the cause of Monophysitism throughout the Church. Despite entreaties to the Emperor Justinian for a fair trial, St Silverius was exiled by Vigilius to the desolate island Palmarola, where he died of starvation a few months later.

63. Vigilius was Pope from 537 to 555. His election followed the death of St Silverius and was achieved through pressure exerted upon the Roman clergy by the Byzantine army then in Italy under General Belisarius. However, after becoming Pope Vigilius underwent an extraordinary turnaround, renouncing Monophysitism. This resulted in his arrest and transfer to Constantinople where he was imprisoned for seven years. It was only after the second ecumenical council of Constantinople in 553 again condemned Monophysitism that Vigilius was allowed by the Emperor Justinian to return to Rome. During the return journey Vigilius died while in Sicily (7 January, 555).

64. Pelagius II was Pope from 579-590. During his reign the Bishop of Milan returned to full communion with the Church and the Visigoths of Spain embraced Catholicism. Pelagius was noted for his generosity, spending his own money to beautify the Basilica of St Peter and converting his private residence into a hospital for the sick. He died in February, 590, during an outbreak of the plague in Rome.

65. St Gregory the Great was Pope from 590-604. He was notable for many significant achievements, including organizing charitable services, re-organizing the Papal land holdings in central Italy to meet the needs of the starving in Rome, preventing a Lombard attack on Rome in 593, issuing pastoral guidelines for bishops (*Liber Regulae Pastoralis*), commissioning St Augustine of Canterbury to evangelize England, and presiding over the form of liturgical music later known as 'Gregorian chant.' St Gregory was also a voluminous writer, authoring nearly a thousand letters, books, commentaries and homilies. Throughout his pontificate, St Gregory remained sincerely humble, calling himself "*Servus Servorum Dei*" ("Servant of the Servants of God").

66. St Martin I was Pope from 649-655. One of his first acts was to call the Council of Lateran to condemn Monothelitism, the heresy that denied the human will of Christ. As a consequence, the Byzantine Emperor, Constans, had St Martin arrested and brought to Constantinople. After years of public humiliations and indignities, St Martin was declared a heretic and a public enemy of the Church and State and exiled to the Crimea, where he died on 16 September, 655.

67. St Sergius I was Pope from 687-701. He was renowned for his humility and holiness. St Sergius rigorously opposed the request of the Byzantine Emperor, Justinian II, to allow the marriage of priests and deacons and added the prayer 'Lamb of God' to the canon of the Mass. Justinian ordered St Sergius' arrest and abduction. However, his attempts were frustrated by the people of Rome. Rather than exploit the anti-Byzantine sentiment, St Sergius endeavored to calm the revolt. He was proclaimed a saint by popular acclaim immediately after his death.

68. St Gregory II was Pope from 715-731. Realizing the growing threat of advancing Islamic armies, he had the walls of Rome repaired. St Gregory sent missionaries (including St Boniface) to Bavaria and Germany and supported the spread of monasticism. He also continued to oppose Monothelitism and wrote letters to a number of bishops in the East opposing the rising Iconoclast ('image breaking') heresy.

69. St Zachary was Pope from 741-752. His great communication skills enabled the Church to have all lands taken by the Lombards restored to her and prevented further attacks against the city of Ravenna. St Zachary greatly supported the missionary work of St Boniface in Germany and converted the heretic Vigilius before making him bishop of Salzburg. He also arranged for the feeding of numerous poor and pilgrims who made their way to the tomb of St Peter and spent Papal monies to buy back Christian slaves being sold to the Moors. In addition, St Zachary commissioned the French bishops to crown Pepin as king of the Franks, laying the foundation for what would later be the Holy Roman Empire.

70. St Leo III was Pope from 795-816. In April, 799, he survived an assassination attempt launched by a jealous aspirant to the Papal chair. It was this Pope who, on Christmas Day, 800, crowned Charlemagne as the first Holy Roman Emperor, making him at the same time protector of the Roman Church. With treasures supplied by Charlemagne, St Leo became a great benefactor to the churches and charities of Rome. He also settled disputes between various episcopal sees in England and gave refuge to various priests and monks who opposed the divorce and remarriage of the Byzantine Emperor.

71. St Leo IV was Pope from 847-855. One of his first acts was to order the rebuilding of churches in Rome damaged by attacks from the Saracens, including St Peter's and St Paul's. He also ordered Rome's defensive walls to be rebuilt and extended to include Vatican Hill and the tomb of St Peter as protection against future Saracen attacks. In 849, St Leo summoned the coastal cities of Naples, Gaeta and Almalfi to form a naval alliance that won a major victory over the Saracen fleet at the Battle of Ostia. St Leo also convoked a synod of bishops in Rome to re-establish discipline, learning and piety among the clergy.

72. St Nicolas I was Pope from 858-867. He was an authentic ascetic who encouraged religious life in Rome and throughout Italy. St Nicolas came to the Papal chair at a time of anarchy both in the Church and the Holy Roman Empire. He determined to restore morality and integrity to the clergy, starting with the excommunication and deposition of the corrupt Archbishop of Ravenna. This was followed with depositions of unworthy bishops throughout France and Germany and the excommunication of royalty who left their legitimate spouses for paramours, including King Lothair II. St Nicolas also opposed and excommunicated the schismatic Photius of Constantinople, compelling the Eastern bishops back into union with Rome.

73. St Leo IX was Pope from 1049-1054. He came to the Papal chair after the disastrous pontificate of the corrupt Benedict IX, which was the zenith of the 'dark age of the Church.' Already known for his outstanding piety as Bishop of Toul in Germany, he entered Rome barefoot and dressed as a monk, and then was immediately proclaimed as Pope by the Roman people and Cardinals. As Pope, St Leo at once attacked the three greatest evils that plagued the Church: simony, clerical immorality and imperial interference. To extend his reform agenda, St Leo toured Italy and other parts of Europe, convoking synods, deposing unworthy bishops, punishing unfit priests, and reforming monasteries. Despite a disastrous military campaign against the oppressive Normans in southern Italy, St Leo managed to convert them and extracted from them a commitment to end their oppression. St Leo died on 19 April, 1054, while Papal legates were on their way to negotiate reconciliation with the Archbishop of Constantinople, Michael Caerularius, who had ordered the removal of St

Leo's name from the Canon of the Mass and closed all Latin churches in the city.

74. St Gregory VII was Pope from 1073-1085. As an administrator, reformer and leader he is considered one of the greatest Popes to ever shepherd the Church. Soon after becoming Pope, St Gregory attacked simony and clerical concubinage. Priests with mistresses or wives were no longer permitted to practise the priesthood. Despite strong opposition from France and Germany, St Gregory refused to relent. In 1075, he forbad any king or emperor to confer investiture on any cleric, reserving that right to himself. King Henry IV of Germany was excommunicated for his defiance and only restored after his humiliation by St Gregory at Canossa. Henry, however, failed to keep his promises and invaded Rome, setting up an anti-Pope (Clement III) in the place of St Gregory. St Gregory fled to Salerno, where on 25 May, 1085, he died. His last words were, "I have loved justice and hated iniquity. Therefore I die in exile."

75. Bl. Urban II was Pope from 1088-1099. He continued the reforms of St Gregory VII with enthusiasm and finesse as well as the struggle against Henry IV and the anti-Pope Clement III. He also excommunicated King Phillip I for his adulterous marriage. In response to the embassy from Byzantine Emperor Alexios Comnenos, Urban called the First Crusade to wrestle Jerusalem and the Holy Land back from the Moslems. Urban was also successful in restoring Sicily to the Christian fold after centuries of Islamic domination.

76. Bl. Eugene III was Pope from 1145-1153. He was a disciple of the great St Bernard of Clairvaux. Immediately upon his election Eugene was faced with demands from Republicans under Arnold of Brescia to forfeit all temporal power in Italy to them. As a consequence of this struggle Eugene was compelled to flee Rome for France, where he stayed for three years. While in France, Eugene campaigned to correct errors, enforce clerical discipline and propagate the faith. Unworthy clerics were deposed, including the Archbishops of York and Mainz. Even after returning to Rome Eugene feared for his life, so he travelled throughout northern Italy, promoting reform wherever he went. After hearing of the fall of Edessa to the Moslems in 1145 he called for a second crusade to

reinforce the threatened Holy Land, a call supported by St Bernard and answered by Louis VII of France and Conrad III of Germany.

77. Innocent III was Pope from 1198-1216. He was a strong Pope during difficult times. He deposed Otto of Brunswick as emperor of Germany for his dishonesty and persecution of the Church. He also placed the Kingdom of France under interdict due to King Phillip II divorcing his wife. King John of England was compelled to accept Innocent's nomination, Stephen Langton, as Archbishop of Canterbury also under threat of interdict. Hungary, Poland and Norway each had their nominated next kings approved by Innocent. In 1208, Innocent called upon Phillip II to suppress the heretical Albigensians, a crusade which ultimately proved successful. Concerning the Islamic threat, Innocent arranged an alliance between Castile, Navarre and Aragon to pursue the Spanish 'reconquista' against the Moslem south. His calling of the fourth crusade to the Holy Land, however, proved to be disastrous, leading to the sack of the cities of Zara and Constantinople without his foreknowledge or approval. On the religious side, Innocent approved the Order of the Friars Minor (Franciscans) in 1209 and convoked the Fourth Lateran Council in 1215.

78. Bl. Gregory X was Pope from 1271-1276. He was elected after a Papal election that lasted a record three years due to divisions between the Italian and French cardinals. At the time of his election, Gregory was in the Holy Land supporting the ninth and final crusade. His first actions as Pope included an appeal for aid for the beleaguered Crusaders in Acre and a letter against the persecution of Jews. Once back in Italy, Gregory summoned an ecumenical Council to meet at Lyons in 1274. The aim of this Council was to heal the East-West schism, consider support for the Holy Land, and to reform abuses within the Church. Bl. Gregory is also noted for legislation governing future Papal elections which remained substantially intact until the pontificate of Paul VI in the 1960s.

79. Boniface VIII was Pope from 1294-1303. His pontificate was a difficult one for him personally and for the Church in general. He faced multiple revolts against his authority led by Cardinals belonging to the Colonna family. On a more positive note, Boniface worked diligently to bring

peace to a number of rival states, including Sicily, Venice, Genoa, France and Germany. On 25 December, 1299, Boniface began a year long Jubilee celebration to commemorate the 1,300ᵗʰ anniversary of the birth of Christ. In 1302, Boniface issued the encyclical *Unam Sanctam* which re-asserted the primacy of the Pope over the whole Church, including the authority to judge kings. For this he was assaulted and imprisoned by representatives of the French King, Philip IV, but remained steadfast in defense of the authority and independence of the Church until his death.

80. St Pius V was Pope from 1566-1572. He was responsible for concluding the Council of Trent and appointing St Charles Borromeo to oversee the enactment of its decrees. Following Trent, St Pius continued the momentum of reform by publishing a new universal Catechism, a new Breviary for priests and a new Sacramentary for Mass. Mass within the Latin Church was standardized and Pius ordered the establishment of seminaries for the training of young men for the priesthood. Pius was severe on heretical bishops and corrupt cardinals. He was instrumental in the formation of the Holy League, whose combined naval force won the great victory over the Ottoman Turks at the battle of Lepanto in 1571. Pius also declared St Thomas Aquinas a Doctor of the Church and patronized the great composer Palestrina.

81. Gregory XIII was Pope from 1572-1585. As a layman and law academic Gregory led a wayward life, living with a mistress and having an illegitimate son. He reformed his life after taking holy orders, eventually becoming a cardinal and participating in the Council of Trent. As Pope, Gregory led a very simple and upright life and pursued reform of the Church with vigor and efficiency. He dispatched missionaries to Asia and Japan and established universities and seminaries throughout Europe, favoring the Jesuits. He also reduced the power of the cardinals and updated the Index of Forbidden Books. Another of Gregory's notable achievements was the reform of the Julian calendar, which because of his involvement became known as the 'Gregorian calendar.'

82. Bl. Innocent XI was Pope from 1676-1689. He was a man of exceptional piety and unselfish devotion to the Church and the poor. Innocent followed a frugal lifestyle and expected the cardinals to do likewise.

Within only two years of being elected, Innocent restored the finances of the Papal treasury by paying off all its debts. He worked hard to ensure purity of faith and morals in the Church through proper education of the clergy, reformation of religious life, and the promotion of modesty of dress. He particularly encouraged the laity to receive the sacraments regularly, especially Holy Communion. As to matters political, Innocent struggled throughout his entire pontificate against King Louis XIV's attempts to control the Church and its revenues in France, meeting with only limited success.

83. Pius VI was Pope from 1775-1799. He made a poor start to his papacy by appointing a nephew as cardinal and granting to another a lavish estate. On a more favorable note, Pius declared the recently suppressed Jesuits innocent of all charges brought against them and that as individuals they could continue their work for the Church. Pius also appointed the first bishop of the newly founded United States (John Carroll) and struggled against Joseph II of Austria in defense of the Church's religious houses and property. On a more tragic note, Pius watched the unfolding of the dreaded French Revolution and the rise of Napoleon Bonaparte. The latter had Pius arrested and imprisoned in Siena and then Florence. It was while Pius was being dragged to France as "the last Pope of the Catholic Church" that he died an old and sickly man.

84. Bl. Pius IX was Pope from 1846-1878. His pontificate was one of the longest in the history of the Church, second only to St Peter's. For many years Pius struggled against political agitations, revolutionary movements and invasions that ultimately led to the loss of the Papal States to the newly formed Italian state. This left Pius a virtual prisoner in the Vatican. Doctrinally, Pius was very conservative, proclaiming as a dogma the Immaculate Conception of Mary in 1854, issuing the *Syllabus of Errors* in 1864 condemning pantheism, nationalism, rationalism communism, liberalism and freemasonry. He convoked the First Vatican Council in 1870 which defined the dogma of Papal Infallibility. Pius was concerned only to appoint men of noted piety and leadership to positions of authority, a major factor in the world-wide growth of the Church during his years. He worked to restore the hierarchy in England and Holland and keenly supported the growth of the Church in the United States.

85. Leo XIII was Pope from 1878-1903. He worked diligently to improve relations with France and Germany and advanced relations with Russia and Switzerland. Doctrinally, he settled the question of Anglican Orders by declaring their invalidity in his encyclical *Apostolicae Curae*. In *Rerum Novarum*, Leo laid out the principles of Catholic social teaching and the relationship between labor and capital, condemning in the process socialism and unbridled capitalism. Leo received the schismatic Uniat Armenians back into full communion and erected 248 new dioceses and vicariates throughout the world. Leo also founded the Pontifical Biblical Commission, reformed the Third Order of St Francis, and strongly promoted devotion to the Sacred Heart of Jesus and the Holy Rosary.

86. St Pius X was Pope from 1903-1914. He inherited a Europe in open revolt against the Catholic Church and determined to tread down the roads of secularism and liberalism. His motto was "Restore all things in Christ." He focused on the sanctification of the faithful through the promotion of daily Holy Communion. In addition, he promoted Marian devotion, Gregorian chant music and religious instruction for adults. Noting the threat of erroneous doctrines, he published the decree *Lamentabili* condemning sixty-five propositions concerning Scripture, inspiration, sacraments and the primacy of the Pope. In his encyclical *Pascendi* Pius warned the faithful against the threat of modernism as "the synthesis of all heresies." During his time, the Church expanded in the United States, Brazil and the Philippines. Pius died in August 1914, lamenting the imminent specter of World War I.

87. Pius XI was Pope from 1922-1939. He worked on settling the 'Roman Question' with Italy by signing the Lateran Treaty of 1929, creating the Vatican City State as a sovereign entity freely administered by the Pope. The 1920s and 30s were dominated by the rise of dictatorships and the world economic depression. Pius responded with the encyclical *Quadragesimo Anno* which condemned socialism, communism and the excesses of capitalism. There were severe difficulties for the Church in Mexico, Spain and Russia during these same years, adding to the burdens of the Pope. Nazism was condemned in 1937 with the publication of the encyclical *Mit Brennender Sorge*. Throughout all this Pius encouraged the growth of the Church in China and Africa. Pius died in February 1939

seeing war clouds gathering again over Europe, a calamity he worked hard to avert.

88. Pius XII was Pope from 1939-1958. He was elected on the eve of World War II and made repeated calls for peace, all of which were ignored. He re-stated the Church's opposition to war and racism and quietly supported the German Resistance and efforts to save Jews from the Holocaust, the latter resulting in the saving of 800,000 lives. Following the War, Pius advocated reconciliation and leniency towards the defeated powers, while condemning Communism and its repression of the Church in Eastern Europe. Pius delivered over 1,000 addresses and radio broadcasts, published forty encyclicals, most notably *Mystici Corporis* (the Church as the Body of Christ), *Mediator Dei* (on liturgical reform), *Humani Generis* (on theology and evolution), and proclaimed the Assumption of Mary as a Dogma of Faith. He was the first Pope to have a majority of Cardinals from non-Italian backgrounds. Pius was made a Servant of God by Pope St John Paul II in 1990 and was declared Venerable by Pope Benedict XVI on 19 December, 2009.

89. St John XXIII was Pope from 1958-1963. His pontificate was characterized by meekness and gentleness, reflective of Christ the Good Shepherd. In all his works he was enterprizing and courageous, visiting his Roman parishes as well as the imprisoned and the sick, welcoming every person of good will, bestowing a fatherly care on all. His most notable encyclicals were *Pacem in Terris* and *Mater et Magistra*, calling for peace on earth and exhibiting the Church as mother and teacher. St John was the first Pope to convoke a Roman Synod of Bishops in centuries, began work on revising and simplifying the Code of Canon Law, and summoned the Second Vatican Council. Throughout, he sustained himself by constant prayer while radiating the peace of one who always trusted in Divine Providence. The faithful saw in him a reflection of God's goodness and called him "the good Pope."

90. St John Paul II was Pope from 1978-2005. His pontificate was one of staggering proportions. Immediately after his election, St John Paul inspired hope in the Polish people and other enslaved peoples living under Communism, leading eventually to the downfall of the Soviet

Empire. St John Paul II worked consistently to improve relations with Judaism, Islam, the Eastern Orthodox churches, and the Anglican Communion. He was relentless in upholding the Church's teachings against artificial contraception, abortion, euthanasia and the ordination of women, while maintaining support for the Second Vatican Council. St John Paul was the most travelled world leader in history, visiting one hundred and twenty-nine countries during his pontificate. He also made one hundred and forty-six pastoral visits within Italy. More than 17,600,000 pilgrims attended 1,160 General Audiences, while countless millions more attended other special audiences and religious ceremonies. His love for young people led him to establish the World Youth Days, bringing together millions of young people from around the world every two-three years. At the same time his care for the family led to the founding of the World Meetings of Families, beginning in 1994. Spiritual renewal was promoted through special yearly celebrations, including the Marian Year and the Year of the Eucharist. As part of providing modern witnesses of holiness, he beatified 1,340 people and canonized 483 saints. His published fourteen Encyclicals, fifteen Apostolic Exhortations, eleven Apostolic Constitutions, and forty-five Apostolic Letters. He also promulgated the *Catechism of the Catholic Church* as the authentic interpretation of Vatican II, gave the world the corpus of teachings later known as the 'Theology of the Body' and completed reform of the Eastern and Western Codes of Canon Law. St John Paul died on 2 April, the Octave of Easter and Divine Mercy Sunday, a feast he established. The faithful have proclaimed him "St John Paul the Great."

91. Benedict XVI was Pope from 2005-2013. As Pope, he defended traditional Catholic doctrine, morals and values. He advocated a return to objective Christian values to counter increasing secularization in the West and the 'dictatorship of relativism.' Benedict also elevated the Tridentine Mass as the "Extraordinary Form" of the Roman Rite and promoted the beauty of art, viewing the use of beauty as a path to the sacred. He published a series of encyclicals on the theological virtues and a three-volume academic series entitled *Jesus of Nazareth*. In general, Benedict's papacy was seen as a continuation of St John Paul II's. On 11 February, 2013, Benedict announced his resignation citing a "lack of strength of mind and body" due to his advanced age. He was the first

Pope to resign his office in nearly six hundred years.

92. Pope Francis was elected to the Chair of St Peter on 13 March, 2013. He has already been noted for his humility, emphasis on mercy and concern for the poor and unemployed. He wishes "a poor Church for the poor." In his prayer life, he practises daily Eucharistic adoration and recitation of the Rosary. He repeatedly speaks out in defense of the unborn and has made it clear that the question of women's ordination is not open for discussion. He speaks often on the reality of the devil, the persecution of Christians throughout the Middle East and the world, and attacks corruption and the Mafia relentlessly. He has taken decisive action to combat the scourge of clerical child abuse and resorts to organizing public prayer vigils for the sake of international peace. He also critiques much of modern Western culture, including its radical individualism, "throw-away mentality" and lack of commitment to permanence, especially marriage. Evangelization is a high priority for Francis, which in his belief can only be carried forward by example. May he continue to reign gloriously.

Chapter 3
Great Councils!

Preliminary

Councils have been an integral part of the life of the Church since the days of the Apostles (Acts 15). They are an important mechanism through which the Holy Spirit guides and preserves the Church throughout the centuries (John 16:12).

Councils occur when the successors to the Apostles, namely the bishops, gather together to discuss, debate and decide important questions relating to faith, morals, discipline, etc. There have been numerous local councils over the centuries and twenty-one 'ecumenical' councils, that is, gatherings to which all the bishops of the world are invited. The first of these ecumenical councils was Nicea I in 325; the last was Vatican II from 1962-1965.

The decrees, canons, dogmas and creeds issued by ecumenical Councils are binding on all the faithful when approved by the Pope and in the case of definitions relating to faith and morals are irreformable. Hence, Councils have been indispensable in ensuring Church unity and guaranteeing certainty in belief, while at the same time enabling an organic 'development of doctrine.'

Councils have issued numerous pronouncements and decrees on hundreds of different questions and issues, including the Trinity, the divinity of Christ and of the Holy Spirit, the true humanity of Christ, the canon of Scripture, the nature of the human soul, Purgatory, the Sacraments, Transubstantiation, Mary as 'Mother of God', Papal Infallibility, just to name a few. Besides defining doctrine, Councils have been instrumental in condemning heresies, healing schisms, effecting re-unions, deposing kings and anti-Popes, reforming discipline and morals, reforming the liturgy, ordering new catechisms, revising translations of the Bible, etc. The list goes on and on.

All faithful Catholics should be thankful that they belong to a church that is served by Councils, for their existence is one of the chief reasons why they can never be *"tossed to and fro and carried about with every wind of doctrine"* (Eph. 4:14).

Reasons

93. Councils have played a major part in the history of the Catholic Church, being an important vehicle through which the Holy Spirit guides the Church in all truth. The consciousness of the Holy Spirit's assistance to the Church is evident in the expression used by the Apostles near the end of the Council of Jerusalem: *"For it has seemed good to the Holy Spirit and to us to lay upon you no greater burden than these necessary things"* (Acts 15:28).

94. The protection offered by the Holy Spirit to Church councils was recognized clearly in the early Church, as evidenced by the following words from St Athanasius: "But the word of the Lord which came through the Ecumenical Council at Nicea remains forever" (*Synodal Letter to the Bishops of Africa* 2, inter 368-372).

95. It was the Catholic Church through the local Councils of Carthage, Hippo and Rome in the late 4th century who gave the world the canons of the Old (forty-six books) and New (twenty-seven books) Testaments.

96. The Catholic faith is a universal faith embodied in creeds formulated in the great early Councils of the Church. These creeds help maintain the world-wide unity of the Catholic faith.

97. The First Council of Nicea (325) affirmed the divinity of Jesus Christ against Arius, namely, that he is "God from God, Light from Light, true God from true God, begotten not made, consubstantial (*homoousios*) with the Father." This Council embodied the faith of the Church in what became known as the *Nicene Creed*.

98. In addition to condemning Arianism, the First Council of Nicea also fixed the date of Easter for both the East and West, healed the Melitian Schism, reconciled the followers of the heretics Novatian and Paul of Samosata, and promulgated twenty disciplinary canons.

99. The First Council of Constantinople (381) re-approved the Nicene Creed and the words "consubstantial with the Father." The Council Fathers also formulated additional words to define the divinity of the Holy Spirit

against the heretic Macedonius: "... the Lord and Giver of life, who proceeds from the Father, who with the Father and the Son together is worshiped and glorified." In addition, the Council Fathers re-affirmed that Christ possessed a human soul (against Apollinaris) and the primacy of the See of Rome over all others. The creed emanating from this Council is the same creed recited by the faithful today.

100. The Council of Ephesus (431) confirmed the validity of the term *Theotokos* ("God-bearer") against Nestorius, defending the teaching that Mary, in virtue of the Incarnation, was the mother of one person, a divine person, namely the God-man Jesus Christ.

101. The Council of Chalcedon (451) affirmed the Nicene Creed and that Christ is one divine person possessing two natures, a human nature and the divine nature, "united and inseparable" in the one divine person. In the course of deliberations one bishop declared, "It is Peter who speaks through Leo." In the process, the beliefs of the heretic Eutyches and the Monophysites (those who asserted that Christ had only one nature, namely divine) were condemned.

102. The Second Council of Constantinople (553) re-affirmed the teaching of Chalcedon and condemned by name those who denied that Christ possessed both a true human nature and the divine nature.

103. The Third Council of Constantinople (680-681) was called to settle the Monothelite controversy, namely the denial that Christ possessed a human will. The Council affirmed against the heretic Sergius that Christ, possessing two natures also possesses two distinct wills, one human, one divine, which were and are always in moral unity.

104. Together, the dogmatic definitions of the six ecumenical Councils from First Nicea to Third Constantinople give Catholics a complete and certain picture of who Jesus Christ is: one divine person with two natures, a human nature and the divine nature. With his human nature Christ possesses a true human body and human spiritual soul with a human intellect and human will. With the divine nature Christ possesses the divine intellect and the divine will. Both Christ's human and divine

natures are 'owned' by the one divine person, namely, the Word, the Second Person of the Blessed Trinity. Being true man, Christ can offer up a perfect sacrifice of himself on the Cross to the Father on behalf of the whole of humanity; being true God, that same sacrifice is infinitely meritorious and therefore adequate to atone for the offense of Adam's original sin and all the sins of humanity.

105. The Second Council of Nicea (787) upheld the efficacy of invoking the prayers of the saints as well as the veneration (as distinct from adoration which is due to God alone) of icons and statues. In the process, the place of sacred art was formally approved in the spiritual life of Christians. In addition, there were also twenty-two disciplinary canons promulgated relating to clerical life and diocesan administration.

106. The Fourth Council of Constantinople (869-870) was convened to settle the dispute between Photius and St Ignatius concerning their respective claims to the see of Constantinople. The Council excommunicated Photius and restored St Ignatius as Patriarch. In the process, relations between the Byzantine Church and the See of Rome were also restored.

107. The First Lateran Council (1123) was convened by Pope Callistus II to confirm the Concordat of Worms that finally ended the age-old controversy between the Holy Roman Empire and the Holy See concerning the investiture of bishops. It also promulgated twenty-two canons relating to disciplinary and moral matters.

108. The Second Lateran Council (1139) was convened by Pope Innocent II to condemn the antipope Anacletus II and end the schism he caused after Innocent's election.

109. The Third Lateran Council (1179) was convened by Pope Alexander III to end the schism caused by the antipope Callistus III. In the process it promulgated a decree requiring the election of future Popes by a two-thirds majority of the College of Cardinals. Each bishop was also required to establish a school for clerical formation.

110. The Fourth Lateran Council (1215) was convened by Pope Innocent III and applied the term "transubstantiation" to describe the mystery of the bread and wine changing into the Body and Blood of Christ during the Mass. In addition, the errors of the Cathars and the Waldenses were specifically condemned.

111. The Fourth Lateran Council also framed a number of general laws for the edification of the faithful, particularly the 'Easter duty' (i.e., sacramental confession at least once a year and reception of the Eucharist also at least once a year, around Easter time).

112. The First Council of Lyons (1245) was convened by Pope Innocent IV to address a number of pressing issues for the Church, including the continued Eastern Schism, the devastation of Hungary by the invading Tartars, clerical incontinence and the strained relations with the Holy Roman Emperor, Frederick II. In addition to promulgating disciplinary legislation, this Council formally deposed Frederick II for sacrilege, suspicion of heresy, perjury and disturbance of the peace.

113. The Second Council of Lyons (1274) was convened by Pope Gregory X and succeeded in establishing a reunion (albeit short-lived) of the Greek Church and the Holy See. In the process it defined the double procession of the Holy Spirit from the Father and the Son and reformed the rules governing the election of the Pope in conclave.

114. The Council of Vienne (1311-1312) was convened by Pope Clement V to deal with the case of the Templars, the business of the Holy Land, and the reform of ecclesiastical morals. On the negative side, the weak Clement obtained the Council's approval to suppress the Templars on trumped up charges brought by French King Philip IV. On the positive side, the Council defined the nature of the human soul as intellectual and constituting the form of the human body, defined the nature of poverty in opposition to the extremist Franciscan 'spirituals', reformed the administration of the Inquisition, and gave impetus to the reform of the clergy.

115. The Council of Constance (1415-1418) deposed or obtained the

resignation of all rival claimants to the Papal throne, thus finally ending the Western Schism that had divided the Church since 1380.

116. The Council of Constance decreed long needed reforms to Church discipline, including forbidding men without ordination to hold ecclesiastical offices, forbidding lay men to collect church taxes, nullifying all elections obtained through simony and excommunicating all those involved. It also condemned the errors of John Wycliffe and John Hus.

117. The Council of Basel-Ferrara-Florence (1431-1445), after lengthy discussions and debates, affected a reunion of the Greeks, Armenians, Copts, Chaldeans, Ethiopians and certain Syrian churches with Rome. In the process, theological disputes concerning the *Filioque*, Purgatory and the supreme authority of the Pope were resolved.

118. The Council of Basel-Ferrara-Florence also provided an enumeration of the books of the Bible and a detailed teaching on the person and natures of Christ.

119. The Fifth Lateran Council (1512-1517) was convened by Pope Julius II in response to the anti-papal Council of Pisa. This Council annulled the decrees of the rebel Council of Pisa, enacted various disciplinary reforms (e.g., forbidding bishops to receive revenues from more than one diocese) and defined the individuality and immortality of the human soul.

120. The Fifth Lateran Council also required bishops to censor all books published by printing establishments within their dioceses, with a view to especially combating the rise of pornographic material.

121. The Council of Trent (1545-1563) re-examined and defined the whole range of Catholic teaching in response to the rise of Protestantism, issuing dogmatic decrees on original sin, justification, the canon of the Bible, the relationship between Scripture and Apostolic Tradition, the Mass, the sacraments, Purgatory, indulgences, sacred images, relics, and the invocation and veneration of the saints. In the process, the novel and variant teachings of the chief Reformers, especially Luther and Calvin, were condemned.

122.The Council of Trent promulgated a comprehensive collection of disciplinary legislation to reform numerous aspects of the Church's life, for example, requiring all bishops, archbishops, cardinals and patriarchs to reside in their dioceses, thereby ending the practice of absentee clerics holding multiple dioceses, abbeys and revenues.

123.The Council of Trent forbad any person being appointed to an episcopal see or abbey not previously in holy orders for at least six months.

124.The Council of Trent forbad bishops and cardinals to provide for their families out of Church income.

125.The Council of Trent required members of religious orders to reside in their houses and be faithful to their rules and vows.

126.The Council of Trent required bishops to visit parishes and take an interest in the spiritual welfare of all the faithful in their diocese.

127.The Council of Trent forbad bishops charging a fee for parish visitations or ordinations.

128.The Council of Trent reserved the announcing of indulgences to the local diocesan bishop only.

129.The Council of Trent required that all marriages take place before a priest and two witnesses and be registered, thus ending the practice of secret marriages.

130.The Council of Trent required that every diocese provide for the proper formation and education of priests in seminaries under the authority of the bishop. In turn, ordained priests and bishops were to give more attention to preaching and teaching.

131.The Council of Trent decreed that bishops living with concubines would automatically forfeit their see and associated income.

132.The Council of Trent gave local bishops greater powers to punish clerics living in concubinage.

133.The Council of Trent ordered bishops to establish high schools with a study program including the study of Scripture.

134.The Council of Trent forbad all duelling under the punishment of *ipso facto* excommunication.

135.The Council of Trent ordered a new Latin translation of the Bible and a new catechism for the universal Church (the *Roman Catechism*).

136. The Council of Trent ordered a revised Breviary for clerics and a standardized Missal for Mass.

137. The Council of Trent ordered a revision of the Index of Forbidden Books to protect the faithful from the explosion of books dangerous to faith and morals.

138.The First Vatican Council (1869-1870) re-affirmed that God's existence can be known through natural reason and that God also reveals himself through supernatural revelation. It also defined the relationship between faith and reason and the nature and gratuity of faith.

139.The First Vatican Council affirmed belief in miracles and prophecies "because they clearly show forth the omnipotence and infinite knowledge of God, (and) are most certain signs of a divine revelation." At the same time, the Council condemned the proposition "that divine revelation cannot be made credible by external signs" ... and that "miracles are not possible, and hence all accounts of them ... are to be banished among the fables and myths."

140.The First Vatican Council declared that it belongs only to the Church "to judge of the true sense and interpretation of the Holy Scriptures", implicitly condemning the notion and practice of private interpretation that has led to countless interpretative contradictions and divisions.

141.The First Vatican Council affirmed the universal primacy of the Bishop of Rome over the whole Church and dogmatically defined the parameters of Papal Infallibility.

142.The Second Vatican Council (1962-1965) was the largest Council convoked in the history of the Church, with 2,540 prelates attending its opening session from all parts of the world.

143.The Second Vatican Council was a 'pastoral council', providing norms and guidance on a myriad of questions and issues for both the Church and humanity in the context of the modern world.

144.The Second Vatican Council promulgated sixteen documents of which four were constitutions, nine decrees and three declarations. Together, they form the largest corpus of conciliar texts dedicated to the reform and renewal of the Church. In the decades that followed Vatican II, Popes Paul VI, St John Paul II and Benedict XVI worked consistently for its proper interpretation and implementation, warning against interpretations that stressed a hermeneutic of rupture rather than continuity with Tradition.

145.After the Second Vatican Council (1965) there emerged the *Catechism of the Catholic Church* (1992), which provided clear and comprehensive teaching in the face of the theological chaos of the time.

Chapter 4
Great Teachings!

Preliminary

The teachings of the Catholic Church have been much-maligned over the centuries for being either non-scriptural, anti-scriptural, unreasonable or just out-of-date. Yet, nothing can be further from the truth. Altogether, the Church's teachings form a great system of inter-connected and consistent beliefs that are firmly based on and supported by Scripture, Apostolic Tradition and reason. If a teaching is not explicitly found in Scripture it is at least somehow materially present therein. Furthermore, no other church has a range of teachings that cover so many areas, teachings that have remained constant in contrast to the never ending change so evident outside her fold. It is these teachings that bring certainty, peace and joy to the Catholic mind.

Most of the teachings outlined in this chapter are what can be called 'Catholic distinctives', teachings peculiar to the Catholic faith and denied by many non-Catholics. For many of these non-Catholics it is unimaginable that these teachings have any support in Scripture, and the same are often shocked when confronted with verses for the first time that seem to contradict what they have always thought.

Many Catholics likewise are ignorant of the scriptural basis of numerous Catholic teachings and often struggle to articulate a defense of their faith when challenged. This is so especially with teachings relating to the Pope, Mary, Purgatory, Indulgences, Images, Justification, Tradition, the Last Times, just to name a few. What Catholics need more than ever is to discover just how scriptural their beliefs actually are and in so doing be in a position to provide an 'eye-opening' service to those who have always thought otherwise. The truth will set them free (John 8:32).

Furthermore, it ought to be remembered that opposition to Catholic teachings is no longer confined to people of other faiths, but is ever more so coming from people with no faith at all. This is most evident as regards the Church's teachings on life, marriage and family. In these areas the Catholic Church remains the last rock of truth and meaning in a world where truth and meaning are increasingly less fashionable.

Reasons

146. Catholic teachings together form a great system of inter-connected and consistent beliefs that liberate the Christian mind from theological relativism, uncertainty and contradiction.

147. The Catholic Church views creation as reflective of the Creator and thus inherently good. Hence, food, drink, sex and procreation are regarded as gifts from God intended for our happiness when used in accord with right reason.

148. The Catholic Church, in opposition to modern liberalizing trends, maintains belief in the fundamental doctrines of Christianity such as the Trinity, the divinity of Christ, the Incarnation, the Virgin birth, the bodily resurrection of Christ, original sin, miracles, the existence of the devil, the eternity of Hell.

149. In affirming belief in the Trinity, the Catholic Church is consistent with the New Testament, in which Christ says to baptize *"in the name of the Father and of the Son and of the Holy Spirit"* (Matt. 28:19).

150. In affirming belief in the divinity of Christ the Catholic Church reflects the opening words of St John's Gospel: *"In the beginning was the Word, and the Word was with God, and the Word was God"* (John 1:1).

151. In declaring the Holy Spirit to be "the Lord, the giver of life" the Catholic Church upholds the divinity of the Holy Spirit as evidenced in the words of St Peter: *"... why has Satan filled your heart to lie to the Holy Spirit ... You have not lied to men but to God!"* (Acts 5:3-4).

152. In affirming belief in Adam and Eve the Catholic Church echoes St Paul who said: *"For as by a man came death, by a man has come also the resurrection of the dead. For as in Adam all die, so also in Christ shall all be made alive"* (1 Cor. 15:21-22).

153. The Catholic belief that each individual person possesses a spiritual soul that is distinct from the body is supported by the following Scripture

passage: *"Watch and pray that you may not enter into temptation; the spirit indeed is willing, but the flesh is weak"* (Matt. 26:41).

154. In upholding belief in original sin as a dogma the Catholic Church maintains the tradition passed on by St Paul: *"Therefore as sin came into the world through one man and death through sin, and so death spread to all men because all men sinned"* (Rom. 5:12).

155. The Catholic Church acknowledges the greatness of human beings as creatures created in the 'image and likeness' of God: *"So God created man in his own image, in the image of God he created him; male and female he created them"* (Gen. 1:27).

156. The Catholic Church teaches that men and women are equal in dignity and are made for each other's happiness: *"... let each one of you love his wife as himself, and let the wife see that she respects her husband"* (Eph. 5:33).

157. The Catholic Church remains steadfast in its refusal to compromise with the agenda of radical feminism, maintaining that men and women are different and have different and complementary roles in the family and in society at large (Gen. 2:18-23; 1 Cor. 11:3-10). Their differences ought to be respected, maintained and encouraged.

158. The Catholic Church teaches that the differences between men and women are what make them attractive to each other and suitable to fulfil the human longing for communion.

159. The Catholic Church continues to assert that males are generally called to be husband and father, and women are called to be wife and mother, and that society is only undermined when such is denied.

160. The Catholic Church continues to staunchly uphold the ideal of fatherhood as a calling of leadership and service that reveals the fatherhood of God.

161. The Catholic Church continues to recognize the work of women in the home as something valuable and irreplaceable and that women who work

in the home should not be less esteemed than those who work outside the home.

162.The Catholic Church recognizes that women who work outside the family home have a vital role in raising and maintaining social ideals, purifying and balancing the political and legal systems, securing a more just administration of public affairs and improving public aid and benefits in support of the family.

163.In contrast to modern-day trends, the Catholic Church steadfastly reveres marriage as an institution that should be *"held in honor among all"* (Heb. 13:4) and is *"a great mystery"* (Eph. 5:32).

164.The Catholic Church sees marriage and family as instituted for the good of the spouses and reflective of the Blessed Trinity as a community in unity.

165.Far from being simply a human or social institution, the Catholic Church sees in the marital union between man and woman an image of the union between Christ and his Church: *"Husbands, love your wives, as Christ loved the church and gave himself up for her"* (Eph. 5:25).

166.The Catholic Church sees marriage as a fruitful institution ordained for the birth and education of children for God: *"Be fruitful and multiply, and fill the earth and subdue it"* (Gen. 1:28).

167.The Catholic Church remains steadfast in upholding marriage as a permanent union between one man and one woman to the exclusion of all others (Matt. 19:5), in contrast to societal trends advocating so-called temporary, polygamous, polyamorous or same-sex marriages.

168.The Catholic Church is alone in teaching that the contraceptive pill is inherently evil and contrary to the word and spirit of Scripture (Gen. 38:8-10; Luke 1:24-25). This teaching is formally found in the encyclicals *Casti Connubii* (1930), *Humanae Vitae* (1968) and *Evangelium Vitae* (1995).

169.The Catholic Church is alone in rejecting all other forms of artificial birth control, including condoms, intra-uterine devices and sterilization, whether of the male or female.

170.The Catholic Church recognizes that there are "well-grounded reasons" allowing married couples to space out births or limit the size of their families through 'periodic abstinence' (or natural family planning). These grounds include grave economic hardship, serious medical or psychological difficulties, or challenging social conditions.

171.The Catholic Church is alone in opposing the use of reproductive technologies that take the fertilization of new human life out of the natural context intended by God, that is, that separates the creation of new human life from the act of natural marital sexual intercourse. Prohibited practices include in-vitro fertilization, artificial insemination, surrogate motherhood and cloning.

172.The Catholic Church recognizes that human dignity and human rights are based on being created in the image and likeness of God, rather than on human laws or human whims.

173.The Catholic Church is virtually alone in upholding the inviolable dignity of the child in the womb (Ps. 139:13-16; Jer. 1:5) and maintaining that abortion is inherently evil and admits no exceptions. Hence, for Catholics the 'right to life' is inviolable from the moment of conception.

174.Defending life from the moment of conception, the Catholic Church prohibits any form of non-therapeutic experimentation with embryoes that results in their freezing, disgarding or destruction. Live embryoes are children and gifts from God, not expendable commodities.

175.The Catholic Church remains steadfast in opposing all forms of infanticide, teaching that there can never be any grounds to justify the deliberate killing of the defenseless and innocent.

176.The Catholic Church recognizes that children belong to the parents rather than the State and consistently defends the rights of parents to choose how their children will be educated.

177.The Catholic Church sees the family as a true society, 'the path of Christians', the fundamental building block of society, that is prior to the State and ought to be protected and supported by the State.

178.The Catholic Church views the family as the 'domestic church', where parents as the first teachers of the faith bring forth new citizens of human society and of the Heavenly kingdom, inculcating them with the moral and social virtues.

179.The Catholic Church continues to oppose the agenda of the 'sexual revolution' which relentlessly seeks to destroy everything related to family and faith and impose a substitute 'culture of lust, selfishness and death.'

180.In a world deluged by sexual and permissive imagery, the Catholic Church continues to recognize the inherent goodness and value of chastity as a means to self-mastery, freedom and happiness.

181.The Catholic Church values the sexual act between man and woman as one that has procreative and unitive functions, hence it must always occur in the context of a permanent marital relationship. Fornication is shunned as desecrating the human body (1 Cor. 6:15-20).

182.Despite the pronouncements of modern-day psychology, masturbation continues to be regarded by the Catholic Church as "an intrinsically and seriously disordered act" which "contradicts the finality of the faculty" (*Catechism of the Catholic Church* #2352).

183.The Catholic Church stands firm in opposing the world-wide trend to recognize homosexuality as a legitimate life-style, to recognize same-sex 'marriage', or to ordain known practising homosexuals.

184.The Catholic Church continues to teach that pornography is a grave sin that enslaves the participant to lust and "immerses all who are involved in the illusion of a fantasy world" (*Catechism of the Catholic Church* #2354).

185.The Catholic Church continues to oppose the practice of euthanasia, whether voluntary or involuntary, upholding human dignity and the inalienable right to life until natural death.

186. Though no longer possessing an Index of Forbidden Books, the Catholic Church still exhorts her leaders to be vigilant to "ensure that in ... writings or in the use of the means of social communication there should be no ill effect on the faith and morals of Christ's faithful." Moreover, Church leaders "have the duty and the right to condemn writings which harm true faith or good morals" (Can. 823 §1).

187. The Catholic Church recognizes conscience as a person's "most secret core ... their sanctuary" (*Gaudium et Spes* #16, 1965), the obligation of each individual to form their own conscience according to objective truth, and the right of each individual to act according to their conscience free from force or coercion.

188. While other denominations increasingly embrace the practice, the Catholic Church remains steadfast in its refusal to ordain women to holy orders, consistent with the witness of both Scripture (Matt. 10:1-4; 1 Tim. 2:11-15; Tit. 1:6) and Tradition.

189. The Catholic Church upholds the meritorious and practical value of virginity and celibacy for the sake of the Kingdom as advocated by both Christ and St Paul (Matt. 19:12; 1 Cor. 7:8, 27, 32-33).

190. Unlike Protestantism, the Catholic Church believes in Scripture *and* Tradition, not Scripture *or* Tradition.

191. Unlike Protestantism, the Catholic Church believes in both faith *and* works, not faith *or* works.

192. Unlike Protestantism, the Catholic Church believes in Jesus *through* Mary, not Jesus *or* Mary.

193. Unlike Protestantism, the Catholic Church believes in preaching *and* the sacraments, not preaching *or* the sacraments.

194. Unlike Protestantism, the Catholic Church believes in private *and* public liturgical prayer, not private *or* public liturgical prayer.

195. Unlike Protestantism, the Catholic Church believes in spontaneous *and* standard prayers, not spontaneous *or* standard prayers.

196. Unlike Protestantism, the Catholic Church believes in Church authority *and* personal freedom, not Church authority *or* personal freedom.

197. Unlike Protestantism, the Catholic Church believes in law *and* grace, not law *or* grace.

198. Unlike Protestantism, the Catholic Church believes in sacramental reality *and* symbolism, not sacramental reality *or* symbolism.

199. Unlike Protestantism, the Catholic Church believes in the communion of saints *and* the individual, not the communion of saints *or* the individual.

200. Unlike Protestantism, the Catholic Church does not teach an exaggerated view of original sin (i.e., 'total depravity'); instead the Catholic Church asserts that human nature still retains some good, though possessing a propensity to sin through the wound of concupiscence.

201. Unlike fundamentalist Protestants, Catholics can enjoy drinking wine and alcohol like those who benefitted from Christ's first miracle at the wedding at Cana (John 2:1-11).

202. Unlike the founders of Protestantism, the Catholic Church acknowledges the reality of human free will and the essential role it plays in having an authentic co-operative and loving relationship with God.

203. The Catholic Church teaches that *"God desires all men to be saved and to come to the knowledge of the truth"* (1 Tim. 2:4). Those condemned to damnation are so damned because of their own fault, not due to any pre-determination by God.

204. Recognizing that God wills all to be saved, the Catholic Church teaches

that God gives sufficent actual graces to all human beings, irrespective of race or religion, to enlighten their intellects and strengthen their wills. Again, only those who wilfully choose not to co-operate with God's graces are damned.

205. While teaching that "outside of the Church there is no salvation", the Catholic Church acknowledges "those who, through no fault of their own, do not know the Gospel of Christ or his Church, but who nevertheless seek God with a sincere heart, and, moved by grace, try in their actions to do his will as they know it through the dictates of their conscience — those too may achieve eternal salvation" (*Catechism of the Catholic Church* #847).

206. The Catholic Church recognizes that the *"born again"* (John 3:3) experience is connected with water baptism: *"Truly, truly, I say to you, unless one is born of water and the Spirit, he cannot enter the kingdom of God"* (John 3:5).

207. The Catholic Church teaches that the justified become "temples of the Holy Spirit" and that their souls are filled with the life of the Blessed Trinity: *"If a man loves me, he will keep my word, and my Father will love him, and we will come to him and make our home with him"* (John 14:23).

208. The Catholic Church teaches that the observance of the Ten Commandments is necessary for salvation as per the following words of Christ: *"If you would enter life, keep the commandments"* (Matt. 19:17).

209. The Catholic Church's teaching that good works done in faith are pleasing to God and merit reward in Heaven is seen in the following words: *"For the Son of man is to come with his angels in the glory of his Father, and then he will repay every man for what he has done"* (Matt. 16:27).

210. The Catholic Church's teaching that good works are necessary for salvation and that they play a vital part in our personal judgment before the throne of Christ is consonant with the following words of St Paul: *"For we must all appear before the judgment seat of Christ, so that each one may receive good or evil, according to what he has done in the body"* (2 Cor. 5:10).

211.In accord with Scripture, the Catholic Church teaches that God differentiates when rewarding Christians for good works done in faith (Matt. 16:27; Rom. 2:6; 1 Cor. 3:8-9; 1 Pet. 1:17; Rev. 22:12).

212.The Catholic Church's teaching that the saints in Heaven vary as to their glory is supported by the following analogy of St Paul: *"There is one glory of the sun, and another glory of the moon, and another glory of the stars; for star differs from star in glory. So is it with the resurrection of the dead"* (1 Cor. 15:40-42).

213.The Catholic Church does not place an artifical barrier between justification and sanctification but sees the latter as an increase of the former in accord with Christ's command to *"... be perfect, as your Heavenly Father is perfect"* (Matt. 5:48).

214.The Catholic Church's belief that salvation is not the result of a one-off event but must be continually worked out over time in co-operation with God's grace is consistent with the teaching and experience of St Paul: *"Therefore, my beloved, as you have always obeyed, so now, not only as in my presence but much more in my absence, work out your own salvation with fear and trembling"* (Phil. 2:12).

215.The Catholic Church's teaching that people can lose their salvation and that only those who persevere until the end will be saved is consistent with the following words of Christ: *"But he who endures to the end will be saved"* (Matt. 10:22).

216.The Catholic Church's insistence on not presuming with absolute certainty that one is saved is consistent with St Paul's attitude expressed to the Corinthians: *"I am not aware of anything against myself, but I am not thereby acquitted. It is the Lord who judges me"* (1 Cor. 4:4).

217.The Catholic Church teaches the value of mortifying the flesh in order to gain the ascendancy of the spirit over the body and to unite with Christ's own self-discipline and suffering (Matt. 10:38; Rom. 8:13, 17; 1 Cor. 12:24-26; 1 Pet. 4:1, 13).

218.The Catholic Church acknowledges that there is a 'redemptive value' in suffering, especially when offered up to God in union with Christ's sufferings for the sake of others or our own souls (2 Cor. 4:10; Col. 1:24; 2 Tim. 4:6).

219.The Catholic distinction between mortal and venial sin is supported by the following words of St John: *"If any one sees his brother committing what is not a mortal sin, he will ask, and God will give him life for those whose sin is not mortal. There is sin which is mortal; I do not say that one is to pray for that. All wrongdoing is sin, but there is sin which is not mortal"* (1 John 5:16-17).

220.It was the Catholic Church that determined and declared which were the four authentic Gospels of the New Testament, sifting through and discarding many spurious and counterfeit writings in the process.

221.The Catholic canon of the Bible is larger than the Protestant canon, containing the following additional books and chapters in the Old Testament: *Tobit, Judith, Wisdom, Sirach (Ecclesiasticus), Baruch,* and *1 & 2 Maccabees,* extra fragments and chapters in *Esther* and *Daniel,* namely, the seven last chapters of *Esther* (10:4 to 16:24), the prayer of Azarias and the canticle of the three children in the fiery furnace (Dan. 3:24-90), the history of Susanna (Dan. 13), and the history of Bel and the Dragon (Dan. 14). All this extra material is contained in the Greek (*Septuagint*) version of the Old Testament.

222.The extra books and chapters contained in the Catholic Old Testament are alluded to over twenty times in the New Testament, for example, Christ alluded to Sirach 27:6, which reads, *"The fruit discloses the cultivation of a tree."* In John 10:22-36, Christ and the disciples observed the key Feast of the Dedication, or *Hanukkah,* which celebrates events recorded only in *1 & 2 Maccabees.* Likewise, St Paul draws from *Wisdom* chapters 12 & 13 in Rom. 1:19-25. Also, in Heb. 11:35 we read of women who *"received their dead by resurrection. Some were tortured, refusing to accept release, that they might rise again to a better life."* This is a reference to the mother and her seven martyred sons in 2 Macc. 7.

223. The Catholic Church acknowledges that Scripture is *"profitable for teaching, for reproof, for correction, and for training in righteousness"* (2 Tim. 3:16) without going to the extreme that it is all-sufficient as per the un-biblical teaching of *sola scriptura*.

224. All distinctive Catholic teachings can be shown to be consistent with Scripture and, though not necessarily formally present, are at least materially present in Scripture.

225. The Catholic Church acknowledges the two-fold nature of the original Gospel message, passed on from generation to generation in oral and written forms: *"So then, brethren, stand firm and hold to the traditions which you were taught by us, either by word of mouth or by letter"* (2 Thes. 2:15).

226. The Catholic Church acknowledges and accepts the value of unwritten traditions for the spiritual life of her members: *"Be imitators of me, as I am of Christ. I commend you because you remember me in everything and maintain the traditions even as I have delivered them to you"* (1 Cor. 11:1-2).

227. The Catholic Church recognizes the distinction between Apostolic Tradition and those traditions, whether doctrines or practices, condemned by Christ in Matt. 15:6 for making God's word and commandments ineffective.

228. Despite the ravages of liberalism, modernism and rationalism the Catholic Church still formally upholds that the Scriptures were "written under the inspiration of the Holy Spirit ... have God for their author, and as such have been delivered to the Church" (Pope Leo XIII, *Providentissimus Deus*, Intro., 1893; *Dei Verbum* #7, 1964; CCC #105, 1992).

229. Despite the ravages of liberalism, modernism and rationalism the Catholic Church still formally upholds the Apostolic origin of the Gospels of Matthew, Mark, Luke and John and that they faithfully hand on what Christ really did and taught (*Dei Verbum*, #19, 1964).

230. The Catholic Church encourages her members to devoutly read the

Scriptures and generously grants a plenary indulgence to any person who does so for at least thirty minutes in any given day.

231. Together with all four lists in the New Testament (Matt. 10; Mark 3; Luke 6; and Acts 1) the Catholic Church acknowledges that St Peter was ranked first among the Apostles.

232. Consistent with numerous verses in the New Testament (Matt. 16:18ff; John 1:42; 1 Cor. 1:12; 1 Cor. 3:22; 1 Cor. 9:12; 1 Cor. 15:5; Gal. 2:7, 11, 14) the Catholic Church does not hesitate to acknowledge that Simon Peter is the firm "rock" on which Christ built his Church.

233. In addition to being the firm "rock", the Catholic Church acknowledges that St Peter was also given power to govern the Church in Christ's name through the bestowal of the "keys": *"I will give you the keys of the kingdom of Heaven, and whatever you bind on earth shall be bound in Heaven, and whatever you loose on earth shall be loosed in Heaven"* (Matt. 16:19).

234. The Catholic Church's teaching concerning the infallibility of the Pope when speaking on faith and morals has implicit support in the following words of Christ: *"Simon, Simon, behold, Satan demanded to have you, that he might sift you like wheat, but I have prayed for you that your faith may not fail; and when you have turned again, strengthen your brethren"* (Luke 22:31-32).

235. The Catholic Church's teaching concerning the infallibility of the Pope when speaking on faith and morals has implicit support in the following words of St Augustine of Hippo: "(On this matter of the Pelagians) two Councils have already been sent to the Apostolic See; and from there rescripts too have come. The matter is at an end; would that the error too might some time be at an end" (*Sermons* 131, 10, inter 391-430).

236. The authority of the Bishops of Rome as successors to St Peter was clearly acknowledged in the early Church. In the words of St Augustine of Hippo: "Run through the list of those priests who have occupied the See of Peter himself; and in that list of Fathers, see who succeeded to whom. This is the Rock which the proud Gates of Hell do not overcome" (*Hymn Against the Donatists* 18, 393).

237. The Catholic Church's belief that St Peter visited and stayed in Rome as its first bishop finds implicit support in the following words from his first epistle: *"She who is at Babylon, who is likewise chosen, sends you greetings; and so does my son Mark"* (1 Pet. 5:13). Babylon was an early Christian code word for Rome.

238. The following Fathers of the Church all wrote mentioning St Peter as having been in Rome: Tertullian (200); Clement of Alexandria (ante 217); Caius (214); Hippolytus (225); St Cyprian of Carthage (250); Firmilian of Caesarea (257); Pope St Julius I (337-352); St Athanasius (358); St Optatus of Milevis (ante 387); Pope St Damasus I (370); St Ambrose (387-390).

239. The Catholic Church teaches that bishops, as successors to the Apostles, also have power to govern their local churches, a power derived from the authority given by Christ to his disciples: *"Truly, I say to you, whatever you bind on earth shall be bound in Heaven, and whatever you loose on earth shall be loosed in Heaven"* (Matt. 18:18).

240. The Catholic Church recognizes that all her members through their baptism belong to the 'baptismal priesthood', offering sacrifices of prayer and praise in line with the following words of St Peter: *"... like living stones be yourselves built into a spiritual house, to be a holy priesthood, to offer spiritual sacrifices acceptable to God through Jesus Christ ... But you are a chosen race, a royal priesthood, a holy nation, God's own people, that you may declare the wonderful deeds of him who called you out of darkness"* (1 Pet. 2:5-9).

241. It is in the Catholic Church that the laity can be truly a 'priesthood of all believers' for it is the Catholic Church that encourages her members to 'take up their cross', to 'drink his cup', to offer up their sufferings as victims, to help orphans and widows, to abstain from the defilements of the world, and to give alms. These are regarded as acts of true worship and as sacrifices *"acceptable and pleasing to God"* (Phil. 4:18).

242. The Catholic Church recognizes Mary to be that *"woman"* and future foe of Satan mentioned in Gen. 3:15: *"I will put enmity between you and the woman, and between your seed and her seed; he shall bruise your head, and you*

shall bruise his heel" (Gen. 3:15).

243.Like St Elizabeth in the Gospels, the Catholic Church recognizes Mary as the 'Mother of God': *"And why is this granted me, that the mother of my Lord should come to me?"* (Luke 1:42-43).

244.In fulfilment of Mary's own prophecy, Catholics belong to those generations who will call her *"blessed"*: *"For behold, henceforth all generations will call me blessed"* (Luke 1:48).

245.The Catholic Church recognizes Mary as the new 'Holy of Holies.' In Old Testament times, the Holy of Holies contained the presence of God (*Shekinah Kabod*), who dwelt within it (1 Kings 6:15-20). The Virgin Mary is the new Holy of Holies in whom dwelt the divine person of Christ.

246.The Catholic Church recognizes Mary as the 'Ark of the New Covenant', carrying within her womb not simply material objects (the tablets of the Ten Commandments, Aaron's priestly rod, a bowl of manna: Heb. 9:4) but the God-man himself, Jesus Christ, the mediator of the *"new covenant"* (Luke 22:20).

247.The Catholic Church recognizes Mary as the 'mother of the Church', a title consistent with the following words of St John the Apostle: *"... the dragon was angry with the woman, and went off to make war on the rest of her offspring, on those who keep the commandments of God and bear testimony to Jesus"* (Rev. 12:17).

248.The Catholic Church recognizes Mary as 'mediatrix.' Christ is the one mediator of redemption; Mary is a universal and powerful mediator of prayer. As St James states, *"The prayer of a righteous man has great power in its effects"* (James 5:16).

249.The Catholic Church recognizes Mary as 'co-redemptrix', which means "with the redeemer." By giving her free consent (*fiat*) to the Angel Gabriel, Mary co-operated with God's plan of redemption. This consent was not only free but also absolutely essential to supply Christ with the necessary human nature to be a son of Adam. Without this human nature, Christ could not have died on the Cross for us; he would not have been eligible to be our Redeemer.

250. The Catholic dogma of the Immaculate Conception of Mary implicitly affirms the reality of original sin, a doctrine denied or ignored by many, even by some professing Christians.

251. The Catholic dogma of the Immaculate Conception of Mary is implicitly found in the book of Genesis, being that *"enmity"* placed by God between the serpent and the woman: *"I will put enmity between you and the woman, and between your seed and her seed; he shall bruise your head"* (Gen. 3:15).

252. The Catholic teaching that Mary did not endure pangs in child-birth (a normal consequence of original sin for women) is supported by the following prophecy from Isaiah: *"Before she was in labor she gave birth; before her pain came upon her she was delivered of a son. Who has heard such a thing? Who has seen such things?"* (Is. 66:7-8).

253. The Catholic teaching of Mary's sinlessness finds support in the book of Revelation, where the *"woman"* who appears in Heaven is *"clothed with the sun"* (symbolizing her fullness of grace) and having *"the moon under her feet"* (symbolizing her victory over sin) (Rev. 12:1-5).

254. As mother of the King of kings, Catholics rightfully acknowledge Mary as the 'Queen Mother', deserving of honor and reverence as Israelites honored the mother of each king in the line of David (1 Kings 14:21, 15:2, 22:42; 2 Kings 8:26, 12:2, 14:1, 15:2, 18:2, 21:1, 22:1, 23:31).

255. Catholic belief in Mary's intercessory role as 'Queen Mother' before the throne of Christ reflects and builds on the practice in ancient Israel wherein the Queen-mother interceded before the throne of her son-king: *"Then she (Bathsheba) said, 'I have one small request to make of you; do not refuse me.' And the king (Solomon) said to her, 'Make your request, my mother, for I will not refuse you'"* (1 Kings 2:20).

256. The Catholic dogma of Mary's bodily assumption into Heaven finds support in the appearance in Heaven of the portentous *"woman"* in Rev.

12:1: *"And a great portent appeared in Heaven, a woman clothed with the sun, with the moon under her feet ..."*

257. Catholics celebrate the bodily assumption of Mary on 15 August, a practice begun by Christians as early as the 5th century. Beginning as a 'memorial of Mary', this primitive celebration eventually evolved into the Feast of the Dormition (falling asleep) of the Virgin and during the 6th century homilies on the Assumption appeared

258. The Catholic teaching of Mary's coronation as 'Queen of Heaven' finds support in the book of Revelation, where the *"woman"* who appears in Heaven wears *"on her head a crown of twelve stars"* (Rev. 12:1).

259. The Catholic dogma of Mary's perpetual virginity is both ancient (St Jerome, *Against Helvidius* 17 & 18, c. 383; Pope St Siricius, *Accepi Litteras Vestras*, 392; Lateran Council, canon 3, 649) and supported by the main founders of Protestantism (Luther, *The Day of the Holy Innocents, Serm. on Matt.*, 2:13-23, 1541; Zwingli, *Opera, Corpus Reformatorum*, Berlin, 1905, in *Evang. Luc.*, vol. 1, p. 424; Calvin, *Serm. on Matt. 1:22-25*, 1562).

260. The Catholic dogma of Mary's perpetual virginity is implicitly inferred in the following events mentioned in Scripture: (i) the return of the Holy Family from Egypt to Nazareth after the death of Herod; (ii) the finding of the Child Jesus in the Temple after being lost for three days; (iii) Christ giving his mother to the care of St John at his crucifixion. Christ was about two, twelve and thirty-three years of age respectively when each of these events occurred. Yet, never is there any mention of brothers or sisters of his being present, which one would expect if they had actually existed.

261. When looking at all the relevant texts of Scripture together (Matt. 10:2; Matt. 12:46; Matt. 13:54-57; Mark 3:16; Mark 15:40; John 19:25; Gal. 1:19; Jude 1:1) it becomes evident that the 'brothers and sisters' of Christ were actually his first cousins, children of Mary and Clopas. The first chronicler of Church history, Hegesippus (c. 170), identified Clopas as the brother of St Joseph. Thus, both Scripture and Tradition support the Catholic dogma of Mary's perpetual virginity.

262. The Catholic belief that cities and countries have guardian angels appointed by God to protect them is supported by the following passage in Scripture: *"The prince (Angel) of the kingdom of Persia withstood me twenty-one days; but Michael, one of the chief princes, came to help me, so I left him there with the prince of the kingdom of Persia and came to make you understand what is to befall your people in the latter days. For the vision is for days yet to come"* (Dan. 10:13-14).

263. The Catholic belief that the people of God together have the archangel Michael appointed by God to protect them is supported by the following passage in Scripture: *"At that time shall arise Michael, the great prince who has charge of your people"* (Dan. 12:1).

264. The Catholic belief that individuals have a guardian angel appointed by God to protect them is supported by the following passages in Scripture: *"See that you do not despise one of these little ones; for I tell you that in Heaven their angels always behold the face of my Father who is in Heaven"* (Matt. 18:10); *"And Peter came to himself, and said, 'Now I am sure that the Lord has sent his angel and rescued me from the hand of Herod and from all that the Jewish people were expecting'"* (Acts 12:11-15).

265. The Catholic belief that the soul lives on after death is supported by the following passage in Scripture: *"The poor man died and was carried by the angels to Abraham's bosom. The rich man also died and was buried; and in Hades, being in torment, he lifted up his eyes, and saw Abraham far off and Lazarus in his bosom"* (Luke 16:22-23).

266. The Catholic belief that the soul is judged immediately after death is supported by the following passage in Scripture: *"... it is appointed for men to die once, and after that comes judgment"* (Heb. 9:27).

267. The Catholic belief that the souls of deceased persons have an eternal destiny either in Heaven or Hell is supported by the following passage in Scripture: *"Then he will say to those at his left hand, 'Depart from me, you cursed, into the eternal fire prepared for the devil and his angels' ... And they will go away into eternal punishment, but the righteous into eternal life"* (Matt. 25:41 & 46).

268. The Catholic belief that the souls of deceased persons are still concerned with what is happening on earth and can pray for us is supported by the following passage in Scripture: *"When he opened the fifth seal, I saw under the altar the souls of those who had been slain for the word of God and for the witness they had borne; they cried out with a loud voice, 'O Sovereign Lord, holy and true, how long before thou wilt judge and avenge our blood on those who dwell upon the earth?' Then they were each given a white robe and told to rest a little longer, until the number of their fellow servants and their brethren should be complete, who were to be killed as they themselves had been"* (Rev. 6:9-11).

269. The Catholic belief that there is a Purgatory, or place of temporary 'fiery' punishment after death for faults or imperfect works performed during one's lifetime is supported by the following passage in Scripture: *"each man's work will become manifest; for the Day will disclose it, because it will be revealed with fire, and the fire will test what sort of work each one has done. If the work which any man has built on the foundation survives, he will receive a reward. If any man's work is burned up, he will suffer loss, though he himself will be saved, but only as through fire."* (1 Cor. 3:13-15).

270. The Catholic belief that Purgatory is God's so-called 'beauty parlour', enabling the righteous to be *"made perfect"* for Heaven is supported by the following passage in Scripture: *"But you have come to Mount Zion and to the city of the living God, the Heavenly Jerusalem, and to innumerable angels in festal gathering, and to the assembly of the first-born who are enrolled in Heaven, and to a judge who is God of all, and to the spirits of just men made perfect"* (Heb. 12:22-23).

271. Catholics can enjoy the kindness of indulgences in the same way the incestuous Corinthian had a penance imposed on him by St Paul (1 Cor. 5:3-5), which was later remitted in part (the 'indulgence') by the same saint (2 Cor. 2:6-11).

272. Catholics recognize that observance of the Old Testament Sabbath is no longer applicable to Christians in accord with the words of St Paul to the Colossians: *"Therefore let no one pass judgment on you in questions of food and*

drink or with regard to a festival or a new moon or a sabbath. These are only a shadow of what is to come; but the substance belongs to Christ" (2:16-17).

273. In place of the Old Testament Sabbath Catholics gather together on a new day of public worship in commemoration of Christ's resurrection from the dead – the *"Lord's day"* (Rev. 1:10).

274. In confessing their sins and receiving the Eucharist on Sundays Catholics imitate the practice of Christians of the 1ˢᵗ century: "On the Lord's Day gather together, break bread and give thanks, after confessing your transgressions so that your sacrifice may be pure ..." (*The Didache* 14, 1, inter 90-150).

275. Catholic churches are decorated by statues and images similar to how the ancient Temple of Jerusalem was decorated: *"The height of one cherub was ten cubits, and so was that of the other cherub. He put the cherubim in the innermost part of the house; and the wings of the cherubim were spread out so that a wing of one touched the one wall, and a wing of the other cherub touched the other wall; their other wings touched each other in the middle of the house"* (1 Kings 6:26-27).

276. Regarding sacred images and art, the mind of the early Christians was clearly a Catholic mind with the treasury of paintings depicting scenes from the lives of Christ, Mary, the Apostles and other persons of the Old and New Testaments found throughout the Catacombs.

277. The Catholic practice of venerating the relics of saints has the support of Scripture which records the marvellous prodigies God rendered through them: *"... as soon as the man touched the bones of Elisha, he revived, and stood on his feet"* (2 Kings 13:21); *"... so that handkerchiefs or aprons were carried away from his (St Paul's) body to the sick, and diseases left them and the evil spirits came out of them"* (Acts 19:12).

278. Catholic veneration of relics is identical to what Christians in the mid-2ⁿᵈ century practised: "When the centurion saw the contentiousness caused by the Jews, he confiscated the body, and, according to their custom, burned it. Then, at least, we took up his bones, more precious than costly

gems and finer than gold, and put them in a suitable place" (*The Martyrdom of St Polycarp* 17, 3, c. 156).

279.Catholics call their priests 'father' in the same way St Paul called himself *"father"* when writing to the Corinthian Christians: *"I do not write this to make you ashamed, but to admonish you as my beloved children. For though you have countless guides in Christ, you do not have many fathers. For I became your father in Christ Jesus through the gospel"* (1 Cor. 4:14-15).

280.The Catholic Church exhorts her members to engage in fasting, a spiritual activity enjoined by Christ and practised in the Apostolic Church: *"The days will come, when the bridegroom is taken away from them, and then they will fast in that day"* (Mark 2:20); *"And when they had appointed elders for them in every church, with prayer and fasting, they committed them to the Lord in whom they believed"* (Acts 14:23).

281.Catholics still abstain from meat on Fridays, a practice the Prophet Daniel on one occasion engaged in: *"In those days I, Daniel, was mourning for three weeks. I ate no delicacies, no meat or wine entered my mouth, nor did I anoint myself at all, for the full three weeks"* (Dan. 10:2-3).

282.Catholics have a great reverence for the cross of Christ, in substance identical to St Paul's: *"But far be it from me to glory except in the cross of our Lord Jesus Christ, by which the world has been crucified to me, and I to the world"* (Gal. 6:14).

283.The Catholic Church rejects 'cessationalism', the belief that miracles ended with the death of the Apostles.

284.While affirming the second coming of Christ, the Catholic Church avoids the rash practise of 'date-setting' with all its accompanying fears, neglects and disappointments.

285.The Catholic Church avoids hysterics about the identity of the Antichrist, preferring to confine herself to basics found in Scripture, namely, that he is an individual who will appear before the second coming of Christ (2 Thes. 2:3), that he will perform pretended signs and wonders with the power of Satan (2 Thes. 2:9), that he will deny that Jesus is the Christ (1 John 2:22-23) and has come in the flesh (2 John 1:7), that he will exalt himself and proclaim himself to be God (2 Thes. 2:4), that the price of accepting his solution to the world's problems will be apostasy and damnation (*Catechism of the Catholic Church* #675), and that the Lord Jesus will destroy him with the breath of his mouth upon his appearing (2 Thes. 2:8).

286. The Catholic Church rejects the notion of a 'secret rapture' as a recent invention contrary to Scripture. The Catholic Church's official teachings on the end-times are contained in the Nicene Creed and the *Catechism of the Catholic Church* ##668-682. In short, the second coming of Christ is associated with the end of the world and the Last Judgment, not with a secret rapture or the establishment of a temporary 'Millennium.' Christ's Second Coming will be triumphant and ever-lasting, not temporal and limited.

287. The Catholic Church has cautiously avoided formally and finally accepting the conclusions of evolutionary science due to the fact that the work of science is still in a state of flux. The current claims of Darwinian science may yet be superseded by later science.

288. Beginning in 1891 with the encyclical *Rerum Novarum*, the Catholic Church offers a body of formal teachings relating to the state and social responsibility that provides Christians with a framework to engage the world, rather than simply leaving a void that is filled by those who disdain or oppose Christianity.

289. The Catholic Church, like Christ, preaches and practises a preferential option for the poor, giving priority to help those downtrodden who cannot help themselves.

290. The Catholic Church recognizes the inherent goodness and value of work, how it is beneficial for humanity, enabling humanity to transform nature and adapt it to its needs. According to Pope St John Paul II in *Laborem Exercens* (1981), work assists humans to achieve fulfilment and perfect themselves as human beings (#9.3).

291. From Pope Paul III in 1537 to Pope Francis today, the Catholic Church has condemned the slave trade, workplace exploitation, child labor, and forced prostitution. The Catholic Church has always supported the right of workers to just wages and to form trade unions.

292. The Catholic Church has always supported the right to private property for guaranteeing the freedom and dignity of persons and to enable them to meet their basic needs. At the same time, the 'universal destination of goods' remains primordial to ensure that the whole human race benefits from the fruits of the earth in a spirit of fraternal solidarity and charity.

293. The Catholic Church has always respected philosophy and esteemed reason. It does not promote blind faith; rather it promotes a "faith seeking understanding." According to G.K. Chesterton, the Catholic Church is an "intelligent institution that has been thinking about thinking for two thousand years."

294. In the encyclical *Fides et ratio* (1998), Pope St John Paul II reaffirmed the existence of absolute truths and the complementary relationship between faith and reason. He also encouraged all people of good will to pursue philosophical studies, especially Thomistic metaphysics.

295. The Catholic teaching on 'Just War' reprobates war conducted for the purpose of conquest, territorial expansion, etc., while tolerating war when conducted in self-defense against an unjust aggressor. 'Just wars' are those conducted by a legitimate authority, in self-defense, using proper means, where the foreseen benefits outweigh the foreseen evils, after all other avenues of preventing aggression have been exhausted. The Catholic Church, therefore, avoids the extremes of pacificism and 'total war' concepts, the latter usually targeting innocent non-combatants.

Chapter 5
Great Prayer!

Preliminary

Prayer is at the heart of any relationship with God. Yet, many accuse the Catholic Church of being spiritually dead, an institution that does not 'feed' its own members with the necessary spiritual food for salvation. Sadly, this is the subjective experience of many who have not been properly catechized or exposed to the numerous rich spiritual traditions found in Catholic spirituality and prayer. At the same time, Catholics are also accused of engaging excessively in 'rote' prayers which come more from the lips than the heart, or in 'dead' liturgy that is lifeless, or, worse still, in idolatrous prayers worshipping creatures such as Mary, the saints, statues or even bread, rather than the Creator God.

The variety of Catholic prayers is truly astonishing, from the simple 'Sign of the Cross' to the great liturgies of Holy Week. Centred on the Mass and the Divine Office, the public worship of the Catholic Church reflects the *"breaking of bread and the prayers"* (Acts 2:42) of the Apostolic Church. In between the simple and the extravagant, Catholics have prayers of adoration, petition, thanksgiving and intercession. There are prayers directly out of the Bible, such as psalms, the Our Father, the *Magnificat* and the *Benedictus*, and others inspired by Scripture such as the Hail Mary and the *Angelus*. There are litanies, novenas, popular devotions galore, as well as prayers associated with pilgrimages and sacramentals. The latter combine the spiritual with the material.

Essentially, the critics of Catholicism seem to believe that all Catholics are spiritually dead and that there are none who practise their faith with any authentic life or enthusiasm. They also fail to see how the uniquely Catholic prayers have any sound justification or foundation in Scripture. This chapter will not provide any justification for badly practising Catholics but it will endeavor wherever possible to provide Scriptural backing for 'contentious' Catholic prayers, as well as build an appreciation of the spiritual variety inspired by the Holy Spirit in and through the Catholic Church over the centuries.

Reasons

296.Catholic prayer acknowledges our utter dependence on God's grace and our need for constant and free co-operation to attain ultimate salvation.

297.The 'Sign of the Cross' is an ancient tradition (beginning in the 2nd century) that testifies to belief in the Holy Trinity and the crucifixion of Christ.

298.The Catholic Church's public liturgy retains elements of mystery, the sacred and the supernatural, thus remaining a barrier to the increasing secularization of modern society.

299.The Catholic Church's public liturgy provides an objective order so that God is appropriately worshiped largely free from the subjective preferences, whims and foibles of private individuals.

300.No matter where Catholics may be, the public liturgy is generally the same, with the same readings, prayers and Eucharistic sacrifice.

301.The public liturgical life of the Catholic Church is one of constant commemoration and celebration, divided into the following seasons: Advent; Christmas and Epiphany; Ordinary Time (1st part); Lent and Holy Week; Easter; Ascension and Pentecost; Ordinary Time (2nd part).

302.The Catholic Church's feast days remind us that we always have someone or something to celebrate: Christmas; Easter; Pentecost; All Saints; All Souls; the Marian feasts; St Joseph; Sts Peter and Paul, etc. The list goes on and on.

303.In the liturgical year of the Catholic Church, Jesus Christ is honored in the following celebrations: his Annunciation (25 March); his Birth (25 December); his Epiphany (2nd Sunday after Christmas); his Presentation in the Temple (2 February); his Baptism (Sunday after 6 January); his Transfiguration (6 August); his Death (Good Friday); his Resurrection (Easter Sunday and every Sunday); his Ascension (Thursday of 6th week of Eastertide); his Universal Kingship (Last Sunday of Ordinary Time); his

Gift of the Eucharist (2nd Sunday after Pentecost); his Sacred Heart (Friday after *Corpus Christi*).

304. In the liturgical year of the Catholic Church, the Virgin Mary is honored in the following celebrations: her Immaculate Conception (8 December); her Birth (8 September); her Presentation (21 November); her Visitation to St Elizabeth (31 May); her Assumption (15 August); her Queenship (22 August); her Divine Motherhood (1 January); Our Lady, Help of Christians (1st Sunday after Pentecost); Our Lady of Sorrows (15 September); Our Lady of the Rosary (7 October).

305. In the liturgical year of the Catholic Church, the Apostles are honored in the following celebrations: Peter (22 February, 29 June); Andrew (30 November); James the Great (25 July); John (27 December); Philip (3 May); Bartholomew (24 August); Matthew (21 September); Thomas (3 July); James the Less (3 May); Simon the Zealot (28 October); Jude Thaddeus (28 October); Matthias (14 May); Paul (25 January, 29 June).

306. During the course of the liturgical year, Catholics dedicate the various months to the following devotions: January to the Holy Name of Jesus; February to the Holy Family; March to St Joseph; May to the Virgin Mary; June to the Sacred Heart of Jesus; July to the Precious Blood of Jesus; August to the Immaculate Heart of Mary; September to Our Lady of Sorrows; October to the Holy Rosary; November to the Holy Souls in Purgatory; December to Our Lady of the Immaculate Conception.

307. The Catholic Church's daily functions of public preaching, the offering of the Mass and the recitation of the Divine Office reflects the core threefold functions of the Apostolic Church: *"And they devoted themselves to the apostles' teaching and fellowship, to the breaking of bread and the prayers"* (Acts 2:42).

308. The Catholic Church's public liturgy makes present on earth the paschal mystery which Christ perpetually offers before the Father through his *"sprinkled blood"* in Heaven (Heb. 12:24).

309. From the writings of St Justin Martyr (*1 Apol.* 65-67, c. 155) it is evident that the Catholic Church's Eucharistic celebration has retained the same basic order for over twenty centuries.

310. The *Kyrie Eleison* is recited as part of the penitential rite at the beginning of Mass in the Roman Liturgy. Used in conjunction with *Christe Eleison*, it directly invokes Christ and implores his mercy. It is one of the remaining prayers of Greek origin in the modern Liturgy.

311. The Catholic Church since time immemorial has called upon her faithful to recite creeds (e.g., the Apostles' Creed, Nicene Creed) when gathered together in public worship as both a sign and a means of expressing the unity of faith.

312. In her public liturgy, the Catholic Church's 'prayers of the faithful' reflect the type of *"supplications, prayers, intercessions and thanksgivings"* encouraged by St Paul (1 Tim. 2:1).

313. In the *Agnus Dei* prayer, Catholics invoke Christ three times in succession under the title given to him by John the Baptist (John 1:29), asking for his mercy and peace before receiving him in Holy Communion.

314. Catholics sing the 'Alleluia' in the Divine Office and during the liturgy, being derived from the Hebrew *hallelujah,* meaning "praise Yahweh."

315. Catholics recite the *Anima Christi* prayer usually after receiving Christ in Holy Communion, asking that he "sanctify", "inebriate", "wash" and "strengthen" our souls so that we may be defended from the "malignant enemy" and one day join the saints in Heaven to praise and adore him forever and ever.

316. In the *En Ego* prayer, Catholics reflect upon the five wounds of Christ, recalling the prophecy of David in Psalm 22:16-17: *"They have pierced my hands and my feet — I can count all my bones."* At the same time, Christ is asked to impress upon our hearts lively sentiments of faith, hope and charity, with true contrition for our sins and a firm resolution of amendment.

317. The practice of midnight Masses reinforces the notion that God is deserving of worship any time of the day or night while reminding us that the two greatest events in salvation history, namely the birth and resurrection of Christ, both occurred in the early hours of the morning.

318. Continuing from Jewish tradition, the Catholic Church incorporates all one hundred and fifty Old Testament Psalms into her public worship, especially in her official prayer known as the Divine Office or the Liturgy of the Hours.

319. With Eucharistic adoration, Catholics acknowledge and adore the perpetual presence of Christ among us, akin to the continued presence of the 'glory cloud' (*Shekinah Kabod*) in the days of ancient Israel.

320. The 'Forty Hours Devotion' engages Catholics in continuous public adoration of the Blessed Sacrament for forty hours in honor of the forty hours Christ rested in the tomb.

321. The practice of 'Benediction' allows Christ in the Blessed Sacrament to be viewed and adored while displayed in public. The faithful on such occasions can receive a special 'Eucharistic blessing.'

322. The custom of 'Eucharistic Processions' is a great form of public expression of faith in Christ's Real Presence among his people, courageously testifying to our belief to a mostly unbelieving world.

323. Catholics privately recite 'Spiritual Communions' when they have been unable to receive Christ in the Eucharist. One form of such a prayer is: "O Lord Jesus, I implore you to come spiritually into my heart with your holiness, your goodness and your grace. O Sacrament most Holy, O Sacrament divine, all praise and all thanksgiving be every moment thine."

324. The Catholic Church recognizes that prayer does not end with death, but that the *"cloud of witnesses"* (Heb. 12:1) in Heaven continue to supplicate before the throne of God: *"O Sovereign Lord, holy and true, how long before thou wilt judge and avenge our blood on those who dwell upon the earth?"* (Rev. 6:10).

325.The 'Stations of the Cross' is a deeply rich and moving devotion that both reminds Catholics of the passion of Christ and how the Christian life is a continuous journey of challenges and struggles that achieves victory only through perseverance and fidelity. The traditional Stations number fourteen, beginning with Christ's condemnation to death by Pilate and finishing with his burial in the sepulcher.

326.The Stations of the Cross devotion is practised in its most public form along the *Via Dolorosa* ('Way of Sorrows') in the Old City of Jerusalem. Every year at Easter time tens of thousands of Catholic pilgrims from all over the world come to re-enact Christ's carrying of his cross along a winding route from the ruins of Antonia Fortress to the Church of the Holy Sepulcher – a distance of approximately 600m. The current enumeration of the fourteen stations is based on a devotional walk organized by the Franciscans since the 14th century.

327.The *Stabat Mater* ("At the Cross her station keeping ...") is a hymn first composed by the Franciscan Jacopone da Todi in the 13th century and describes and honors Mary's sorrows at the foot of the Cross on Good Friday. It enables the Christian to share Mary's sentiments and weep with her before the crucified Lord.

328.The 'Our Father', given to us by Christ himself (Matt. 6:9-13; Luke 11:1-4), is considered the most important of all the Church's prayers and is used extensively both in public and private worship. Whatever we could ever properly ask for is contained in this prayer. As St Augustine of Hippo says: "We cannot but utter that which is contained in Our Lord's prayer, if we pray in a suitable and worthy manner" (*To Proba*, Ep. 130, 412).

329.The Holy Rosary of the Blessed Virgin Mary is a wonderful private devotion that combines an act of faith with prayers of adoration, petition, contrition and thanksgiving.

330.In the recitation of the Holy Rosary, the Catholic faithful also meditate on twenty great events in the lives of Jesus and Mary under the groupings of 'Joyful', 'Luminous', 'Sorrowful' and 'Glorious' mysteries.

331. The fact that there are ten Hail Marys for each 'decade' of the Holy Rosary gives ample time to the devotee to meditate on the mystery in question, mysteries which all relate to the lives of Jesus and Mary.

332. In the Hail Mary, Catholics praise Mary with the same words used by the Angel Gabriel and St Elizabeth: *"Hail, full of grace, the Lord is with you"* (Luke 1:28); *"Blessed are you among women and blessed is the fruit of your womb!"* (Luke 1:42).

333. In the Hail Mary, Catholics ask Mary to pray to God the Father through the priestly intercession of Christ: "pray for us sinners, now and at the hour of our death. Amen."

334. In praying the Hail Mary, Catholics pray a prayer recommended and praised by Martin Luther: "We can use the Hail Mary as a meditation in which we recite what grace God has given her. Second, we should add a wish that everyone may know and respect her ... He who has no faith is advised to refrain from saying the Hail Mary" (Weimer, *The Works of Luther*, Pelikan, Concordia, vol. 43, pp. 39-41).

335. In the 'Glory be', Catholics praise and adore the Holy Trinity, Father, Son and Holy Spirit ... "in the beginning, is now, and ever shall be, world without end."

336. In the 'Fatima Prayer', Catholics ask Christ for forgiveness of their sins and that he "lead all souls to Heaven, especially those in most need of ... mercy."

337. The ashes received by Catholics on Ash Wednesday are a timely reminder of our need for repentance, of the temporal nature of this life and the reality of the next.

338. In the *Confiteor* (Confession of sin) said during the Mass, Catholics publicly confess their sins before Almighty God and petition the Virgin Mary, the angels, saints and our fellow brothers and sisters in Christ on earth "to pray for me to the Lord our God."

339. In 'Acts of Contrition', Catholics beg God for forgiveness of their sins, praise God's goodness, and petition him for the grace not to sin again.

340. In 'Acts of Faith', Catholics declare their faith in one God in three divine persons, Father, Son and Holy Spirit, and in Jesus Christ who became man and died for our sins. We also affirm belief in all the truths which the Catholic Church teaches, because in revealing them God can neither deceive nor be deceived.

341. In 'Acts of Hope', Catholics rely on God's almighty power and infinite mercy and promises to obtain pardon of our sins and life everlasting, through the merits of Jesus Christ, our Lord and Redeemer.

342. In 'Acts of Love', Catholics declare their love of God above all things "because God is all-good and worthy of all love." We also declare our love of neighbor as ourselves for the love of God.

343. In 'Acts of Acceptance', Catholics declare their willingness to accept death calmly and resign themselves to the will of God: "O Lord God, at this moment I accept readily and willingly whatever kind of death you may please to send me, with all its pains, penalties and sorrows. Amen."

344. In 'Morning Offerings', Catholics offer the Lord all their prayers, works, joys and sufferings of each day for his glory and the good of the world.

345. In the 'Evening Prayer', Catholics give thanks to God for all the blessings and graces received during the day and ask that "your holy angel may protect me during the night."

346. In the 'Jesus Prayer', Catholics simply and humbly beg the Lord's forgiveness for their sins: "Lord Jesus Christ, Son of God, have mercy on me, a sinner."

347. In the prayer known as 'The Divine Praises', Catholics praise God, God's holy Name, the Name of the Lord Jesus, Jesus' Sacred Heart, Jesus in the Blessed Sacrament, the Holy Spirit, the great Mother of God and her prerogatives, St Joseph, and God in all his angels and saints.

348. In prayers before and after meals, Catholics bless and thank the Lord for all his gifts which come to us out of his goodness.

349. In praying the 'Come, Holy Spirit' prayer, Catholics call upon the Holy Spirit to fill our hearts, enkindle in us his love, and "renew the face of the earth."

350. In the *Veni Creator* prayer, Catholics invoke the Holy Spirit and implore that he come and dwell in our souls and grant us his grace and heavenly aid.

351. The *Te Deum Laudamus* is a long and majestic Catholic prayer comprised of portions of the psalms said to be chosen by Sts Ambrose and Augustine in the late 4th century. Sung usually on great feasts or on joyful occasions, this prayer gives great glory and praise to God and Christ while asking for their mercy and a place with them in eternal glory.

352. In the 'Sacred Heart' prayer, Catholics ask Christ to make their hearts like his own, namely, meek and humble. At the same time, they behold the Heart that has loved humanity so much and has received very little love in return.

353. In the *Magnificat* prayer, Catholics join with Mary to praise God as our Creator and Savior in the very words used by her when visiting St Elizabeth to assist her before the birth of John the Baptist: *"My soul magnifies the Lord, and my spirit rejoices in God my savior"* (Luke 1:46-55).

354. In the *Benedictus* prayer, Catholics recite the words of Zachariah in praise of the God of Israel for fulfilling his promise to send that prophet (John the Baptist) who would *"go before the Lord"*, the one who would make known to us our salvation and *"guide our feet into the way of peace"* (Luke 1:68-79).

355. In the *Angelus* prayer, Catholics recall how the Angel Gabriel announced to the Virgin Mary that she was chosen by God to be the mother of the Messiah and rejoice in the mystery of the Incarnation, viz., how the Eternal Word became flesh and dwelt among us in Jesus Christ.

356. In the *Regina Caeli* prayer, Catholics join with the Virgin Mary as 'Queen of Heaven' to rejoice in the resurrection of Christ and invoke her prayers that we too may be brought to the joys of eternal life "through Christ our Lord."

357. The *Akathist Hymn* is a profound and beautiful Marian devotion originating in the Byzantine Rite sometime during the 5th century. It is made up of twenty-four sections and sings praises to Mary for her role in the Incarnation, the infancy of Christ, and her virginal motherhood. Traditionally, this hymn is publicly sung in part on the first four Saturdays of Lent and in full on the fifth Saturday.

358. In the *De profundis* prayer, Catholics recite Psalm 130 (or 129) in a spirit of contrition and call upon the Lord not to remember our sins for he is merciful and possesses "plenteous redemption."

359. Catholics often pray 'litanies', which are structured forms of prayer involving a series of petitions and fixed responses. All litanies contain invocations of the Persons of the Trinity, petitions relating to a specific theme, three invocations of the Lamb of God, and a short closing prayer. The most well known litanies are: the Holy Name, the Sacred Heart, the Precious Blood, Our Lady of Loreto, St Joseph, the Saints, the Dying.

360. Catholics often pray 'novenas', a form of devotional prayer for a specific intention stretching over nine consecutive days. There are many different types of novenas (to the Holy Spirit, the Sacred Heart of Jesus, the Immaculate Heart of Mary, etc.). The first novena was prayed by the infant church in Jerusalem for the coming of the Holy Spirit in the nine days between Christ's ascension into Heaven and Pentecost Day (Acts 2).

361. Catholics often use chaplets to assist them in their devotional prayers. The word 'Chaplet' means 'little crown' and is usually applied to hand-held strings of beads that assist the person praying to count prayers of repetition. The most well known chaplets include: the Chaplet of Divine Mercy; the Chaplet of the Sacred Heart; the Chaplet of the Precious Blood; the Chaplet of the Holy Spirit; the Chaplet of St Michael; the Chaplet of St Therese, etc.

362.When engaging in an examination of conscience, Catholics invoke the Holy Spirit to help recall their sins before reciting an act of contrition or receiving the sacrament of Penance.

363.When praying to their Guardian Angels, Catholics invoke their protection knowing that God has assigned them to protect us in all our comings and goings: *"For he will give his angels charge of you to guard you in all your ways"* (Ps. 91:11).

364.In the 'Prayer to Saint Michael', Catholics call upon the Archangel Michael to "defend us in the day of battle" and "by the power of God" cast into Hell "Satan and all the other evil spirits who prowl about the world seeking the ruin of souls."

365.In the 'Breastplate' prayer of St Patrick, Catholics call upon Christ to be "with me", "within me", "behind me", "before me", "beside me", "beneath me", "above me", "in the hearts of all who love me", and in the "mouth of friend and stranger."

366.In the 'St Francis prayer', Catholics ask the Lord to make us into instruments of peace that sow love, pardon, faith, hope, light and joy in opposition to hatred, injury, doubt, despair, darkness and sadness.

367.In the 'Canticle of the Sun' prayer composed by St Francis of Assisi just before his death, Catholics praise God in poetic language for the gift and beauty of all his creation.

368.In the prayer of St Thomas Aquinas, Catholics ask God for understanding, diligence, wisdom, a way of life that is pleasing, perseverance, "and confidence that I shall embrace you at the last."

369.In the prayer of St Ignatius Loyola, Catholics pledge to serve Christ "as you deserve: to give and not to count the cost; to fight and not to heed the wounds; to work and not to seek for rest; to labor and not to ask for any reward, save that of knowing that we do your holy will."

370. In the ministry of exorcism, prayers of exorcism and liberation are recited to deliver individuals from the effects of magic, occultism and Satanism.

371. The forty days of Lent remind Catholics of Christ's forty days in the wilderness (Luke 4:1-2) and inspires Catholics to practise meritorious self-sacrifice through prayer, fasting and alms-giving.

372. Abstaining from meat on Fridays is a practice that reinforces self-sacrifice and discipline, while reminding Catholics of how Christ sacrificed his own flesh on Good Friday.

373. Palm Sunday is a wonderful day whereby Catholic families can re-enact Christ's triumphant entry into Jerusalem as the son of David and King of the Jews.

374. Holy Thursday commemorates Christ's gifts of the priesthood and the Eucharist to the Church; it also provides a poignant lesson in humility through the 'washing of the feet' ceremony.

375. Good Friday ceremonies allow Catholics to re-live Christ's glorious passion and death on the Cross. At the same time, abstinence and fasting enable Catholics to unite their own sacrifices to Christ's.

376. The Saturday Easter Vigil enables Catholics to proclaim Christ as the 'Light' and welcome new members formally into the Church.

377. During the Easter Saturday Vigil, both the candidates for baptism as well as those in the congregation pronounce their baptismal promises to renounce Satan, together with his pomps and works, followed by a threefold affirmation to serve God and Jesus Christ faithfully in the one, holy, Catholic church.

378. Easter Sunday celebrates the day of 're-creation', or the 'eighth day', Christ's glorious resurrection from the dead. Christ's resurrection is continually celebrated every Sunday.

379.'Holy Days of Obligation' call upon Catholics to publicly commemorate the most important events and mysteries of the Christian story: *"He who observes the day, observes it in honor of the Lord"* (Rom. 14:6).

380.The 'Precepts of the Church' encourage Catholics to integrate into their spiritual lives regular Mass attendance on Sundays and 'Holy Days of Obligation', reception of the sacraments of Holy Communion and Penance, fasting and abstinence, works of piety and charity, support for the Church and her works, and to enter valid and holy marriages.

381.'Friday abstinence' is the regular practice whereby Catholics chose to abstain from meat on Fridays in honor of Christ's passion and death which occurred on a Friday. Compulsory abstinence from meat is now confined to Ash Wednesday and Good Friday, however, all Fridays remain days of penance requiring either abstinence from meat or an alternative voluntary penance.

382.Many prayers are said during pilgrimages. Pilgrimages have been undertaken by Catholics to places of special significance since the first centuries of Christianity. Those undertaking a pilgrimage do so for various reasons, either as an act of penance or thanksgiving, or in the hope of a cure or conversion, or any other important request or favor. The most significant pilgrimage sites include Rome, Jerusalem, Bethlehem, Santiago de Compostela, Assisi and Marian shrines such as Guadalupe, Lourdes and Fatima.

383.The tradition of visiting seven churches after the Mass of the Lord's Supper on Holy Thursday is an ancient Catholic practice originating in Rome. Pilgrims visit the seven major basilicas (St John Lateran, St Peter's Basilica, St Mary Major, St Paul-outside-the-Walls, St Lawrence-outside-the-Walls, St Sebastian-outside-the-Walls, and Holy Cross-in-Jerusalem) as penance and pray before the altar of repose in each church. This custom was revived in the 16th century by St Philip Neri.

384.The *Scala Sancta* are the stairs trod by Christ leading up to the praetorium of Pontius Pilate. They were brought to Rome in 326 by St Helena and are located in a building near the basilica of St John Lateran. Many pilgrims to Rome climb these stairs on their knees in honor of Christ's passion. No specific prayer is obligatory when ascending, though specific prayers have been composed for each step. A small prayer booklet is available from the Passionist Fathers who are the custodians of the shrine.

385. In 'vocation' prayers, Catholics ask God to reveal his will for our lives, how we can best serve him in this world, what will bring us the greatest happiness in this life and salvation in the next.

386. Catholics often say prayers for protection while they sleep. One such prayer reads, "Save us, Lord, while we are awake; protect us while we sleep; that we may keep watch with Christ and rest with him in peace."

387. In times of difficulty and trouble, Catholics traditionally resign themselves to the will of God. One example of a prayer of resignation reads, "In all things may the most holy, the most just, and the most lovable Will of God be done, praised, and exalted above all forever."

388. Catholics traditionally pray for 'a good death', namely, that they may be ready and willing to die when the Lord so wills, and so to die in a state of friendship with God, prepared to encounter Christ in judgment with the hope of receiving everlasting life.

389. Catholics continue to offer up prayers for the dead in accord with Old (2 Macc. 12:39-45) and New Testament practice: *"May the Lord grant mercy to the household of Onesiphorus, for he often refreshed me; he was not ashamed of my chains, but when he arrived in Rome he searched for me eagerly and found me – may the Lord grant him to find mercy from the Lord on that Day – and you well know all the service he rendered at Ephesus"* (2 Tim. 1:16-18).

390. Catholics continue to offer up Masses for the dead in accord with the practice of the early Church: "The Sacrament of the Eucharist, which the Lord commanded to be taken at meal times and by all, we take even before daybreak in congregations, but from the hand of none others except the presidents ... We offer sacrifices for the dead on their birthday anniversaries ... We take anxious care lest something of our Cup or Bread should fall upon the ground" (Tertullian, *The Crown* 3, 3-5, 211).

391.In the spirit of Christ's own prayer (John 17:22), Catholics pray for Christian unity, recognizing the good will that exists in many of those who live outside the visible Catholic Church, invoking Christ's aid that "all be united in one faith under one Shepherd."

392.There are numerous 'popular devotions' practised by Catholics which foster a great variety of prayer and piety. One of the most well-known and practised devotions is that to the Sacred Heart of Jesus. The Church dedicates the month of June to the Sacred Heart with a special feast day in its honor celebrated after *Corpus Christi*. The purpose of this devotion is to foster love for the Heart that has loved us so much and to imitate this love in our own lives: "*... learn from me; for I am gentle and lowly in heart*" (Matt. 11:29).

393.Catholics have devotion to the Holy Child Jesus, which fosters veneration of Christ's sacred infancy and the virtues of child-like innocence. Some of the most renowned Catholic saints had a strong devotion to the Divine Child, including St Francis of Assisi, St Anthony of Padua, St Teresa of Avila and St Therese of the Child Jesus.

394.Catholics have devotion to the Holy Face of Jesus to contemplate more deeply another aspect of the Incarnation, namely, that the infinite and eternal God deigned to take on human nature and undergo his passion and death out of love for humanity. In the words of St Therese of the Child Jesus: "O Jesus, Who in Thy bitter Passion didst become 'the most abject of men, a man of sorrows', I venerate Thy Sacred Face whereon there once did shine the beauty and sweetness of the Godhead."

395.Catholics have devotion to the Holy Name of Jesus as "the name that is above all names." The Church dedicates the month of January to the Holy Name of Jesus, with a special feast day on 3 January. The name itself means "Yahweh saves" and it is in Jesus' name that all Christian prayers should end. In the words of St Paul: "*... at the name of Jesus every knee should bow, in Heaven and on earth and under the earth*" (Phil. 2:10). Catholics through this devotion also seek to make amends for improper use of the Holy Name.

396.Catholics have devotion to the Precious Blood of Jesus shed on Mount Calvary as the price of redemption for the world. The Church dedicates the month of July to the Precious Blood with a special feast day on the first Sunday of that month. Devotion to the Blood of Christ is as old as the Church itself, as evident in the following words of St Clement of Rome (96): "Let us fix our gaze on the Blood of Christ and realize how truly precious it is, seeing that it was poured out for our salvation and brought the grace of conversion to the whole world."

397.Catholics have devotion to the Five Wounds of Jesus which he received during his Passion and which remain in his glorified resurrected body. Together with the shedding of his blood, Christ's wounds illustrate his love for humanity and the price he was willing to pay for our salvation: *"... he was wounded for our transgressions, he was bruised for our iniquities; upon him was the chastisement that made us whole, and with his stripes we are healed"* (Is. 53:5). Remaining in his glorified body, Christ's wounds are trophies of his victory over sin and death.

398.Catholics have a particular Good Friday devotion known as *Tre Ore*, or three hours, which honors Christ's time spent on the Cross between midday and 3.00pm. During this time, the preaching is based on the seven last words of Christ. After the final sermon, a priest detaches the corpus of Christ from the Crucifix and places it in an elaborate casket for veneration. In some Latin American countries noises are made and flashing powder ignited to simulate the thunder and lightning of the original Good Friday.

399.Catholics have devotion to the Holy Spirit through both prayers and novenas. The novena to the Holy Spirit prayed every year during the nine days from Ascension Thursday to Pentecost Sunday is considered the principal novena of the Church. In the words of St Alphonsus de Liguori: "The novena to the Holy Spirit is the chief of all novenas, because it was the first that was ever celebrated, and by the holy Mother of God with the Apostles in the upper-room."

400.Catholics have a devotion to the Holy Family as the perfect example of family life for all Christians. The Church dedicates the month of February to the Holy Family. In the words of Pope Leo XIII: "Nothing truly can be more salutary or efficacious for Christian families to meditate upon than the example of this Holy Family, which embraces the perfection and completeness of all domestic virtues."

401.Catholics have a devotion to the Immaculate Heart of Mary, acknowledging her perfect sinlessness and love of God. This devotion involves daily recitation of the Rosary, the reception of Holy Communion on the first Saturdays of the month in reparation for sins committed against Mary's Immaculate Heart, monthly meditation on the mysteries of the Rosary for fifteen minutes, and monthly confession.

402.Catholics have devotion to the Seven Sorrows of Mary with the aim of uniting oneself to the sufferings of Christ through the sufferings the Virgin Mary endured as Mother of God. The Church honors the Seven Sorrows of Mary on 15 September. The Seven Sorrows are all events found in Scripture and include the following: the prophecy of Simeon; the flight into Egypt; the 'loss' of Jesus and his finding in the Temple after three days; the meeting of Jesus and Mary along the Way of the Cross; the Crucifixion; the taking down of the body of Jesus from the Cross; Jesus laid in the tomb.

403.Catholics have a devotion to St Joseph, both as a model of authentic fatherhood and faithful spouse and for his intercession to obtain the grace of a happy and holy death: "O St Joseph, foster father of the Child Jesus and true spouse of the Blessed Virgin Mary, pray for us and for the dying of this day (or night). Amen." The Church honors St Joseph with a Feast Day on 19 March.

404.Catholics have a devotion to St Michael the Archangel as the special protector of the Church against the 'wickedness and snares of the devil': "Saint Michael the Archangel, defend us in the hour of battle. Be our safeguard against the wickedness and snares of the devil. May God rebuke him, we humbly pray, and do thou, O Prince of the Heavenly host, by the power of God cast into Hell Satan and all the other wicked spirits that prowl about the world seeking the ruin of souls. Amen." The Church honors St Michael with a Feast Day on 29 September.

405. Catholics have a devotion to the Holy Souls in Purgatory in order to relieve them of their sufferings and reduce their time in Purgatory. The Church dedicates the month of November to the Holy Souls, with a special feast day on 2 November. It is a great act of charity to assist the faithful departed, particularly through prayers, good works and the Holy Sacrifice of the Mass. According to Scripture: *"But if he was looking to the splendid reward that is laid up for those who fall asleep in godliness, it was a holy and pious thought. Therefore he made atonement for the dead, that they might be delivered from their sin"* (2 Macc. 12:45).

406. Often associated closely with prayer is the use by Catholics of 'sacramentals', usually some form of blessed material object that is an aid to prayer, devotion, or an instrument of grace. One popular form of sacramental is Holy Water, which is water that has been blessed by one in Holy Orders. Holy Water for thousands of years has been used for blessings (cf. Num. 5:17) and for Christians is a reminder of our baptism. St Teresa of Avila (+1582) once said, "I know by frequent experience that there is nothing which puts the devils to flight like Holy Water."

407. Another often-used sacramental are Holy Oils. In the Old Testament, oil symbolized abundance and joy and was used to anoint kings, priests and prophets. In the Catholic Church, blessed oils are used to anoint catechumens, the baptized, and the ordained to symbolize the anointee's calling as an anointed follower of Christ. When used sacramentally, e.g., in Confirmation and Anointing of the Sick, the oil is an instrument of added grace and healing.

408. Catholics traditionally accompany incense with their prayers, especially during the liturgy. Incense symbolizes how our prayers should be sweet-smelling and ascend Heaven-ward: *"And another angel came and stood at the altar with a golden censer; and he was given much incense to mingle with the prayers of all the saints upon the golden altar before the throne; and the smoke of the incense rose with the prayers of the saints from the hand of the angel before God"* (Rev. 8:3-4).

409. Catholics traditionally light 'votive candles' as a sign of one's intention to offer up prayer for another person. Lighted candles symbolize Christ as the "light of the world", the one who is the "*lamp to my feet and a light to my path*" (Ps. 119:105). In the words of Dom Prosper Guéranger, OSB, "St Anselm, Archbishop of Canterbury ... bids us consider three things in the blessed candle: the wax, the wick, and the flame. The wax, he says, which is the production of the virginal bee, is the flesh of our Lord; the wick, which is within, is his soul; the flame, which burns on top, is his divinity."

410. Palm branches are sacramentals distributed to the faithful on Palm Sunday to commemorate Christ's entry into Jerusalem (Matt. 21:1-11) and to honor his glory and kingship. Palms and olive branches are often kept in Catholic homes as a witness to faith in Christ as the messianic king. Individual Catholics also wear palm crosses during Holy Week to remind them of the need to carry our daily crosses patiently.

411. Rosary beads are one of the most well-known forms of sacramental. Most practising Catholics possess a set of Rosary beads that has been blessed by a priest. They symbolize a 'crown of roses' and assist the user to keep count of the prayers while they meditate on the great events in the lives of Jesus and Mary.

412. Catholics wear the Medal of Saint Benedict with the intention of calling down God's blessing and protection upon them, upon their homes and possessions, particularly through the intercession of St Benedict. Around the rim of the reverse side of the medal are the letters V R S N S M V - S M Q L I V B, which are the initial letters of a Latin prayer of exorcism against Satan: *Vade retro Satana! Nunquam suade mihi vana! Sunt mala quae libas. Ipse venena bibas!* ("Begone Satan! Never tempt me with your vanities! What you offer me is evil. Drink the poison yourself!").

413. One of the most popular medals worn by Catholics is the 'Miraculous Medal' fashioned after the apparition of the Virgin Mary to St Catherine Labouré in 1830. The front of the medal depicts the Virgin Mary standing on a globe with outstretched hands emitting rays of light surrounded by the words, "O Mary, conceived without sin, pray for us

who have recourse to thee." Mary promised great graces to those who wear this medal, especially if worn around the neck. Many thousands of miracles have been attributed to the medal.

414. The Brown Scapular is a miniature religious habit akin to the fully-sized scapulars worn by religious of the Carmelite Order. Devotion to the Brown Scapular originated in the 13th century stemming from the Virgin Mary's promise to St Simon Stock: "Whosoever dies wearing this scapular shall not suffer eternal fire. It shall be a sign of peace and a safeguard in times of danger." The Scapular is a reminder of Mary's special prayers and protection. In order to receive the benefits of the Scapular one must strive to live a holy life centred on Christ and Mary's intercession.

415. The Green Scapular consists of a single piece of green felt on a cord, with a picture of the Virgin Mary on one side and an image of Mary's Immaculate Heart pierced with a sword on the other. Those who wear or carry the Green Scapular are required to recite the following prayer daily: "Immaculate Heart of Mary, pray for us now and at the hour of our death." Use of this Scapular is renowned for graces of healing, especially the seriously ill, and conversion of loved ones and the obstinate.

416. The devotion to the Cord of St Joseph began in the 17th century following the miraculous cure of an Augustinian nun named Sr Elizabeth who had suffered for years from excruciating pains due to distemper. Devotion to the Cord and its associated prayers was formally approved by the Church in 1859. Every year, Cords are blessed in the Church of St Nicholas, Verona, especially for hospital patients. In addition to being worn as a remedy against physical ailments the Cord is also worn as a preservative of the virtue of purity.

417. Catholics traditionally use blessed salt to preserve them from demonic influence under the guise of sin, sickness, or other manifestation. Salt may be sprinkled in bedrooms, homes and cottages to prevent burglary, in vehicles and boats for safety, etc. A few grains sprinkled in drinking water or in food have been known to produce astonishing spiritual and physical benefits. Salt also reminds the Catholic that we are called to be *"the salt of the earth"* (Matt. 5:13), flavoring the world with the spirit of Christ.

418. An *Agnus Dei* is a sacramental made of wax blessed by the Pope and having the image of a lamb on one side and the Papal Coat of Arms on the other. It symbolizes Christ as Savior and is traditionally used as a protection against sickness, temptation, fire, storms and sudden death. Pregnant women also use it to obtain graces for safe delivery.

419. Blessed wedding rings are worn by Catholics as sacramentals, symbolizing the love and union of the husband and wife. As rings have no beginning or end, they also symbolize the 'never-ending' nature of marriage. An indulgence may be gained by couples who kiss a blessed ring and recite the following prayer: "Grant us, O Lord, that loving you, we may love each other and live according to your holy law."

420. Many young Catholics wear 'Chastity Rings' as a sacramental to signify their free pledge to abstain from all kinds of sexual activity until marriage. Many of these Catholics also commit themselves to the counter-cultural 'True Love Waits' movement.

421. Holy Cards have been used by Catholics as sacramentals and as aids to prayer since the 15th century. Holy Cards can serve multiple functions, including as a keepsake, a piece of art, or a stimulant to devotion. When Holy Cards have prayers on the back they are useful for teaching children or adults new prayers. Parishes usually distribute Holy Cards to promote devotion to the patron saint of the church or to pray for a certain intention or to commemorate a significant event, ordination or death.

Chapter 6
Great Sacraments!

Preliminary

Sacraments play an important role in the life of the Catholic Church and in the life of individual faithful Catholics. However, for many outside the Catholic fold sacraments are problematic, either because they seem to have little or no support in Scripture, or look as if they are mechanical 'works' rather than acts of faith, or appear to be obstacles to a direct personal relationship with Christ. There are also those who reject sacraments because they oppose the very idea that material objects can ever be vessels of spiritual grace.

Catholics, on the other hand, can point to passages in both the Old and New Testaments that together provide clear scriptural underpinnings for all seven sacraments, as well as numerous references in the writings of Church Fathers that testify to the importance of the sacraments in the life of the early Christians. Rather than being obstacles to a relationship with Christ, the sacraments are visible encounters with him through which Christians can receive his grace in all the important moments of life from cradle to grave. Being visible rites involving words and actions, sacraments conform to human nature which relates to the same. Involving material objects (water, oil, bread, wine), sacraments testify to the inherent goodness of material creation and the power of God to make such instruments of spiritual gifts.

Sacraments are also Christ's gifts to the Church so that the Church can continue to do his work of sanctification in the world. Through the sacraments, Christians receive sanctifying grace, the theological and moral virtues, the gifts of the Holy Spirit and actual graces to assist them to fulfil their specific vocation. Also, the Christian receives these graces irrespective of the worthiness of the minister, as Christ himself is the principal minister of all the sacraments.

Finally, while God binds himself to bestow grace every time a sacrament is properly administered he is not limited by the sacraments. God is still free to give grace as he chooses to whom he chooses outside of the sacraments, usually in response to our daily prayers and good works.

Reasons

422. Catholicism is fundamentally sacramental, using water, oil, bread and wine as instruments of God's grace. This illustrates Catholicism's recognition of the goodness of creation as both a gift and sign of God.

423. In connecting the bestowal of grace with material things such as water, oil, bread and wine, Christ gives to his people the consoling certainty through the senses of the precise moment when grace is bestowed. The sacraments are thus appropriately fitted to our human nature comprised of body and soul.

424. There are seven recognized sacraments in the Catholic Church, viz., Baptism, Confirmation, Blessed Eucharist, Penance, Anointing of the Sick, Holy Orders and Holy Matrimony. Baptism gives the soul birth to the supernatural order and a participation in God's own life; the Eucharist gives daily supernatural nourishment and strength through union with Christ's Body, Blood, Soul and Divinity; Confirmation gives the seven gifts of the Holy Spirit in added strength to lead the life of an adult Christian courageously; Penance restores the Christian to the life of grace after it has been lost through mortal sin; Holy Matrimony gives the Christian couple the grace to raise and educate their children for God in a life-long indissoluble union modelled on Christ's union with the Church; Holy Orders enables the clergy to faithfully carry out their mission on earth as 'other Christs'; and Anointing of the Sick assists the Christian to meet sickness and death with resignation, courage and peace of mind. The sacraments therefore provide grace for every individual and community need from the cradle to the grave.

425. According to Catholic teaching, three of the sacraments, namely Baptism, Confirmation and Holy Orders, confer a 'character.' A character is an indelible mark imprinted on the soul that, so-to-speak, demands, and where there is no obstacle, gives grace to the soul, as well as a right to actual graces. It can never be removed, not even by mortal sin. The characters given by Baptism, Confirmation and Holy Orders show that one belongs to Christ and respectively invest the Christian with a special office in the Church to receive, defend and administer divine things.

78

426. According to Catholic teaching, it is not essential that the minister of the sacrament be in a state of grace or even personally believes in the rite. This is due to the fact that the virtue of the sacrament comes not from the human minister but from Christ himself. As St Augustine says: "As for the proud minister he is to be ranked with the devil. Christ's gift is not thereby profaned: what flows through him keeps its purity, and what passes through him remains clear and reaches the fertile earth" (*Homilies on the Epistle of John* 5, 15, c. 416). This provides peace of mind to the recipient that he/she will receive Christ's grace irrespective of the minister's dispositions.

427. Catholics who live a sacramental life replicate the way of life of the early Christians, according to the witness of Tertullian of North Africa: "The flesh, then, is washed, so that the soul may be made clean. The flesh is anointed so that the soul may be dedicated to holiness. The flesh is signed, so that the soul too may be fortified. The flesh is shaded by the imposition of hands, so that the soul too may be illuminated by the Spirit. The flesh feeds on the Body and Blood of Christ, so that the soul may be nourished on God" (*The Resurrection of the Dead* 8, 3, c. 210).

428. Catholics are baptized *"in the name of the Father, and of the Son, and of the Holy Spirit"*, according to Christ's command to the Apostles (Matt. 28:19).

429. The Catholic Church recognizes the reception of baptism as fulfilling Christ's injunction to be *"born of water and the Spirit"* (John 3:5). Being 'born again' through baptism we become children of God and are given the right to inherit God's Kingdom.

430. Consistent with Scripture, the Catholic Church teaches that baptism is necessary for salvation: *"He who believes and is baptized will be saved ..."* (Mark 16:16); *"... unless one is born of water and the Spirit, he cannot enter the Kingdom of God"* (John 3:5).

431. The Catholic Church upholds belief in baptismal regeneration (spiritual washing by the Holy Spirit) consistent with the words of St Paul: *"But you were washed, you were sanctified, you were justified in the name of the Lord Jesus Christ and in the Spirit of our God"* (1 Cor. 6:11).

432. Through baptism, Catholics receive sanctifying grace to remove all stain of sin, original and actual (mortal and venial) (Acts 2:38; Acts 22:16).

433. Through baptism, Catholics also receive the supernatural infused virtues of faith, hope and charity, the seven gifts of the Holy Spirit (wisdom, understanding, counsel, fortitude, knowledge, piety, and fear of the Lord), and sacramental grace, that is, the right to actual graces of union, light and fruitfulness to enable us to live the Christian life.

434. Through baptism, Catholics are mystically incorporated into Christ, his death and resurrection (Rom. 6:3-7).

435. The Catholic Church's practice of baptizing the candidate by sprinkling water over the head (as distinct from full immersion in water) fulfils the Old Testament prophecy relating to water baptism found in Ezek. 36:25: *"I will sprinkle clean water upon you, and you shall be clean from all your uncleannesses, and from all your idols I will cleanse you."*

436. The Catholic Church's practice of baptizing children finds implicit support in the following injunction of St Peter: *"Repent, and be baptized every one of you in the name of Jesus Christ for the forgiveness of your sins; and you shall receive the gift of the Holy Spirit. For the promise is to you and to your children ..."* (Acts 2:38-39).

437. Infant baptism allows new-born children to be placed into God's grace as soon as possible through the faith of the parents, a practice evident in the early Church: "Baptize first the children; and if they can speak for themselves, let them do so. Otherwise, let their parents or other relatives speak for them" (St Hippolytus of Rome, *The Apostolic Tradition* 21, c. 215).

438. All baptized children have a sponsor chosen for them to make a profession of faith in the name of the baptized child during the ceremony and, together with the parents, help it to grow in and live a Christian life. A sponsor must be a confirmed Catholic not less than sixteen years of age living a life of faith befitting the role to be undertaken.

439. In addition to sacramental water baptism, the Catholic Church recognizes the efficacy of 'Baptism of Desire' and 'Baptism of Blood.' A person has a baptism of desire when he or she has perfect contrition for their sins and desires to do all necessary for salvation. This doctrine is proved from the following words of Christ: *"Therefore I tell you, her sins, which are many, are forgiven, for she loved much"* (Luke 7:47); *"Truly, I say to you, today you will be with me in Paradise"* (Luke 23:43). A person has a baptism of blood when he or she is put to death for the Faith, that is, dies as a martyr. Christ has promised salvation to those who give their lives for him: *"He who finds his life will lose it, and he who loses his life for my sake will find it"* (Matt. 10:39); *"So every one who acknowledges me before men, I also will acknowledge before my Father who is in heaven"* (Matt. 10:32).

440. The Catholic Church retains the sacrament of Confirmation (Acts 8:17), a sacrament discarded long ago by most non-Catholic denominations.

441. Through Confirmation, Catholics receive a further outpouring of the seven gifts of the Holy Spirit which strengthens and equips them fully to carry out Christ's mission as 'soldiers of Christ' (Acts 8:14-17).

442. The sacrament of Confirmation was administered in the early Church, as evidenced by St Hippolytus of Rome: "The bishop, imposing his hands on them ... Then pouring the consecrated oil into his hands and imposing it on the head of the baptized, he shall say: 'I anoint you with holy oil in the Lord, the Father Almighty and Christ Jesus and the Holy Spirit.' And signing them on the forehead he shall kiss them and say: 'The Lord shall be with you.' And he that has been signed shall say: 'And with your spirit.' Thus shall he do with each" (*The Apostolic Tradition* 22, c. 215).

443. Each candidate for confirmation has a 'sponsor' who should be a confirmed Catholic in good standing, at least sixteen years of age, and who is not a parent of the candidate. The sponsor is responsible to do what he or she can to ensure that the candidate behaves as a true witness of Christ and faithfully fulfils the duties inherent in this sacrament.

444. In celebrating the Mass, Catholic priests fulfil what Christ commanded at the Last Supper: *"Do this in remembrance of me"* (Luke 22:19).

445. The Catholic Church celebrates the Mass on an altar, in the same way the early Christians gathered around *"an altar from which those who serve the tent have no right to eat"* (Heb. 13:10).

446. The Mass is a 're-presentation' of the Sacrifice of Calvary, making that same sacrifice present to Christians today in an unbloody and sacramental form.

447. The Mass makes the glorified High Priestly Christ present among Christians today, the same Christ who is the *"mediator of a new covenant, and to the sprinkled blood that speaks more graciously than the blood of Abel"* (Heb. 12:24).

448. The Catholic Church celebrates the Eucharist every Sunday and more (not monthly or quarterly), as was the case in the days of the Apostles (Acts 2:42).

449. The Eucharist not only bestows grace but contains the very Author of Grace himself — Jesus Christ!

450. The Eucharist is the new 'manna' from Heaven, providing a greater spiritual benefit than the Old Testament manna: *"Your fathers ate the manna in the wilderness, and they died. This is the bread which comes down from heaven, that a man may eat of it and not die"* (John 6:49-50).

451. The Catholic Church only obliges reception of the Eucharist once a year, at or about Easter time (Fourth Lateran Council, 1215), though daily reception is highly encouraged in imitation of the early Christians: "And we ask that this bread be given us daily, so that we who are in Christ and daily receive the Eucharist as the food of salvation, may not ... be withheld from the Heavenly Bread, and be separated from Christ's Body" (St Cyprian of Carthage, *The Lord's Prayer* 18, 251-252).

452. The Catholic Church allows any Catholic who has reached the age of reason, is validly baptized, and has been properly instructed in its nature to receive the Eucharist.

453. In receiving the Eucharist, Catholics receive *"the food which endures to eternal life"* (John 6:27).

454. In receiving the Eucharist, Catholics eat that bread which Christ calls *"my flesh"* (John 6:51).

455. In receiving the Eucharist, Catholics eat the "flesh" and drink the "blood" of Christ (John 6:53).

456. Through faithfully eating the flesh and drinking the blood of Christ Catholics enjoy *"eternal life"* and the promise of being raised up *"at the last day"* (John 6:54).

457. Christ's teachings on the Eucharist are *"a hard saying"* (John 6:60). Catholics, on the other hand, profess the faith of Simon Peter who answered, *"Lord, to whom shall we go? You have the words of eternal life"* (John 6:68).

458. Like St Paul, Catholics recognize that the *"cup of blessing"* blessed during the Eucharistic liturgy is *"a participation in the blood of Christ"* and the *"bread"* that is broken is *"a participation in the body of Christ"* (1 Cor. 10:16).

459. Like the early Christians, Catholics who *"eat this bread and drink the cup ... proclaim the Lord's death until he comes"* (1 Cor. 11:26).

460. The Catholic Church encourages her members to *"examine"* themselves before receiving the Eucharist as per St Paul's exhortation (1 Cor. 11:28).

461. The Catholic Church encourages faithful reception of the Eucharist through her teaching that the grace received is often in proportion to the faith and charity of those partaking of it.

462.The Catholic Church acknowledges that those who receive the Eucharist *"in an unworthy manner will be guilty of profaning the body and blood of the Lord"* (1 Cor. 11:27).

463.Worthy reception of Holy Communion gives Catholics an increase of sanctifying grace and the aid of actual graces to help live the life of holiness. Holy Communion nourishes the soul by giving it new energy, fervor and vitality and helps it to resist sin by stifling our carnal appetites, weakening our sensual and worldly desires, and opening our eyes and minds to a love of the things of God.

464.The Catholic Church reserves consecrated Holy Communion hosts in the 'Tabernacle' of each church, enabling Christ to continue his presence in a most special way among his faithful akin to how Yahweh perpetually dwelt among the Israelites (*Shekinah Kabod*) in the days of the Tabernacle and the Temple.

465.Catholics who attend Mass and receive the Eucharist worthily imitate the earliest Christians according to the testimony of St Ignatius of Antioch: "Take care, then, to use one Eucharist, so that whatever you do, you do according to God: for there is one Flesh of Our Lord Jesus Christ, and one cup in the union of his Blood; one altar, as there is one bishop with the presbyters and my fellow servants, the deacons" (*Letter to the Philadelphians* 4, 1, c. 110).

466.The Catholic Church continues to forgive sins through her ordained ministers (bishops and priests) using the power of the Holy Spirit given by Christ to his Apostles immediately after his resurrection: *"'Peace be with you. As the Father has sent me, even so I send you.' And when he had said this, he breathed on them, and said to them, 'Receive the Holy Spirit. If you forgive the sins of any, they are forgiven; if you retain the sins of any, they are retained'"* (John 20:21ff).

467.In having their sins forgiven through the sacrament of Penance, Catholics rejoice that God has *"given such authority to men"* (Matt. 9:8). In describing this same gift, St Paul says that God *"gave us the ministry of reconciliation"* (2 Cor. 5:18).

468. The sacrament of Penance is in the words of St Jerome "a second plank" (*To Demetrius*, Epistle 130:9, 414) or second chance for those who fall into serious sin after baptism.

469. Catholics who confess their sins in the sacrament of Penance imitate the earliest Christians according to the testimony of St Cyprian of Carthage: "I beseech you, brethren, let everyone who has sinned confess his sin while he is still in this world, while his confession is still admissible, while satisfaction and remission made through the priests are pleasing before the Lord" (*The Lapsed* 29, 251).

470. In the sacrament of Penance, Catholics who sincerely repent enjoy the great consolation of hearing that their sins are forgiven: "Through the ministry of the Church may God give you pardon and peace; and I absolve you of your sins in the name of the Father and of the Son and of the Holy Spirit. Amen."

471. In addition to having their sins forgiven through the sacrament of Penance, Catholics can also obtain genuine peace of mind. Experience testifies as to how many mental difficulties that arise from great guilt or fear of death and judgment are prevented or eradicated by frequent confession.

472. Catholics who go to confession to confess all venial sins and faults committed receive grace to avoid future venial sins, as well as a total or partial remission of the debt of temporal punishment.

473. The sacrament of Penance for Catholics is also an excellent means of obtaining sound spiritual advice from one experienced in the direction of souls.

474. Catholics who confess their sins in the sacrament of Penance are guaranteed anonymity by some of the strictest laws of the Church: "A confessor who directly violates the sacramental seal incurs a *latae sententiae* (automatic) excommunication reserved to the Apostolic See" (*Code of Canon Law* #1388). This seal applies not only to the priest, but also to anyone who overhears or learns of confessional sins in any way.

475. The Catholic Church anoints the elderly, sick and dying in the sacrament of Anointing of the Sick as commanded by Christ (Mark 6:13) and practised by the Apostles: *"Is any among you sick? Let him call for the elders of the church, and let them pray over him, anointing him with oil in the name of the Lord; and the prayer of faith will save the sick man, and the Lord will raise him up; and if he has committed sins, he will be forgiven"* (Jas. 5:14-15).

476. The sacrament of Anointing of the Sick is not only available to those who are at the point of death but also to any of the faithful in danger of death from sickness or old age.

477. Through the sacrament of Anointing, Catholics receive forgiveness of sins and spiritual peace of mind in preparation for meeting Christ. All mortal and venial sins are remitted; the 'Apostolic Blessing' given in conjunction with the sacrament remits the debt of temporal punishment due to sin.

478. When fruitfully received, Anointing of the Sick gives an increase in sanctifying grace and, through actual grace, enables the recipient to endure more easily the sufferings and pains of sickness, and to resist with greater fortitude the last attacks of the devil.

479. The Catholic Church continues to ordain her leaders through a visible rite of ordination: *"While they were worshiping the Lord and fasting, the Holy Spirit said, 'Set apart for me Barnabas and Saul for the work to which I have called them.' Then after fasting and praying they laid their hands on them and sent them off"* (Acts 13:2-3).

480. The Catholic rite of ordination through the laying on of hands is again evident in the writings of St Paul: *"I remind you to rekindle the gift of God that is within you through the laying on of my hands ..."* (2 Tim. 1:6).

481. The Catholic priest is 'another Christ', visibly continuing in the world Christ's work of teaching, sanctifying and governing as *"stewards of the mysteries of God"* (1 Cor. 4:1).

482. The Catholic Church retains the orders of deacon, presbyter and bishop as evident in the writings of St Paul (1 Tim. 3:1; Tit. 1:5; 1 Tim. 3:8).

483. The Catholic Church's priestly hierarchy is substantially identical to that of the early Church as evident in the writings of St Ignatius of Antioch: "You must all follow the bishop as Jesus Christ follows the Father, and the presbytery as you would the Apostles. Reverence the deacons as you would the command of God. Let no one do anything of concern to the Church without the bishop" (*Letter to the Smyrnaeans* 8, 1, c. 110).

484. In offering up the Eucharist to God the Father in the Holy Sacrifice of the Mass, the Catholic priesthood fulfils the prophecy of the "pure offering" uttered by the Prophet Malachi four centuries before Christ: *"I have no pleasure in you, says the Lord of hosts, and I will not accept an offering from your hand. For from the rising of the sun to its setting my name is great among the nations, and in every place incense is offered to my name, and a pure offering; for my name is great among the nations, says the Lord of hosts"* (Mal. 1:10-11).

485. By virtue of the sacrament of Holy Orders Catholics can enjoy the spiritual benefit of blessings given "in the name of the Father and of the Son and of the Holy Spirit" by deacons, priests or bishops.

486. In having a distinct ministerial priesthood, the Catholic Church fulfils the prophecy uttered by Isaiah concerning the Gentiles: *"And they shall bring all your brethren from all the nations as an offering to the Lord, upon horses, and in chariots, and in litters, and upon mules, and upon dromedaries, to my holy mountain Jerusalem, says the Lord, just as the Israelites bring their cereal offering in a clean vessel to the house of the Lord. And some of them also I will take for priests and for Levites, says the Lord"* (Is. 66:20-21).

487. The Catholic Church continues to uphold marriage as a sacrament, consistent with Scripture (Matt. 19:4-5; 1 Cor. 7:14; Eph. 5:25-33) and 2,000 years of tradition.

488. Faithful Catholics who enter the sacrament of Holy Matrimony enter a covenantal relationship of total mutual self-giving that attracts God's graces to assist both parties to faithfully carry out the duties of the married state. This assistance begins with the blessing bestowed by the celebrant (deacon, priest or bishop) during the wedding ceremony.

489. When Catholics enter into a sacramental marriage a 'marital bond' is formed that makes the couple a living image of Christ and the Church, and urges them to imitate this relationship in their own lives.

490. Though opposed to divorce, the Catholic Church permits a separation of husband and wife in certain cases where moral necessity requires, e.g., cruelty, adultery, anti-Catholic activity, apostasy, living a criminal and disreputable life, but neither party may marry again during the lifetime of the other.

491. The Catholic Church recognizes the *Pauline Privilege* (1 Cor. 7:12-15) which allows separation and remarriage in the case when one member of an unbaptized couple converts and is baptized and the other partner inhibits the practise of their new faith. In such circumstances the baptized partner is free to leave the unbaptized spouse and enter a sacramental marriage.

492. Understanding the covenantal and sacramental nature of Holy Matrimony, the Catholic Church allows 'annulments' where it is ascertained that some essential element was absent at the time of marriage. Grounds for annulment include, e.g., psychological immaturity or incapacity, consent extracted through force or fear, deceit or fraud perpetrated to secure consent, an intention to have no children, an intention to exclude fidelity or permanence.

Chapter 7
Great Miracles!

Preliminary

In Scripture, miracles served as 'signs' to give credibility to the claims of Jesus of Nazareth that he was the divine Son of God. Before he ascended into Heaven, Christ gave the Church power to do the same miraculous works as he did, as a proof of her divine authority.

Some ask, "How come miracles happened only in the past? Why don't we see miracles happening today?" Despite the claims of some, miracles did not cease with the death of the Apostles. Miracles have occurred in every age, and are still occurring in our own days.

There are 'divine' miracles that evidence the existence of God; there are 'Christian' miracles that evidence the truth of Christianity; and there are 'Catholic' miracles that testify to the truth of distinctly Catholic beliefs. The purpose of this chapter is to outline many examples of miracles that prove the truth of Catholicism.

There are many types of 'Catholic' miracles. There are miracles that testify to the efficacy of relics as instruments of God's grace. There are 'stigmata' and incorrupt bodies that testify to the sanctity of living and past followers of Christ. There are Eucharistic miracles that prove that the Host consecrated by the priest during Mass has become something different, has become the Body and Blood of Christ. There are miracles resulting from the invocation of deceased saints. There are miracles associated with the Marian Shrine of Our Lady of Lourdes in France, as well as miracles involving statues and images of Christ and the Virgin Mary. Finally, there are 'miscellaneous' miracles which do not fit into any of the above categories but are each significant in their own right. All these miracles have undergone numerous scientific and medical tests, including the most rigorous in modern times, concluding that something with no natural explanation has undoubtedly occurred.

Together, all these miracles form an impressive testimony that God still works among us and does so through the Catholic Church. This is modern 'good news' that should be known by all Catholics and people of good will. Let us proclaim this good news to all and sundry.

Reasons

493.St Januarius was a bishop martyred during the Diocletian persecution in 305. Three times a year (beginning on the first Sunday in May, 19 September and 16 December), the relic of St Januarius' blood, contained as powdery and solid elements in a silver and glass vial, liquefies without any scientific explanation. This miracle is repeated each year, being first recorded in 1389.

494.St Pantaleon died a martyr during the Diocletian persecution in 305. The Monastery of the Incarnation in Madrid, Spain, houses a phial of St Pantaleon's blood, permanently kept in a glass capsule, which remains solid throughout the year except on his Feast Day, 27 July, when it liquefies for twenty-four hours. Thousands come to witness this event every year; some are miraculously healed of infirmities. According to pious legend, failure of the blood to liquefy portends disaster.

495.Stigmatas are an extremely rare phenomenon in which the five wounds of Christ suddenly manifest in the body of an individual. The Church recognizes stigmata as a particular favor from God to men and women of noted holiness enabling them to participate intimately in the passion of Christ. The first man and woman recorded to have received the gift of stigmata were St Francis of Assisi and St Catherine of Siena.

496.St Gemma Galgani first received the stigmata of the wounds of Christ on 8 June, 1899, the Vigil of the feast of the Sacred Heart of Jesus. They were witnessed and carefully examined by her spiritual director and biographer. The wounds would appear every week at 8.00pm on Thursday night and continue until 3.00pm the following Friday. Intense pain and blood flow would accompany each appearance of the stigmata. This phenomenon lasted until early 1900, when it stopped at the command of St Gemma's spiritual director.

497.St Pio of Pietrelcina first received visible signs of stigmata on 17 September, 1915. On 5 August, 1918, his side was mystically pierced, followed on 20 September with further piercings of his hands and feet. Blood would henceforth flow continuously from these wounds. These five wounds remained visible in his body for the next fifty years, disappearing mysteriously a few moments after his death on 23 September, 1968.

498.Bl. Anne Catherine Emmerich from 1802 until her death bore the wounds of the Crown of Thorns and, after 1812, the full stigmata of Christ, including a cross over her heart. These wounds were judged as authentic by a diocesan commission of doctors and clergy. At the end of 1818 Emmerich was partially granted her prayer to be relieved of the stigmata, with the wounds in her hands and feet closing. However, on each Good Friday all these wounds reopened again.

499.Therese Neumann was a German mystic favored with visions and the stigmata, which bled on Fridays and during the final two weeks of Lent. She also received miraculous interventions on the beatification and canonization days of St Therese of the Child Jesus, curing her respectively of blindness and paralysis in 1923 and 1925. From 1927 she ate no food at all, surviving solely on daily Holy Communion until her death in 1962. No official Church statement has yet to be released concerning her.

500.Numerous Eucharistic miracles have occurred over the centuries. In the late 6th century, while celebrating Mass in the church of St Peter, Pope St Gregory the Great noticed that among the congregation was a woman laughing out loud. She happened to be the same woman who had prepared the hosts for Mass. On being challenged by the Pope as to why she laughed, the woman stated she could not bring herself to believe how the very bread she had prepared with her own hands was now the Body and Blood of Christ. St Gregory then forbad her from receiving Communion and began to pray for her enlightenment. He had just completed his prayer when he saw one of the Hosts turn into flesh and blood. Witnessing this herself, the woman repented, fell upon her knees, and began to weep. Relics from this miracle are still preserved to this day at the Benedictine Monastery in Andechs, Germany.

501.During Mass celebrated by a priest-monk of the Order of St Basil around the year 700, the Host suddenly turned into a circle of human flesh and the wine turned into visible human blood. The latter eventually dried into five stone-sized pellets. For the next twelve centuries the Host and the pellets remained housed in an elaborate reliquary in the town of Lanciano, Italy. In 1971, a detailed medical and scientific investigation found that the Host was indeed human heart muscle and the pellets were human blood, both blood type AB. This miracle in currently housed and viewable in the Tabernacle above the high altar of the Church of St Francis in Lanciano.

502. Around the year 1000, a non-Christian woman, pretending to be a Christian, stole a consecrated Host during Mass and proceeded to take it home. She placed the Host onto a pan containing boiling oil and began to fry it over a fire. Suddenly, the Host became flesh and such a flow of blood poured forth that it spilled onto the floor. The woman, now terrified, screamed and shouted repeatedly until she drew the attention of the whole neighborhood, including the civil and Church authorities. The relic of this Eucharistic miracle is currently preserved in the Church of St Andrew at Trani in the Puglis region of Italy.

503. In his own words, the great Doctor of the Church, St Peter Damian, describes a Eucharistic miracle he witnessed: "This is a Eucharistic event of great importance. It took place in 1050. Giving in to a horrible temptation, a woman was about to take the Eucharistic Bread home to use the Sacred Species for sorcery. But a priest noticed what she had done and ran after her, taking away from her the Host she had sacrilegiously stolen. Then he unfolded the white linen cloth in which the sacred Host had been wrapped and found that the Host had been transformed in such a way that half had become visibly the Body of Christ, while the other half preserved the normal look of a Host. With such a clear testimony, God wanted to win over unbelievers and heretics who refused to accept the Real Presence of the Eucharistic mystery: in one half of the consecrated bread the Body of Christ was visible, while in the other the natural form, thus highlighting the reality of the sacramental transubstantiation taking place at the Consecration."

504. In the town of Blaine, France, in 1153 a young girl by the name of Agnes refused to believe in the Real Presence of Christ in the Blessed Sacrament. During the High Mass of the feast of the Holy Spirit

celebrated by Archbishop Anculphe de Pierrefonds, Agnes and the entire congregation witnessed the Host suddenly change into an image of the Infant Jesus. This occurred precisely at the moment of elevation. Agnes converted immediately and founded a convent where the miraculous Host was housed for centuries until the French Revolution.

505. During Mass on Easter Sunday, 1171, in the Italian city of Ferrara, at the moment when the Host was broken into two, a stream of blood suddenly gushed forth sprinkling the marble vault behind the altar, while the Host visibly turned into human flesh. News of the miracle spread rapidly and the Bishop of Ferrara and the Archbishop of Ravenna rushed to the scene to verify the event. All agreed that the flesh and blood were the flesh and blood of Christ. To this day the crimson colored miraculous blood is still visible on the marble vault which is located in a splendid setting in the city's basilica of St Mary in Vado.

506. In 1194 in the city of Augsburg, Germany, a woman clandestinely removed a consecrated Host after Mass for private adoration in her home. Troubled in conscience, the same woman returned the Host five years later to the priests of the church of the Holy Cross. After receiving the Host, the priests noticed that part of it had changed into flesh with clearly evident red streaks. The Host was then transferred to the city cathedral where a second miracle took place: it expanded and became blood-red. At the suggestion of the Bishop, the miraculous Host was placed in a crystal container and returned to the church of the Holy Cross. It remains there to this day in perfect condition, and every year on 11 May a solemn feast is observed in commemoration of the miracle.

507. In 1228 in the Italian town of Alatri, a young woman, desperate to win back the love of her fiancé, consulted a sorceress who advised her to steal a consecrated Host and use it to concoct a love potion. Upon returning home with a stolen Host wrapped in a cloth, the woman was shocked to discover that it had transformed into bleeding flesh. The woman and the sorceress then returned the Host to the local bishop, begging for his pardon. In a Papal Bull dated 13 March, 1228, Pope Gregory IX acknowledged the miracle and declared that it was a sign from God confirming the truth of the Real Presence against the heresies prevalent at

the time. The miraculous Host is today still preserved intact in the town's cathedral of St Paul the Apostle.

508. On 30 December, 1230, a priest named Uguccione, having finished celebrating Mass for a group of nuns, did not realize that he had left several drops of consecrated wine in the chalice. The next day Fr Uguccione returned to find at the bottom of the chalice drops of coagulated blood. These were shown to the nuns, the clergy, the bishop, and then to the Florentine locals. The Bishop placed the miraculous blood in a crystal cruet and again showed the people. Eventually, the miraculous blood was returned to the nuns for safe-keeping near the Basilica of St Ambrose. The miraculous blood is still visible today, conserved in a reliquary inside a white marble Tabernacle.

509. In the same Basilica of St Ambrose of Florence, this time on 24 March, 1595, a second Eucharistic miracle took place after the main altar cloth caught fire, damaging the altar and the Tabernacle. In the commotion, a pyx with six consecrated Hosts was knocked to the ground, with the Hosts falling onto the smouldering carpet. The heat of the carpet fused the six Hosts together and caused them to become twisted and curled; otherwise, they remained intact. In the years that followed, the Hosts remained incorrupt, and were officially declared to be miraculously so by the Archbishop of Florence in 1628. Every May, these Hosts, together with the coagulated blood of 1230, are exposed for public adoration during the Forty Hours devotion.

510. In 1239, the Spanish Christian cities of Daroca, Teruel, and Calatayud joined forces to reconquer the castle of Chio Luchente from the Moors. Before the battle, Mass was celebrated, in the course of which six Hosts were consecrated for the six leading captains. A surprise attack by the Moors forced Mass to be suspended and the six consecrated Hosts were hurriedly wrapped in the corporal and hidden under a rock. The Moors were repelled, and after the battle the corporal was recovered, whence it was discovered that the six Hosts were soaked in blood. The commanders, interpreting this as a great sign of divine favor, consumed the Hosts and tied the blood-stained corporal to a lance so as to make a standard. They then proceeded to attack the Moors and reconquered the castle of Chio

Luchente. Afterwards, a church dedicated to the Virgin Mary was built at Daroca together with a precious reliquary, where to this day it is still possible to venerate the blood-stained corporal.

511. In 1242, the Tartars were ravaging the countryside of Moravia and turned their sights to conquering the city of Olmütz. Jaroslas of Sternberg led an army of 12,000 men in defense of the city. The day before the battle he made confession of his sins and received the Eucharist. His army followed suit. Jaroslas also arranged five consecrated Hosts to be placed in a ciborium and carried into battle with a priest on horseback. The ensuing battle resulted in a great triumph for the Christians, with the leader of the Tartars being killed and their remaining forces vacating Moravia. On returning the Hosts after the battle, the priest opened the ciborium only to find that all five of them exhibited a shiny rosy-colored circle. This was taken as a sign that it was the hand of God that gave them the victory.

512. In 1247, a woman living in the Portuguese town of Santarem was unhappy because she believed her husband was unfaithful to their marriage vows. Desperate to win back her husband's affection, the woman was convinced by the town witch that she could recover her husband's love in return for a stolen consecrated Host. Agreeing reluctantly, the woman stole a Host from the parish church of St Stephen and then placed it in her head scarf. While on her way to the house of the witch, the Host began to bleed. Panicking, the woman hid the Host at the bottom of a wooden chest in her house, only to see brilliant rays of light shining therefrom during the night, waking the woman and her husband. Both saw angels adoring the bleeding Host and then joined them kneeling in adoration and reparation. The next morning they informed the parish priest, who returned the Host to the Church of St Stephen in a solemn procession. The Host remains intact today, irregularly shaped and with delicate veins running up and down its length, and contained in a pear-shaped monstrance with a quantity of miraculous blood at the bottom. The church of St Stephen is now named the "The Church of the Holy Miracle."

513. In 1254, in the town of Douai, France, a consecrated Host was accidentally dropped to the ground while communion was being

distributed to the faithful. Seeing the dropped Host, the priest moved to pick it up, only for it to suddenly fly up and rest on the purificator. A short time later, a lovely Child appeared at the same spot, seen by all the faithful and religious present. To this day on every Thursday in the church of St Peter of Douai numerous faithful gather in prayer before the miraculous Host.

514. In 1263, a German priest, Peter of Prague, stopped at Bolsena while on pilgrimage to Rome. He was a pious priest but was troubled with doubts about the Real Presence of Christ in the Eucharist. While celebrating Mass in the church of St Christina, blood began to drip from the Host and trickle over his hands onto the altar and the corporal. Fr Peter was confused and attempted to hide the blood, but then ended the Mass and made his way to the neighboring city of Orvieto, where Pope Urban IV was then residing. The Pope heard Fr Peter's account and absolved him and then ordered an immediate investigation. When all the facts were verified, the Pope ordered that the Host and the blood-stained corporal be brought to Orvieto. Amid great pomp, the relics were placed in the cathedral. One year later, Urban IV instituted the feast of *Corpus Christi*. The linen corporal bearing the spots of blood is still enshrined and exhibited in the Cathedral of Orvieto, while the blood stains are still visible on the paved floor of the church of St Christina in Bolsena.

515. In 1280, in the town of Lanciano, a woman named Richiarella went to a witch and asked her how she could recover her husband's love. The witch advised her to steal a consecrated Host, cook it until it became powder and then sprinkle the powder into her husband's food. The Host, however, was transformed into living flesh. Horrified, Richiarella wrapped the bloodied Host in a linen handkerchief and buried it under the manure in her husband's stable. Seven years later, Richiarella confessed her sin to the prior of the Augustinian priory in Lanciano, Giacomo Diotallevi, a native of Offida. The priest went to the stable and recovered the Host. The reliquary containing the miraculous Host is today exposed in the Church of St Augustine in Offida. Every year on 3 May the people of Offida commemorate the anniversary of the miracle.

516. In Aninon, Spain, around the year 1300, a fire ravaged the Church of Our Lady of Castile. Everything in the church was destroyed, including the main altar and the Tabernacle. However, lying amidst the ruins were five bleeding Hosts and a sixth Host stuck to the pall. In response, the people constructed a new church to honor the miraculous Hosts to which they flocked in adoration over the ensuing centuries. On 23 November, 1613, the Vicar General of Tarazona approved the miracle.

517. On Easter Sunday, 1290, a man named Jonathas, who opposed the Catholic faith and denied the Real Presence of Christ in the Holy Eucharist, managed to obtain a consecrated Host. In his fury, Jonathas stabbed the Host with his knife and it began to bleed. Terrified, Jonathas threw the Host into the fire, but it miraculously arose from it. Desperate, he then threw the Host into boiling water, only for it to again arise, hovering in mid-air. Finally, Jonathas placed the Host in the bowl of a parishioner of Saint-Jean-en-Grève who brought it to her parish priest. There it remained for centuries in a small reliquary until it was destroyed during the French Revolution.

518. In 1317, a priest in Viversel, Belgium, was asked to take Holy Communion to a sick man in the village. The priest arrived with a consecrated Host in a Ciborium. He placed the Ciborium on a table and then went to speak to some members of the sick man's family. Meanwhile, another relative saw the Ciborium and moved by curiosity lifted the cover and held the consecrated Host. The Host then began to bleed. Frightened, he threw the Host back into the Ciborium and scurried away. When the priest went to give Holy Communion to the sick man he found the Host stained with blood. The priest told his bishop of the event and the bishop ordered him to take the Host to the church of the Cistercian nuns in Herkenrode. The Sacred Host remained there until 1796, when the nuns were expelled by French revolutionaries. In 1804, the Host was removed from its hiding place and carried in solemn procession to the Cathedral of St Quentin in Hasselt. The Reliquary with the sacred Host remains perfectly preserved and continues to receive the adoration of the faithful to this day.

519.In 1330, a priest was asked to bring Holy Communion to a sick peasant. The priest, however, irreverently placed a consecrated Host between two pages of his breviary and made his way to the peasant's home. After hearing the peasant's confession, the priest opened up his breviary only to find that the Host was stained with living blood, enough to soak through the two pages between which it had been placed. The priest, confused and repentant, set out to the Augustinian monastery in Siena to seek the counsel of a Fr Simon Fidati, a monk well-known for his piety. Fr Simon absolved the priest and asked if he could keep the two pages stained with the precious blood. The relics of the two pages are today preserved in the Basilica of St Rita in Cascia.

520.On Easter Sunday, 1331, Mass was offered by Fr Hugues de la Baume, the vicar of Blanot. One of the parishioners to receive Holy Communion was a woman named Jacquette. Fr Hugues placed the Host on her tongue, but it fell from the woman's mouth and landed upon the cloth that covered her hands. The priest immediately approached the railing, but instead of finding the Host, he saw a spot of blood the same size as the Host. When the Mass was completed, the priest took the cloth and placed the stained area in a basin of water. After washing the spot and scrubbing it numerous times he found that, instead of becoming smaller and lighter, it had become larger and darker. The priest then took a knife and cut from the cloth the piece bearing the imprint of the blood. This square piece of cloth was reverently placed in the Tabernacle. To this day, each year on Easter Monday, according to ancient custom, the relic is solemnly exposed in the church of Blanot.

521.On 12 March, 1345, a devout Catholic man in Amsterdam, Holland, became very ill. He told his family he wanted to receive Holy Viaticum. Immediately after receiving Communion the man vomited and the family disposed of the contents in the fire. The next morning the Blessed Sacrament was found in the midst of the ashes, with a light surrounding it. The woman who rescued the Host found that it was cold. She then took it home and asked a priest to come and have a look at it. The priest notified the clergy of Amsterdam and a procession was held to carry the Host to the church. The sick man's home soon became a chapel and from 1360 public processions and pilgrims traveled to the site. One pilgrim was

Archduke Maximilian, later Emperor, who came and received a cure in 1480. In thanksgiving, the Archduke added a beautiful window to the chapel. The original chapel no longer exists; however, devotion to this Eucharistic miracle still takes place on 12 March each year at the church nearest the site.

522. In 1356, an anonymous priest in the city of Macerata, Italy, harbored strong doubts about the doctrine of transubstantiation. During Mass on 25 April, immediately after the priest broke the Host, blood began to drop and fall onto the corporal and chalice. The priest immediately informed his bishop, Nicholas of San Martino, who ordered a regular canonical process, which quickly declared the miracle as authentic. The Bishop then ordered that the blood-stained corporal be housed in the Cathedral of Holy Mary Assumed and St Giuliano. Since the mid-14th century, the corporal has been carried in solemn procession through the city, enclosed in a crystal and silver urn. To this day, the relic of the "corporal marked by blood" is preserved under the Most Holy Sacrament altar, together with the original parchment on which the miracle is described.

523. On 4 October, 1369, a golden ciborium containing sixteen consecrated Hosts was stolen from the church of St Catherine in Brussels, Belgium. The instigator of the theft, a wealthy anti-Christian merchant by the name of Jonathon, was murdered two weeks later. Fearing that his murder was punishment for the theft, Jonathon's wife disposed of the Hosts to friends of her husband, who were also violently anti-Christian. On Good Friday, 1370, these friends gathered together and began hurling verbal and physical abuse upon the Hosts, including stabbing them with knives. To their horror the Hosts began to bleed. In their fear, the desecrators entrusted the surviving Hosts to a Christian woman named Catherine, who eventually returned them to the curate of the Bishop of Cambrai and Brussels. Three of the Hosts were eventually brought in solemn procession and housed in the Cathedral of St Michael. For centuries afterwards a feast in commemoration of the miracle was celebrated every 15 July. The history of the miracle is depicted in the Cathedral's stained-glass windows, paintings and tapestries which continue to be displayed annually during the months of July and August.

524. During Lent of 1374 in the town of Middleburg a servant named Jean, who had not gone to confession for many years, attended Mass at the request of his new employer. As he received Holy Communion on his tongue, it suddenly turned into bleeding flesh. Shocked, Jean spat the Host out of his mouth, as blood from the Host trickled onto the cloth which covered the altar railing. The priest immediately placed the miraculous Host on a tray inside the Tabernacle. Jean, repenting, confessed his sins in front of all present. The Archbishop, after detailed investigations, approved the miracle and the devotion surrounding it. A part of the Host is still preserved today in the monastery of the Augustinian Fathers in Louvain. The other part is kept at the Church of St Peter in Middleburg.

525. On Holy Thursday in 1384, in the small town of Seefeld, Oswald Milser, Lord of Schlosberg, pridefully demanded to receive the large Host like that of the celebrating priest. However, at the moment he was about to receive Communion, the ground under him began to shake and brake apart. Desperate, Oswald grasped the altar and the priest immediately retrieved the Host from his mouth. The shaking stopped, whereupon blood began to flow from the Host. All those present witnessed the miracle and soon the news of it spread across the country. Today, the precious relic of the Host, stained with blood, is exposed in the church of St Oswald, surrounded by many paintings depicting the miracle.

526. In 1430, in Monaco, a lady purchased a monstrance from a dealer in second hand goods. It was probably stolen as it still contained a consecrated Host. Ignorant as to the nature of the Eucharist, the lady removed the Host with a knife. To her great surprise, blood began to flow from it, leaving on the Host an imprint of Christ enthroned with instruments of the Passion at his side. News of the event quickly spread, even reaching Pope Eugene IV, who donated the miraculous Host to Duke Phillip of Borgogna, who in turn donated it to the city of Dijon. The miraculous Host was burned and destroyed in 1794 by anti-Catholic French revolutionaries devoted to the 'goddess of Reason.' Today, in the Cathedral of Dijon a stained glass window faithfully portrays the image of Christ as it originally appeared on the miraculous Host.

527. In 1597, a thief stole twenty-four consecrated Hosts together with other precious items from a church near the town of Alcalá, Spain. A few days later, the thief returned with remorse and confessed his sins to a Jesuit priest named Padre Juarez. Padre Jaurez absolved the man and asked him to return the Hosts. However, for fear that the Hosts were laced with poison they were not consumed, but stored away in the church's pantry to be destroyed by water or fire after they had naturally decayed. However, after eleven years the Hosts were still perfectly intact, leading the authorities to make medical and theological investigations, which in 1619 declared the preservation miraculous. In 1936, communist revolutionaries attacked the cathedral housing the Hosts, which were taken by the priests and hidden to prevent them being desecrated. The priests who hid the Hosts were then murdered. Since then, the hiding place of the Hosts has remained undiscovered.

528. In 1608, on the Vigil of the Feast of Pentecost, the monks of the Benedictine Abbey of Faverney held exposition and adoration of the Blessed Sacrament. As the monstrance was so large the monks placed two Hosts within it. After Vespers the monks left the monstrance exposed on the provisional altar. The next morning, the sacristan returned to find the provisional altar burnt to ashes and the church full of smoke. After the smoke cleared, the monks beheld the monstrance suspended in the air and the Hosts unharmed. The monstrance only descended after a new provisional altar was prepared. On 10 July, the Archbishop of Besançon declared the miracle authentic. The miracle rekindled the faith of many. To this day it is possible to see and venerate the relic containing one of the two Hosts. The other Host, however, after it was donated to the nearby Church of Dole, was destroyed by French revolutionaries in 1794.

529. As per the annual custom in Siena, Italy, on 14 August, 1730, festivities were held in honor of the Assumption of the Virgin Mary. During the festivities, thieves broke into the empty church of St Francis and stole the ciborium containing 348 consecrated Hosts and six halves. The theft caused the cancellation of the traditional Assumption festivities, with public prayers of reparation substituted in their place. Two days later the Hosts were discovered in the offering box in the church of St Mary of Provenzano. After the Hosts were returned to the church of St Francis in

solemn procession, the priests were unable to consume them, due to the continuous flow of people coming daily to adore them. As time passed, and to the amazement of all, the Hosts did not decay as normal, but remained fresh. Numerous detailed scientific tests on the Hosts were conducted in 1780, 1789, 1914, 1922. On each occasion the Hosts were found to be perfectly intact and free of any deterioration. One professor, Siro Grimaldi, declared: "The holy particles of unleavened bread represent an example of perfect preservation ... A singular phenomenon that inverts the natural law of the conservation of organic material. It is a fact unique in the annals of science." To this day the miraculously preserved Hosts are publicly displayed on the 17th day of each month.

530. In January, 1772, robbers escaped with two containers holding consecrated Hosts from the church of St Peter at Paterno. About a month later, mysterious rays of light and a dove appeared over the place where the stolen Hosts were buried, being the estate of the Duke of Grottotelle, under a pile of manure. The Hosts were found to be still entirely intact. After a two year canonical investigation by the diocesan Vicar General, Monsignor Onorati, the event was approved as miraculous. In more recent times, Dr Domenico Cotugno of the Royal University of Naples declared that, "The intact preservation of the Hosts cannot be explained with physical principles and they surpass the power of natural agents. Therefore, they must be considered as miraculous." In 1972, Professor Pietro de Franciscis, teacher of human physiology at the University of Naples, confirmed the above statement.

531. In 1822, in the Church of St Eulalia in Bordeaux, France, Christ appeared in the Host immediately after Abbot Delort gave the benediction with the Blessed Sacrament. For more than twenty minutes numerous of the faithful beheld an apparition of Christ blessing the congregation. In addition, Christ could be heard saying, "I Am He Who Is." This event was approved by the Archbishop of Bordeaux, Monsignor D'Aviau, who personally interviewed all the witnesses. To this day one can visit the chapel of the miracle and venerate the relic of the monstrance of the apparition.

532. In the small hamlet of Stich, Germany, on the evening of 9 June, 1970, Mass was celebrated by a visiting priest from Switzerland. After the consecration, the celebrant noticed that a small reddish spot had appeared on the corporal where the chalice had been resting. After completing the Mass the priest inspected everything on the altar but could find no source for the reddish stain. He locked the stained corporal in a safe place. After discussing the event with the parish priest, the corporal was photographed and sent to the Clinical Institute for Radial Therapy and Nuclear Medicine and the Polyclinical Institute of the University of Zurich for chemical analysis. The results of four separate analyses indicated that the stain was human blood that contained biochemical markers of a man in agony. On 14 July, the phenomena repeated itself with four stains appearing on the corporal after the consecration. The largest of these stains had a cross appearing distinctly on it. Several days later, the parish priest sent the stained corporal to the District Hospital at Cercee for analysis. Again, the results indicated that the stains were human blood. The results of both examinations were forwarded to the Bishop of Augsburg, Joseph Stimpfle.

533. On 8 December, 1991, the Feast of the Immaculate Conception, Fr Otty Ossa Aristizabal was celebrating midnight Mass when immediately after breaking the consecrated Host into four pieces a red substance began to ooze from the remaining pieces on the plate on the altar. Fr Otty placed the bleeding Host in a Chalice and put it in the Tabernacle. When Fr Otty looked at the Host the next morning it was still bleeding, so he placed it in a Monstrance and showed it to the people attending Mass. They all saw the Host bleeding and blood accumulating at the bottom of the Monstrance. Some filmed it on their video camcorders. The local bishop, Ricardo of Los Teques, ordered the Host to be tested in Caracas. The investigation determined that the red substance was human blood, type AB. Today, the miraculous Host is housed in the convent of the Augustinian Nuns in Los Teques, where it is adored by visiting pilgrims.

534. On 18 August, 1996, a priest in Buenos Aires was given a Host that had been abandoned in a candle holder in the church. Because it was covered in dirt the priest placed it in a water bowl and put it in the Tabernacle. Eight days later on 26 August the priest opened the Tabernacle to

discover that the Host had turned red and was oozing a blood-like substance. The priest informed the then Auxiliary Bishop Jorge Bergoglio (now Pope Francis), who asked a professional photographer to take photos of the Host, first on 26 August and then again on 6 September. Later, as Archbishop of Buenos Aires, Jorge Bergoglio asked a Bolivian-born atheist professor, Dr Ricardo Castañon, to conduct an investigation. Dr Castañon removed a small piece of the Host and some of the liquid, which were then sealed and labeled for forensic analysis. In April, 2004, Dr Frederick Zugibe of New York, a heart specialist and forensic pathologist, without knowing the origin of the sample, declared that he was looking at human heart tissue of a male, type AB blood, specifically from the left ventricle. Moreover, the heart was inflamed as if it had been recently injured. Even more remarkable was the presence of white blood cells, which could only exist if the sample had been taken from a living person. Dr Zugibe stated, "How or why a communion host could change its character and become living human flesh and blood is outside the ability of science to answer."

535. Eucharistic miracles have also manifested themselves in the lives of the saints through extraordinary fasts: St Angela of Foligno (d. 1309) lived solely on the Eucharist for twelve years; St Catherine of Siena (d. 1380) lived solely on the Eucharist for twenty-five years from the age of eight until her death at thirty-three; St Lidwina of Holland (d. 1433) spent the last nineteen years of her life living solely on the Eucharist; St Nicholas of Flüe (d. 1487) ate and drank absolutely nothing, except the Eucharist once a month, for over twenty years; St Joseph of Cupertino (d. 1663) spent five years eating nothing and went fifteen years without drinking, sustained during these times solely by the Eucharist; Anne Catherine Emmerich (d. 1824) lived twelve years solely on the Eucharist; Alexandrina da Costa (d. 1955) lived three years solely on the Eucharist; Therese Neumann (d. 1962) took no food or water, except the Eucharist, from 1926 to 1962. The Eucharist would remain in her for about twenty-four hours, but near the end of the day she would feel herself dying, until she received the Eucharist again.

536. There have been to date sixty-nine cures formally examined by medical experts and approved by the Church as miracles connected with the

Marian Shrine of Lourdes. To qualify for Church approval as a miracle, the cure needs to be complete, rapid, lasting and occurring without the aid of any treatment. The first of the 'Lourdes miracles' involved Catherine Latapie who, on 1 March, 1858, was instantly cured of paralysis of the last two fingers of her right hand after bathing it in the hollow which had begun to collect water from the newly flowing spring.

537. Louis Bouriette was cured in March, 1858, of total blindness in the right eye, an injury resulting from a quarry accident nineteen years earlier. Bouriette's cure occurred immediately after repeatedly bathing his right eye in the waters of the Lourdes spring while praying to the "Lady of the Grotto."

538. Blaisette Cazenave was cured in March, 1858, of "chronic infection of the conjonctivae and eyelids, with bilateral ectropion", a condition which at that time was completely incurable. After two applications of the Lourdes' water by Cazenave over her eyes they returned "to a normal healthy state by a rapid regrowth of the tissues."

539. Henri Busquet was cured in 28 April, 1858, of multiple ailments, including tuberculosis, an enormous septic ulcer at the base of his neck, and inflamed lymph glands. After applying to his neck a dressing soaked in water brought by a neighbor from the Lourdes Grotto, Busquet discovered the next morning that his infection had subsided, his ulcer had scarred over, and his lymph glands had disappeared. No relapse occurred after this sudden and complete cure which was described as "beyond the laws of nature."

540. Justin Bouhort was cured in early July, 1858, when just two years of age. A feeble, puny and disabled boy, Justin was dying of consumption when his desperate mother immersed him in the freezing waters of the Lourdes Grotto. After being brought home, Justin quickly recovered and for the first time in his life began to walk. As an elderly adult Justin attended the canonization of St Bernadette of Lourdes in Rome on 12 August, 1933.

541. Madelaine Rizan was cured on 17 October, 1858, of paralysis to the left side of her body caused by an "attack of choera" twenty-six years earlier.

Doctors had long since abandoned all hope of a cure and on 16 October death seemed imminent. Next morning, Rizan drank Lourdes water brought by her daughter and applied some to her face and body. Immediately her paralysis vanished and her strength returned. She led a normal life until her death eleven years later.

542. Marie Moreau was cured on 9 November, 1858, of an inflammatory disease of the eyes which caused virtual blindness. Moreau's father had travelled to Lourdes to get some water from the Grotto. On the evening of 8 November, 1858, the young Moreau soaked a bandage with the Lourdes water and tied it over her eyes. Upon removing the bandage the next morning Moreau found that her sight was fully restored.

543. Pierre de Rudder was cured on 4 July, 1875, of a fracture of his left leg sustained eight years earlier that would never heal. Pseudoarthrosis had set in at the site of the fracture, preventing any chance of his bones re-uniting. De Rudder had set out from his home town as an invalid to make a pilgrimage to a replica of the Grotto of Lourdes in the Belgian town of Oostacker. He returned in the evening of the same day without crutches or wounds. The bones in his left leg had united without any shortening or deviation from the vertical axis.

544. Joachime Dehant was cured on 13 September, 1878, of a ten year old gangrenous ulcer that covered two-thirds of her right leg and left her with permanently contracted muscles and a club foot. After taking two baths in Lourdes water, all trace of the ulcer disappeared. Dehant's flesh and tendons had returned to normal and her skin was restored and rose-colored. After a third bath some time later, Dehant's foot was restored to its normal position.

545. Elisa Seisson was cured on 29 September, 1882, of "chronic bronchitis with severe organic heart disease." For over six years Seisson's condition resisted all treatment and she was categorized as hopelessly incurable. On her first day in Lourdes, Seisson visited the baths and emerged very much improved. After a restful night's sleep she woke up completely cured. Seisson remained in good health for the next thirty years.

546.Sister Eugenia was cured on 21 August, 1883, of multiple ailments, including an abscess from the appendix, peritonitis, bilateral phlebitis and a "longstanding chronic infection in the right iliac fossa, with vesical and colonic fistulae." At death's door, Sr Eugenia departed for Lourdes and on arrival received Holy Communion from which she sensed some relief. After visiting the Baths in the afternoon of the same day Sr Eugenia felt completely cured. She emerged on her own and all signs of illness had vanished. There was no change in her thriving state of health throughout the next twenty-four years.

547.Sister Julienne was cured on 1 September, 1889, of pulmonary tuberculosis. X-rays showed that the condition was incurable, however, after emerging from the Lourdes Baths the pulmonary lesion had completely disappeared. Sr Julienne remained perfectly well afterwards.

548.Sister Josephine Marie was cured on 21 August, 1890, of "tuberculosis with gross apical lesions." Ill for many years and now moribund, Sr Josephine travelled to Lourdes under obedience. Upon arrival, she immediately entered the Baths. The next day, Sr Josephine entered another two times, after which she felt "infinitely better." A week later her doctor pronounced that "the disease had completely disappeared." Sr Josephine resumed her religious life and had no need of a doctor for the next twenty-eight years.

549.Amelie Chagnon was cured on 21 August, 1891, of tubercular osteo-arthritis of the knee and second metatarsal of the left foot. Chagnon's illness had resisted all treatment for over a year when she decided to visit the Lourdes Shrine. Chagnon returned from Lourdes enjoying free and normal leg movements without pain. Two weeks later Chagnon's doctors certified that the disease was completely cured.

550.Clementine Trouve was cured on 21 August, 1891, (on the very same day Amelie Chagnon was cured), of tuberculous osteoperiostitis of the right calcaneum. Trouve's doctor was of the opinion that her illness warranted "a radical operation ... or else, some other lengthy treatment." After Trouve's cure in the Baths the same doctor certified "that she only bore the scarred mark" of her former illness which "was now cured."

551.Marie Lebranchu was cured of pulmonary tuberculosis on 20 August, 1892. Previously, she had been homeless and the hospital was practically her home. When entering the Lourdes Baths she was in her terminal stages and weighed less than twenty-five kilograms. After returning from Lourdes, Lebranchu's doctor examined her twice and was left astonished. A third examination by another doctor confirmed that the tuberculosis had completely disappeared. The name of Marie Lebranchu was removed from the books of the hospital and she went on to live until 1920.

552.Marie Lemarchand was cured on 21 August, 1892, of severe pulmonary tuberculosis which had reached its terminal stages. At the time she entered the Lourdes Baths she also had deep and repulsive tuberculous ulcerated areas on her face, quite resistant to all treatment. She returned home completely cured and later married and had eight children.

553.Elisa Lesage was cured on 21 August, 1892, of tuberculosis of the right knee. She had been suffering of "white swelling" for more than a year before entering the Lourdes Baths. Her complete recovery was confirmed on the same day by the Medical Bureau of Verifications "without any sequelae or ankylosis."

554.Sister Marie of the Presentation was cured on 29 August, 1892, of chronic gastro-enteritis, a condition that had slowly worsened over twelve years to the point where she was in "a state of absolute starvation, which would undoubtedly end in death." The first sign of improvement occurred while Sr Marie traveled to Lourdes in the train. This improvement allowed her to eat a little. It was while praying in the Rosary Basilica that Sr Marie experienced "stomach pains far worse than she had ever felt before." Suddenly, a complete cure occurred with no subsequent relapse.

555.Father Cirette was cured on 31 August, 1893, of various conditions, including an inability to walk, mental confusion, and difficulty with speech and memory. All treatments had hitherto proved ineffective. Fr Cirette entered the Lourdes Baths two days after arriving but at first nothing extraordinary happened. Suddenly, he had an urge to go to the Grotto and set off without the aid of any walking sticks. Fr Cirette had been cured in a sudden, unexpected and lasting manner and after his return home was able to carry out all normal priestly functions.

556. Aurelie Huprelle was cured on 21 August, 1895, of cavitating pulmonary tuberculosis. Upon arriving at Lourdes by train, she was carried to the Baths to bathe. She felt immediately better, so much so that she considered herself totally cured. Upon her return home, Huprelle's physician, utterly astounded, verified "the reality of this complete and sudden cure."

557. Esther Brachman was cured at Lourdes on the 21 August, 1896, of tuberculosis. On her arrival she was taken straight to the Grotto and from there to the Baths. Emerging from the water, Brachman felt no more pain and the swelling of her abdomen had subsided. She could walk and was hungry. Over the next two days she could participate in the spiritual exercises of the pilgrimage and follow the Stations of the Cross. On returning home, Brachman's embarrassed doctors kept her under observation for a year. Eventually, they issued a certificate confirming her inexplicable cure.

558. Jeanne Tulasne was cured on the 8 September, 1897, of tuberculous peritonitis which had caused multiple ailments, including destruction of vertebrae and a marked curvature of the dorsolumbar spine, a bone abscess in the left thigh, muscular atrophy and clubfoot. At Lourdes, Tulase joined in the Blessed Sacrament procession led by her own Bishop. All of a sudden she felt cured. Multiple medical examinations over the next twelve months confirmed Tulasne's cure as sudden, complete, and lasting.

559. Clementine Malot was cured on 21 August, 1898, of tuberculosis with spitting of blood. She came to Lourdes in desperation and was taken to the Baths on arrival. However, nothing immediately happened. But the next day and bath Malot felt a sudden and marked improvement in health. After multiple examinations over the next twelve months Malot's cure was confirmed and upheld as certain.

560. Father Salvator was cured on 25 June, 1900, of pulmonary tuberculosis peritonitis. His condition was so serious that his doctors considered further treatment a waste of time. On arrival at Lourdes he was taken immediately to the Baths. A few minutes later, he emerged so transformed that no one could doubt his cure. That same evening Fr Salvator ate heartily and slept well again. Subsequent medical examinations could find no sign of his former illness.

561. Sister Maximilien was cured on 20 May, 1901, of a hydatid cyst of the liver with phlebitis of the left leg. This condition left her unable to walk and was incurable. On arrival at Lourdes Sr Maximilien was taken immediately to the Baths. A few minutes later, she emerged walking and cured. All swelling of her abdomen and leg had disappeared. The doctor who had treated Sr Maximilien for many years was compelled to write, "I am bound to say in all sincerity, that Sr Maximilien returned from Lourdes completely cured."

562. Marie Savoye was cured on 20 September, 1901, of complications due to rheumatic fever, namely heart disease, with all the signs of a mitral lesion, and an almost complete loss of appetite and spitting of blood. Her weakness was so pronounced that no one dared to lower her into the Baths. However, during the Benediction of the Blessed Sacrament all Savoye's symptoms suddenly disappeared, as well as the bed-sore on her back. Savoye's cure was so complete that she could spend the next seven years helping others at the Lourdes Grotto.

563. Mrs Johanna Bezenac was cured on 8 August, 1904, of progressive cachexia, tuberculous in nature, which attacked the skin of her face, gradually spreading into the hair roots. The condition resisted all treatment. Bezenac's cure occurred over a two day period in which she applied the spring water as a lotion. Two months later, her doctor verified the "absolute cure of her general condition and localized lesions."

564. Sister Saint Hilaire was cured on 20 August, 1904, of chronic gastroenteritis that was resistant to all treatment. The illness left her grossly emaciated and asthenic, with an ever-more frequent loss of blood in the stools. After the first bath, she felt reinvigorated and recovered her

appetite. A few hours later Sr Hilaire realized that she had been totally cured. Within three months she had gained twenty kilos in weight and was engaged in "a life of hard work" with her community.

565. Sister Saint Beatrix was cured on 31 August, 1904, of laryngeal-bronchitis, causing gross emaciation. For eight years she suffered from general weakness, loss of weight, coughing with blood, pus in the sputum, and cachexia. On the morning of her arrival in Lourdes, Sr Beatrix visited the Baths and felt an immediate change. Examined by doctors two days later, no sign of illness was found, either in her larynx or chest. A year later, Sr Beatrix returned to Lourdes and received another cure, this time of the visual disturbances which had plagued her for fifteen years.

566. Marie-Therese Noblet was cured on 31 August, 1905, of Pott's Disease, or tuberculosis of the spine. Noblet was cured the instant she entered the Hospital of Notre-Dame des Douleurs, after attending the Blessed Sacrament Procession. She was examined by doctors the following morning, as well as by her family doctor over the course of the next year. Never again was there any evidence of pain, deformity or restricted movement.

567. Cecile Doubille de Franssu was cured on 21 September, 1905, of "white swelling" of the knee, loss of appetite, fever, and progressive consumption, all due to tuberculosis. With no improvement in sight, she was taken to the Lourdes Baths, from where she emerged totally cured. On the same evening she was examined by doctors who found no sign of the disease, past or present. Franssu went on to celebrate her one hundredth birthday in 1985.

568. Antonia Moulin was cured on 10 August, 1907, of an abscess of the right leg with phlebitis and lymphangitis. Her first journey to Lourdes in 1905 proved fruitless, leaving without any improvement at all. Moulin's condition continued to worsen over the next two years with the wound on the right thigh increasing in size and her knee becoming grossly enlarged and ankylosed. On the second day of her 1907 trip Moulin was carried to the Baths again. After her return it was noticed that her wound had scarred over, and that she could use her limb again. The local doctors

immediately confirmed her cure while her personal doctor in late September signed a certificate stating, "This cure is scientifically inexplicable."

569. Marie Borel was cured on 21-22 August, 1907, of six discharging fistulae and lesions that obstructed the normal path of the stools. Borel arrived in Lourdes in a pitiful condition. On the morning of 21 August, Borel emerged from the Baths with four of the fistule closed and their dressings clean and dry. The following day, Borel's two remaining fistulae closed after coming out of the Baths a second time. The doctors on site verified that all fistulae had closed and the stools now followed their normal course. This sudden cure was re-checked by different doctors from 1907-11, and remained in the minds of all experts as scientifically inexplicable.

570. Virginie Haudebourg was cured on 17 May, 1908, of cystitis and nephritis, a urinary infection tuberculous in origin and eventually fatal. In May, 1906, she made her first pilgrimage to Lourdes, resulting in no change in her condition. Further deterioration in the early months of 1908 left Haudebourg unable to get up and walk. On the third day of her second Lourdes visit, during the Blessed Sacrament blessing, she felt violent pain. After a peaceful night's sleep she presented herself for urine tests which showed her health inexplicably restored. For the next fifty years Haudebourg evidenced no sign of any relapse.

571. Mrs Marie Bire Lucas was cured on 5 August, 1908, of multiple illnesses and afflictions, including gangrene of her left forearm and hand, with excruciating pain and vomiting, intracranial hypertension, and blindness. After attending Mass at the Grotto, Lucas' eye-sight suddenly returned, even though she still showed signs of "retinal pallor of cerebral origin." In the weeks that followed, further examinations by three ophthalmologists revealed that "evidence of optic atrophy no longer present and the cure is complete."

572. Aimee Allope was cured on 28 May, 1909, of "four enormous abscesses from which pus ran freely and showed no sign at all of healing." Upon arriving at Lourdes, Allope was in a terrible state, weighing only forty-four kilograms. No improvement occurred during the first days of her

pilgrimage. However, after receiving Holy Communion at the Grotto, her suffering suddenly ceased, her wounds closed, and her appetite returned. Within twelve months Allope gained ten kilograms in weight.

573. Juliette Orion was cured on 22 July, 1910, of multiple ailments, including tuberculosis, pleurisy, bronchitis, loss of weight, left mastoiditis with meningeal involvement, laryngitis, oscillating fever and comatose episodes. Her doctors viewed her case as hopeless. Orion applied to join the Diocesan Pilgrimage to Lourdes but was denied a place. During the night of 22-23 July, Orion decided to pray to Our Lady of Lourdes. Suddenly, she felt much improved. By the following morning she had recovered her voice and asked for food. Her doctor was summoned, who confirmed a complete cure for which "he did not claim the least credit."

574. Mrs Marie Fabre was cured on 26 September, 1911, of a uterine prolapse, dyspepsia and mucomembranous-enteritis. This digestive disorder prevented her from eating normal food and led to her anaemia and debility. All prescribed treatment had proved futile. She was so feeble she could not enter the Lourdes Baths on arrival. After taking part in the Benediction of the Blessed Sacrament, she felt better, spoke, sat up on her couch, and asked for food and ate, something she had not done for two years. Henceforth Fabre lived a normal life.

575. Henriette Bressolles was cured on 3 July, 1924, of "Pott's disease of the spine with total paraplegia and double incontinence." On the afternoon of her arrival at Lourdes, Bressolles was taken to the Blessing of the Sick, and afterwards to the Grotto. After experiencing something like "a very painful crack" she felt cured, and for the first time in six years could sit up on her couch. The next day her spine moved freely without pain. Three months later, three separate examinations conducted by physicians and surgeons confirmed that "the cure was complete and stable, and was obtained in Lourdes."

576. Lydia Brosse was cured on 11 October, 1930, from bone disorders due to tuberculosis. Several operations left her exhausted and emaciated while intestinal and nasal haemorrhages left her in an anaemic state. No improvement occurred in her condition while at Lourdes. However, on

her return journey Brosse found the urge and strength to raise herself up, while her fistulae suddenly closed. Three months later her weight had risen by twelve kilograms. Doctors a year later declared that "this cure, by its rapidity, defies current concepts of the laws of biology."

577. Sister Marie Marguerite was cured on 22 January, 1937, of numerous ailments, including renal and kidney disease, pyelo-nephritis, generalized phlyctenular oedema of both lower limbs, frequent cardiac crises with dyspnoea, and facial neuralgia. These entirely prevented her from leading a normal life. Her Community began a novena to Our Lady of Lourdes during which Sr Marie replaced all her medication with Lourdes' water. On the last day of the Novena, Sr Marie suddenly sensed a great relief at the moment of the elevation of the Host during Mass. The oedema instantly vanished; she could wear shoes and began to walk. This cure was verified by her doctor, who continued to visit her for the next eight years.

578. Louise Jamain was cured on 1 April, 1937, of pulmonary, intestinal and peritoneal tuberculosis. After being in hospital with this disease for seven years, Jamain decided to go to Lourdes. The journey was very difficult and she was given the last sacraments on 30 March. Suddenly, on the morning of 1 April, Jamain felt perfectly rested and asked for food. The medical examination on 3 April found no evidence of any lesion or bacteria. The cure was certain. The staff at the Parisian hospital from which Jamain had set off were utterly amazed. Some years later Jamain married and had two children.

579. Francis Pascal was cured on 31 August, 1938, of paralysis of the lower and upper limbs, and loss of vision due to meningitis. The child was taken in this state to Lourdes by his parents. It was after the second bath that Francis' sight was restored and his paralyses disappeared. When he returned home, he was examined by three doctors who had previously seen him. They all acknowledged a definitive cure that "medically ... could not be explained."

580. Gabrielle Clauzel was cured on 15 August, 1943, of a rheumatic condition of the vertebrae, associated with painful visceral and functional disorders, and myoclonic contractions due to spondylitis, with nerve-root

compression. Clauzel was bed-ridden and had to be carried to church, which was one hundred meters away. After Mass on the Feast of the Assumption, to the amazement of all present, Clauzel got up and walked home herself. She attributed her cure to praying to Our Lady of Lourdes. For the next thirty-nine years Clauzel enjoyed good health and never experienced a relapse.

581. Yvonne Fournier was cured on 19 August, 1945, of a traumatized left arm with intolerable pain, oedema, and trophic lesions, rendering it virtually useless. Nine operations had failed to improve function. After her first washing in the Lourdes Bath, Fournier felt power in her left arm return, with freedom from pain and movement. She was examined by the medical team on site and later by two of the surgeons who had previously operated on her, all recognizing that the cure was medically inexplicable.

582. Mrs Rose Martin was cured on 3 July, 1947, of pelvic metastases (tumor). She was taken to Lourdes in a semi-comatose state. After her third bath, Martin arose with no pain and could move about normally. There was no longer any trace of tumor. After returning home she gained seventeen kilograms in ten months. Following medical tests more than a year later, Martin's complete cure was recognized as "without either a medical or natural explanation."

583. Mrs Jeanne Gestas was cured on 22 August, 1947, of abdominal difficulties causing frequent vomiting and painful pseudo-ulcers. At one point she weighed no more than forty-four kilograms. Her first visit to Lourdes proved fruitless, though she began to pray. Gestas then developed adhesive peritonitis, which gave her little rest and stifled all activity. She decided to revisit Lourdes and after her second bath felt much better, with all malaise disappearing. Gestas' appetite and zest for life returned. Examinations over the next few years confirmed that her cure was "real and inexplicable."

584. Marie-Therese Canin was cured on 9 October, 1947, of tuberculosis of the spinal column and abdomen and associated ailments, including oedema of both lower limbs, a vaginal fistula, and very frequent collapses. She arrived at Lourdes weighing only thirty-eight kilograms. After the

Procession of the Blessed Sacrament, she felt much better, moving about and eating a full meal. Examinations the next day showed that Canin was completely cured. A year later she weighed fifty-five kilograms. A subsequent examination in 1949 confirmed that "there was no natural or scientific explanation for this cure."

585. Maddalena Carini was cured on 15 August, 1948, of tuberculosis of the pleura, dorsal spine, peritoneum, pericardium and the right femur. Despite years of treatment she was in a deplorable condition, weighing only thirty-two kilograms. When in front of the Lourdes Grotto, Carini experienced a sudden and notable improvement, but she did not tell anyone until during the return journey the next day. Several doctors verified the lasting nature of the cure, concluding that "we are in the presence of a cure contrary to all logical reasoning, taking into account the past history of the patient."

586. Jeanne Fretel was cured on 8 October, 1948, of tuberculous peritonitis, which left her emaciated, unable to get out of bed, and with a high oscillating fever. Her prognosis was hopeless. In her death throes, Fretel was taken to Lourdes. On the third day, after receiving Holy Communion and then being taken to the Grotto, her stomach returned to normal, the fever and pains disappeared, and she could get up, walk and eat. The medical examination that followed declared, "No explanation of this cure can be given. It is beyond the natural laws."

587. Thea Angele was cured on 20 May, 1950, of a disorder of the central nervous system that caused sensory and motor loss and poor coordination. Her condition steadily deteriorated until she was semi-conscious, unable to communicate, and virtually dying. Within a few hours after being dipped in the Lourdes Baths, Angele recovered her speech, muscle power, ability to walk, and appetite. All subsequent medical examinations agreed that the cure was "medically inexplicable." Angele later entered a religious order in Lourdes and never exhibited any recurrence of the disease.

588. Evasio Ganora was cured on 2 June, 1950, of Hodgkin's Disease, a malignant disease of the glands. Treatment with cytotoxic drugs,

radiotherapy and transfusions all proved futile. Ganora could only just make the journey to Lourdes on a stretcher. After his first bath, he felt cured, and the next day began pushing the carriages of other invalids. Four years later, medical examinations confirmed that he had certainly received an inexplicable cure, beyond the laws of nature.

589. Edeltraud Fulda was cured on 12 August, 1950, of Addison's Disease, causing pyonephrosis, pigmentation of the skin, anaemia, and hypotension. For very many years Fulda was sustained by a daily dose of a suprarenal hormone named Percontin. After her first bath in Lourdes, Fulda felt cured. Doctors both at home and at Lourdes confirmed the cure as "sudden and lasting."

590. Paul Pellegrin was cured on 3 October, 1950, from an amoebic abscess of the liver causing a profuse purulent discharge. All therapeutic measures had to date proved ineffective. After his second bath at Lourdes, Pellegrin's fistula suddenly dried up. An anticipated relapse never occurred. Medical examinations following gave a unanimous verdict: "a medical explanation could not be given ... it defied the natural laws."

591. Brother Leo Schwager was cured on 30 April, 1952, of disturbances of speech, sight and balance due to multiple sclerosis. Upon arriving at Lourdes, all these symptoms suddenly vanished in an instant during the Blessed Sacrament procession. He could now stand, walk, speak, see and eat normally, all in full view of doctors present at the time. Subsequent medical examinations all agreed that "the circumstances of this cure remain medically inexplicable."

592. Mrs Alice Couteault was cured on 15 May, 1952, of multiple sclerosis. This illness rendered her a permanent invalid, unable to cope without the assistance of her husband. At the Baths, Couteault experienced a discernible change, and in the afternoon recovered her speech and ability to walk. Her doctor confirmed a complete cure. Afterwards, Couteault and her once sceptical husband visited Lourdes twice a year to assist other patients.

593. Marie Bigot was cured on 8 October, 1953, of arachnoiditis of the posterior fossa, with adhesions, causing deafness in the right ear and virtual blindness in both eyes. She was also hemiplegic. No improvement followed Bigot's first visit to Lourdes, despite her hopefulness. On her second visit a year later she recovered her ability to walk; on her third visit the next year she recovered her hearing at the end of the Procession and her vision on the train during the return journey. Her cure was recognized as inexplicable by all doctors.

594. Ginette Nouvel was cured on 21 September, 1954, of thrombosis of the sub-hepatic veins. This condition left her extremely weak and emaciated and requiring her ascites drained every ten days. Upon arriving at Lourdes, Nouvel followed all the ceremonies, with no apparent benefit. However, from that day she no longer required draining of her ascites and gradually began to live a normal life. Examinations over the next five years confirmed a lasting cure that was extraordinary and inexplicable.

595. Elisa Aloi was cured on 5 June, 1958, of multiple tuberculous lesions in various bones and joints with accompanying fistulae. Aloi's first visit to Lourdes proved fruitless, and afterwards her condition only worsened. On her second visit, Aloi was encased in a pelvis-to-foot plaster cast, with four fistulae drained through it. Her dressings were soaked in Lourdes' water, resulting in a complete cure. All subsequent examinations confirmed the same. Aloi would go on to safely give birth to four children.

596. Juliette Tamburini was cured on 17 July, 1959, of tuberculous infection, resulting in fistula formation and repeated epistaxes (nose bleeds). Numerous operations were to no avail. After Lourdes water was applied to the fistulous tract, the discharge dried up, the fistula closed and even the bleeding ceased. No relapse or recurrence ever followed. Three detailed examinations over the next four years confirmed the cure as "medically inexplicable."

597. Vittorio Micheli was cured on 1 June, 1963, of a malignant tumor, or sarcoma, resulting in total destruction of his left hip joint. He bathed at Lourdes encased from pelvis to foot in a plaster cast, but no noticeable

immediate change occurred. Six months later, Micheli was experiencing excellent health and was able to walk with no pain. More remarkably, his left hip had undergone an astonishing reconstruction. Medical specialists examining Micheli were left dumbfounded, admitting that it was "impossible to give any medical explanation for this cure."

598. Serge Perrin was cured on 1 May, 1970, of right hemiplegia due to thrombosis in the left carotid artery, at times causing a loss of consciousness. Perrin's first trip to Lourdes proved fruitless, followed by a marked deterioration involving cerebral eclipses and visual disturbances. He visited Lourdes a second time at the insistence of his wife. After attending the Ceremony of Anointing the Sick, Perrin began to feel sensation return and by the afternoon of the same day could walk freely and see clearly. Thorough medical examinations confirmed that Perrin's cure was "certain, instantaneous and lasting."

599. Miss Delizia Cirolli was cured in December, 1976, of a malignant tumor in the shin bone of her right leg. Doctors had informed Delizia's parents that her only hope of survival was to have the leg amputated. Delizia's father decided to take her to Lourdes in August, 1976, but no change occurred. The parents, however, continued to pray to Our Lady of Lourdes for a cure. One morning in December, 1976, Delizia got out of bed and began to walk as if she had never been ill. Medical examinations determined that Delizia's cure was "perfect and definitive."

600. Jean-Pierre Bély was cured in October, 1987, of paralysis due to multiple sclerosis. He was medically classified as a total invalid at the time he went to Lourdes, and those accompanying him feared he would not survive the journey. At the end of the pilgrimage he received anointing of the sick. After returning home Bély was able to walk and all traces of the illness had disappeared. Bély's doctor, an agnostic, admitted that there was "no scientific explanation for what occurred."

601. Anna Santaniello was cured in 1952 of a fatal form of rheumatic heart disease known as Bouillaud's Disease. Her condition had deteriorated to the point where she was bed-ridden and barely able to breathe. The same illness had killed one of her brothers and a sister. Upon being lowered by

stretcher into the icy cold Lourdes' waters, Santaniello felt a "hot explosion" in her chest. Minutes later, she was able to get out of her stretcher and walk. A heart specialist back in Italy pronounced her perfectly healthy. In 1964, the Church declared her case an "extraordinary healing" and in 2005 "miraculous."

602. Serge Francois was cured on 13 April, 2002, of paralysis in his left leg due to complications following two operations that left him with a herniated disc. After praying at the Lourdes' Grotto, Francois went to the spring to drink the water and wash his face. There followed a "rapid functional healing." Medical specialists declared Francois' recovery as "sudden, complete, unrelated to any particular therapy and durable." Afterwards, Francois made a 1,560km pilgrimage to Santiago de Compostela, Spain, to give thanks for his recovery.

603. Danila Castelli was cured in May, 1989, of severe complications arising from a tumor in the rectal, bladder and vaginal regions. In an effort to save her life, Danila underwent a hysterectomy, an annexectomy and a partial pancreatectomy. Her doctor husband wanted to take her to America for further treatment, but Danila convinced him to travel to Lourdes instead. Danila emerged from the Baths feeling extraordinarily well and afterwards presented herself to the Lourdes Office of Medical Observations. All agreed that Danila had been cured in a complete and lasting way, unrelated to any treatments or surgeries.

604. There are over another 2,500 miracles that have occurred connected with Lourdes that are awaiting ecclesiastical approval. Two of the most famous of these are the cures of Gabriel Gargam and Jack Traynor. Gargam was cured on 20 August, 1901, of total paralysis resulting from a major train accident. He had wasted away to a mere skeleton and could only receive nourishment from a tube once a day. An atheist, Gargam only agreed to go to Lourdes at the insistence of his mother and aunt. He arrived at Lourdes on the point of death. The first miracle was spiritual, with Gargam deciding to go to confession and receive Holy Communion. Later that same day, after Gargam was blessed with the Blessed Sacrament, he sat up and said, "Help me. I can walk! I feel I can walk." Sixty prominent doctors then examined Gargam and all agreed that he

was entirely cured. For the next fifty years Gargam consecrated himself to the service of the invalids at Lourdes.

605. Jack Traynor was a British World War I veteran who as a result of war injuries suffered from the following afflictions: epilepsy; paralysis of the radial, median and ulnar nerves of the right arm; atrophy of the shoulder and pectoral muscles; a 2.5cm trephine opening in the right parietal region of the skull; absence of voluntary movement in the legs and loss of feeling; lack of bodily control. All these afflictions totally disappeared on 25 July, 1923, after Traynor was blessed with the Blessed Sacrament on his fourth day at Lourdes. Traynor's cure led to numerous conversions in and around Liverpool.

606. The next series of 'great miracles' are those obtained through the invocation and intercession of Blesseds which have been accepted by the Church as the 'second miracle' needed for their formal canonization. There are thousands of such miracles. The following are just ten examples associated with saints canonized in recent decades. The first of these involves Marco Fidel Rojas, the former mayor of the town of Huila, Colombia, who was cured of Parkinson's disease during the night of 27 December, 2010, after praying the following prayer: "Venerable Father John Paul II: Come and heal me; put your hands on my head."

607. In 1937, a Lebanese blacksmith named Iskandar Oubeid lost sight in one eye due to a work accident that left his pupil destroyed. Thirteen years later, he took the advice of friends to visit the tomb of Fr Charbel Makhlouf. On returning home he had a dream in which a monk appeared, promising to cure him. The next morning he found he could see perfectly out of both eyes. No medical explanation could be found. A canonical inquiry was convened which verified the miracle which was later accepted by the Sacred Congregation for the Causes of the Saints.

608. On 27 July, 1976, Br Heriberto Webber completed a novena invoking the intercession of Bl. Marcellin Champagnat. Previously, Br Heriberto had been suffering high fevers and severe spinal pains due to a serious pulminary infection. Doctors had diagnosed him as incurable. Immediately after the novena, Br Heriberto felt a sudden and unforeseen

improvement. On 21 March, 1998, the Church recognized Br Heriberto's cure as "very rapid, complete and lasting ... scientifically inexplicable."

609. In 1987, the two-year old Teresa Benedicta McCarthy ingested nineteen times the lethal dose of Tylenol (acetaminophen). The child was left near death with total kidney failure and a deteriorating liver. Desperate, the McCarthy family organized a 'prayer chain' invoking Bl. Edith Stein's intercession. Shortly thereafter, the infant Teresa began to sit up completely healthy. Dr Ronald Kleinman, who treated Teresa Benedicta, later testified, "I was willing to say that it was miraculous."

610. On 7 December, 1988, Marcela Antúnez Riveros was pulled out of a swimming pool completely blue, her tongue hanging from her mouth, and her stomach inflated. She had been under water for five minutes. Ordinarily, Marcela should have suffered severe neurological damage, leaving her in a permanent vegetative state. After being pulled from the water, Marcela's friends began begging the intercession of Bl. Teresa of the Andes. Immediately she let out a guttural sound. Four days later she was released from hospital completely recovered with no ill effects.

611. In November, 1992, Dr Manuel Nevado was suffering from cancerous chronic radiodermatitis, an incurable disease, affecting his fingers due to over-exposure to x-rays. Dr Nevado began praying for a cure through the intercession of Bl. Josemaria Escriva. From that day onwards his hands began to improve. Within two weeks his lesions had completely disappeared and his cure was complete. In January, 1993, Dr Nevado returned to perform surgical operations without any problems.

612. Kathleen Evans, a middle-aged Australian wife and mother of five children, was diagnosed with aggressive lung cancer and secondary brain cancer in 1993. Her doctors were convinced that the condition was inoperable and so Kathleen was sent home to die. Family, friends and the Sisters of St Joseph prayed to Ven. Mary MacKillop for a cure. Less than a year later an x-ray found that all traces of cancer had disappeared. It was a complete and permanent cure.

613. On 5 October, 1995, an American priest named Fr Pytel was suddenly cured of a congenital heart condition which had left his left ventricle permanently damaged. His cardiologist believed that he would never be able to work normally as a priest. The cure occurred after Fr Pytel venerated a relic of Sr Faustina Kolwalska on the anniversary of her death. For fifteen minutes afterwards Fr Pytel lay on the ground unable to move. During his next check-up, Fr Pytel's heart was found to be normal. A medical team evaluated the change as "scientifically unexplainable."

614. On 20 January 2000, Matteo Pio Colella started to shiver and develop a fever. He rapidly grew worse, developing fulminant meningitis with acute respiratory distress syndrome and multi-organ failure. The mortality rate for such a condition is usually 100%. Meanwhile, prayers for his recovery were being offered through the intercession of Padre Pio. Matteo attests that while he was asleep he was visited by an old man with a white beard and a long brown garment accompanied by three angels. This man gave Matteo his hand and said, "Matteo, don't be worried, you will soon be healed." By midday Matteo began to improve and within a few weeks his recovery was complete. His restoration was medically inexplicable and was declared a miracle by the Congregation for the Causes of the Saints.

615. In 2003, Elisabeth Arcolino was sixteen weeks pregnant with her fourth child when she sustained a tear in the placenta, resulting in the loss of amniotic fluid. The baby's chances of survival were nil. Providentially, Bishop Diogenes Silva Matthes of Franca, Brazil, was visiting a friend in the same hospital and advised Arcolino not to have an abortion. At home the bishop prayed to Bl. Gianna Molla, "The time for your canonization has arrived. Intercede to the Lord for the grace of a miracle and save the life of this little baby." Despite the lack of amniotic fluid, Elisabeth delivered a healthy baby girl, Gianna Maria, on 31 May, 2003.

616. The next series of 'great miracles' that are publicly verifiable involve the phenomena of 'incorrupt bodies.' The bodies of over two hundred and fifty Catholic saints since the 2nd century remain mysteriously preserved. The first known incorrupt body is that of St Cecilia who died a virgin and martyr in 177. Her body was discovered incorrupt in the catacomb of St Callistus in 1599. During public exposition before its re-internment, St

Cecilia's body emitted a mysterious and beautiful flower-like odor. It is now located in the Church of St Cecilia in Trastevere, Rome.

617. St Agatha died in 251 a virgin and martyr after being brutally tortured and mutilated. Her body was discovered incorrupt in the city of Catania, Sicily, in the 11th century and then dismembered. Her principal relics are still preserved today and are venerated three times a year in the cathedral of St Agatha in Catania.

618. St Etheldreda died in 679. Buried in a wooden coffin, she was found seventeen years later to be entirely intact and fresh, together with her clothes. The saint remained in such a condition until the Reformation, when her shrine was destroyed and her relics scattered. However, in 1811 her left hand was discovered in what was formerly a priest's hiding hole. The hand remains in a remarkably preserved state and now rests in the church of St Etheldreda in Ely, England.

619. St Edward the Confessor died in 1066. After his death his body was exhumed many times, including in 1098 when it was first found to be incorrupt. St Edward's incorrupt body came to rest finally in Westminster Abbey on 13 October, 1269, where it still lies today.

620. The great Franciscan preacher and miracle-worker St Anthony of Padua died in 1231. In 1263, his sarcophagus was opened and his tongue was found to be incorrupt. It was removed by St Bonaventure and is now on public display in a golden reliquary in St Anthony's Basilica in Padua.

621. St Clare of Assisi died in 1253 and was buried the following day. Seven years later, when being translated to the Church of Saint Clare in Assisi, her body was found to be totally incorrupt. When it came again to translate her remains to another new crypt in the 19th century, it was discovered that St Clare's clothing and flesh had disintegrated, though her skeleton was still in perfect condition. Now in the crypt at Santa Chiara, Assisi, St Clare's intact skeleton lies in a state of repose, covered in a wax likeness of her and clothed in the habit of her Order.

622. St Albert the Great died in 1280. On the occasion of his translation to the Dominican church of Cologne in 1283 his remains were found to be in a state of perfect preservation and exhaling a sweet odor. They remained so for another two hundred years. Even after the remains of the saint were reduced to bones they still diffused a delightful perfume. The remains are today wrapped in silk and rest in the crypt of St Andrew's church in Cologne.

623. St Catherine of Siena died in 1380. Fifty years later her body was found to be incorrupt. Various parts of her body, including a hand, a foot, fingers, and a shoulder blade, were distributed to different churches throughout Italy and England. St Catherine's head was placed in a reliquary of gilded copper and eventually made its way to the church of St Dominic in Siena, where it is on display today.

624. St Rita of Cascia died in 1457. Her whole body rests in a glass sacophagus in the Basilica of St Rita in Cascia. It lies virtually intact, with only slight discoloration and a dislodged eyebrow. Pilgrims on ocassions testify to seeing her eyes open and close unaided, her whole body levitate or move position within the sacophagus. A sweet odor is also discernible at times.

625. St Catherine of Bologna died in 1463. Her body was exhumed eighteen days later because of reports of miracles and a sweet smelling odor emanating from her grave. Her body today remains intact in a seated position in the chapel of the Poor Clares in Bologna, though her skin has become dark through exposure to nearby burning candles over the centuries.

626. St Francis Xavier died in 1552. He was buried on Sancian Island off the coast of China in a wooden coffin with two layers of quicklime to accelerate decomposition. Two and a half months later, the body was exhumed and found totally incorrupt. The same was discovered during the body's sea journey to Goa via Malacca. St Francis' right arm and another arm bone are now kept in reliquaries respectively in Rome and Macau. The rest of the incorrupt body is contained in a silver and glass casket in the Basilica of Bom Jésus in Goa.

627.St Teresa of Avila died in 1582. Afterwards, the nuns noticed a sweet fragrance coming from her grave. When her coffin was opened in mid 1583 the body was found to be firm and entirely intact, though the coffin lid had rotted. The majority of St Teresa's remains are today located in the Carmelite convent of Alba de Tormes in Spain, though her intact heart, hands, right foot, right arm, left arm and a part of her jaw are housed in other sites throughout the world.

628.St Charles Borromeo died in 1584. When his body was exhumed in 1607 it was found to be intact, even though the cover of the double casket was corroded in different places. Another examination of the body in 1880 found it still preserved. The still incorrupt body now rests in a majestic reliquary in the great Duomo Cathedral in Milan, Italy.

629.St John of the Cross died in 1591. His tomb was opened twice in the eighteen months following and the body found still perfectly preserved, even though it had been placed under a layer of lime. It also gave off a powerful perfume. A leg and an arm were later removed and sent elsewhere for veneration. Further exhumations in 1859, 1909 and 1955 revealed that the head, torso, arm and leg remained intact, moist and flexible, though now slightly discolored. These can be seen today in the Carmelite monastery in Segovia, Spain.

630.The Venerable Mother Mariana de Jesus Torres of Quito, Ecuador, died in 1635. After death, her body remained flexible, her facial skin rosy, and she appeared to carry a charming smile as if still alive. To this day her body remains intact and her casket emanates a sweet scent of flowers.

631.The Venerable Mary of Agreda died in 1665. Her body was first exhumed in 1909 and found to be completely incorrupt. Another examination in 1989 found the body "had absolutely not deteriorated at all in the last eighty years." Her body remains on display in the Convent Chapel of Agreda in Spain.

632.St Lucy Filippini died in 1732. Her body was exhumed in 1926 and found almost entirely incorrupt with all her bones still intact and covered in soft and flexible tissue. She looked "like a person just after death."

Today, only the saint's face has suffered a little as she rests in a crystal reliquary in St Margaret's Cathedral in Montefiascone, Italy.

633. St Teresa Margaret of the Sacred Heart died in 1770. She was buried in a double casket in a wall of the convent in which she lived. Nevertheless, a sweet odor was evident. In 1783, the body was exhumed and found to be perfectly incorrupt. The same was the case in 1805. Today, her body remains incorrupt, though darkened and dry, and resides in a glass case in the Convent of St Teresa, Florence, Italy.

634. St John Vianney died in 1859. In 1904, his body was exhumed and found dry and darkened, but perfectly entire. The body now rests in a golden reliquary above the main altar in the Basilica at Ars in France. The perfectly preserved heart was enclosed in a separate reliquary in 1905 and placed in another building called 'The Shrine of the Curé's Heart.'

635. St Catherine Labouré died in 1876. Her body was exhumed in 1932 and found to be totally incorrupt with the arms and legs perfectly supple. Even her eyes were still shining blue. Today, St Catherine's body can be viewed in the chapel Rue du Bac 140 in Paris and still appears the same as it did the day after she died.

636. St Bernadette Soubirous died in 1879. Exhumations in 1909 and 1919 found her body incorrupt, though somewhat emaciated, while the arms and face were in perfect condition and with their natural skin tone. Since 1919, St Bernadette's face has become slightly discolored due to washing, otherwise the entire relic remains in a remarkable state of preservation and can be viewed in the Chapel of St Bernadette in Nevers.

637. St Paula Frassinetti died in 1882. In 1906, her body was exhumed and found to be perfectly preserved, with flexible joints and undamaged clothing. It remains incorrupt today, though somewhat darkened and dry, and rests in the Dorothean Motherhouse of St Onofria in Rome.

638. St Frances Xavier Cabrini died in 1917. In 1931, her remains were exhumed and found to be partially incorrupt. She now rests under the altar in the chapel at St Francis Cabrini Shrine in New York City.

639. St Charbel Makhlouf died in 1898. Four months after his death his body was exhumed and found to be perfectly preserved, even though it had been subject to floods and was floating in muddied water. For the next sixty-seven years it was necessary to change his habit twice a week because of the mysterious secretion of perspiration and blood from his pores. This remained the situation until his beatification in December, 1965, after which his body succumbed to natural deterioration. However, oils continued for a time to exude from his bones, which to this day remain reddish in color.

640. Pope St Pius X died in 1914. Before he died, he explicitly forbade any preservation of his body, but when it was exhumed thirty years later in 1944 it was found to be in such a well preserved condition that his limbs were still flexible. Today, the incorrupt body of St Pius X rests under the Chapel of the Presentation in St Peter's Basilica.

641. Blessed Jacinta Marto died in 1920. Her body was exhumed in 1935 and 1951 and on both occasions the face was found to be incorrupt. The priest present at the 1935 exhumation stated, "The expression on Jacinta's face was that of great peace ..." Bl. Jacinta has since been re-entombed and lies buried in the Basilica of Our Lady of Fatima in Fatima, Portugal.

642. St Pio of Pietrelcina (Padre Pio) died in 1968. Forty years later his body was exhumed. Archbishop Domenico D'Ambrosio explained what he saw: "The top part of the skull is partly skeletal but the chin is perfect and the rest of the body is well preserved. The knees, hands, mittens and nails are clearly visible." He went on to say that the hands "looked like they had just undergone a manicure." The robes were also found still intact and his feet visible. However, due to some degree of deterioration, Padre Pio's face was reconstructed with a life-like silicone mask.

643. There have also been countless miracles relating to images and statues of Christ and Mary. The first of these occurred as early as AD 40 when the Apostle St James the Great, while preaching along the Ebro River in Spain, was visited by the Virgin Mary in a vision. The Virgin Mary asked St James to build an oratory and then return to Jerusalem. Mary in the

vision stood upon a pillar surrounded by angels. The pillar still exists today in the Basilica of Our Lady of the Pilar in Zaragoza topped with a wooden statue of Our Lady and the Christ Child. Scientists have been unable to match the granite of the pillar with any known stone substance in the world. Furthermore, no dust ever settles on it, so the statue miraculously never requires any cleaning.

644. The image of Our Lady of Good Success was made at the command of the Virgin Mary herself given to the Ven. Mother Mariana de Jesus Torres on 16 January, 1599. Due to various difficulties suffered by Mother Mariana, the statue's construction was delayed for years and only miraculously completed by the Archangels Michael, Gabriel and Raphael. The statue immediately afterwards became animated as Mary walked into it and began to sing the *Magnificat*. Over the centuries the statue has become renowned for its numerous miracles. Presently, it resides in the Conceptionist Convent in Quito, Ecuador.

645. The image of Our Lady of Good Counsel with the Christ Child arrived mysteriously in the Italian town of Genazzano on 25 April, 1467, carried upon clouds — a prodigy witnessed by thousands of the townsfolk. It is believed the image escaped before the invading Turks then overrunning Albania and came to rest in the unfinished church of Our Lady of Good Counsel. Since its arrival, hundreds of miracles have been granted to those visiting the image. Today, the image rests on its base, unsupported by any other object, defying gravity for over five hundred years.

646. The image of Our Lady of Perpetual Help has its origins in the 13th or 14th century. It was brought to Rome in the late 15th century and since 1866 has resided in the church of St Alphonsus de Liguori. Private and public veneration of this image has been associated with numerous miraculous favors and graces, including dramatic healings of the seriously ill, the paralyzed and those near death.

647. The oil painting of Our Lady of Sorrows, Quito, Ecuador, depicts the Virgin Mary carrying the crown of thorns and the three nails. From 20 April, 1906, during a period of heightened anti-clerical activity, many students of St Gabriel's Academy in Quito and others saw Our Lady's

eyes become animated, opening and closing repeatedly for extended periods of time. At times she also appeared sad and holding back tears. In all, there were over forty witnesses. A diocesan investigation conducted with the utmost rigor declared on 3 June, 1906, that the events in question were historically certain, inexplicable according to the laws of nature, and free of any diabolical influence.

648. The image of Our Lady of Czestochowa is otherwise known as the 'Black Madonna' due to the color of Our Lady's face, or Our Lady of Jasna Gora after the name of the monastery where it has been kept for six centuries. The image has three cuts to it, the first in the throat inflicted by the arrow of a Tartar in 1382, the other two caused by the sword of a Hussite heretic in 1430. These three slashes have always reappeared after artistic attempts to repair them. Since the defeat of the invading Swedes in 1655, the image of Our Lady of Czestochowa has been the symbol of Polish unity and nationhood.

649. The image of Our Lady of Guadalupe depicts the Virgin Mary as a pregnant half Aztec-half Spanish young woman. It first appeared in 1531. The image on cactus fibre is not painted on but is mysteriously impregnated into the threads and the pigments have no known source. The image still exists today unaffected by wind, humidity, nitric acid and bomb attacks. The base material should have decayed within twenty years, but it remains intact after nearly five hundred. Modern photography has also revealed that three men are reflected in Our Lady's eyes, one of them being St Juan Diego.

650. The image of Our Lady of Las Lajas ("the Rocks") is a beautiful image of Mary carrying the Christ Child with two male religious standing below. It was first discovered in the 18th century by a native Indian in a cave above the Guaitara River in Colombia. The image is said to be an *achiropita*, meaning not made by human hands, but rather by the angels. It is three-dimensional and set 122cm into the rock and contains no dye or pigment. Over fifty scientists from twelve countries have studied the rock and have been unable to provide any scientific explanation.

651. The image of Our Lady of Pompeii depicts the Virgin Mary sitting on a high throne with the Infant Jesus on her lap and a Rosary in her left hand. To her right and left are the kneeling figures of St Dominic and St Catherine of Siena. This image has been restored three times, the last being in 1965. Since 1883, it has been housed in the Shrine of the Virgin of the Rosary in Pompeii, which has been the site of hundreds of healings and miracles, all officially recorded at the sanctuary.

652. There are two international 'pilgrim statues' of Our Lady of Fatima carved under the supervision of Sister Lucy, the eldest of the three seers of Fatima. These statues are continually taken around the world by faithful promoting devotion to Our Lady of Fatima and her message. While in New Orleans on 17 July, 1972, one of these pilgrim statues began to weep inexplicably and continued to do so until the next morning. This event was witnessed by the statue's custodian, Fr Joseph Breault, a Fr Romagosa, as well as photographers and reporters.

653. The image of Our Lady of Akita is a statue approximately 90cm tall of Our Lady standing upon a globe and before a cross, her arms at her side with the palms of her hands facing forward. From 4 January, 1975, until 15 September, 1981, the image wept one hundred and one times. On some occasions it also perspired sweat and blood from the hands. These phenomena were witnessed on no less than ninety-six occasions, by both Catholics and non-Catholics. Rome approved the cult of veneration of Our Lady of Akita on 20 June, 1988.

654. The 'Shroud of Turin' is a linen cloth depicting the front and back of a crucified male human figure. Despite doubts over its authenticity since the late 14th century, modern scientific examination has provided no explanation for how the image came to be imprinted on the cloth, as well as the traces of human blood, type AB. Because of the remarkable similarity to the picture of the crucified Christ provided in the Gospels, the Shroud remains an inspirational and acceptable object of veneration for the faithful.

655. The 'Sudarium' is a face-cloth believed to be the one placed over the face of Christ during his burial. It contains three stains of type AB blood and

lymph. In 1969, NASA scientists placed the image of the Sudarium and that the Shroud of Turin over each other and found that they match perfectly, establishing that both cloths touched the same head after death. The Sudarium is housed in the Cathedral of San Salvador in Oviedo, Spain, where it has been since the early 9th century.

656. The 'Manoppello' is a transparent veil made of ancient byssus on which the face of Christ appears. It is said to be the original 'Veronica's veil' used to wipe the face of Christ during his carrying of the Cross. How the image appears on the cloth remains a mystery to scientists and artists alike. Tests in 1978 concluded that the face image on the 'Manoppello' and that on the Shroud of Turin are precisely super-imposable.

657. During three consecutive nights in 1533, the inhabitants of the village called Molochiello, Italy, saw a celestial vision and two lights in the middle of a dense hedge. The inhabitants set fire to the hedge but to their surprise the flames would not burn that section where the two lights had been seen. When the fire went out they saw a crucifix lying at the place where the lights had been, completely untouched by fire. The news travelled to the city of Terranova where a solemn procession of clergy and people went to the site of the crucifix and then carried it with reverence to the Mother Church. The crucifix survived the great earthquake of 1783, though most of the church containing the crucifix and the town of Terranova were destroyed.

658. The image of the 'Lord of the Miracles' of Lima, Peru, was painted in the 17th century by an unknown African slave. It miraculously survived two earthquakes in 1655 and 1687, which both left all the other walls of the chapel in ruins. Many healings have been associated with devotion to this image. The annual procession in October with a copy of the image is the largest religious gathering in Peru, numbering many hundreds of thousands.

659. In 1753, a Colombian Indian woman living in the town of Buga had saved 70 reales to buy a crucifix. One day she saw a man being sent to prison because he could not pay his debt of 70 reales. She decided to donate her savings to set the man free. Later, while washing some clothes

in a river a crucifix floated towards her. She took it home and put it in a box. To her surprise, the crucifix began to grow and eventually reached over 180cm. The bishop was informed and placed the crucifix on public veneration. Years later, fearing superstition the bishop decided to burn it. However, the crucifix was completely untouched by the flames. The miraculous wooden crucifix of Buga also regularly shatters the blades of those who attempt to hack at it. The feast of the 'Lord of Miracles' is on 14 September.

660. The miraculous Crucifix of Limpias is located in the 16th century Church of St Peter in Santander, Spain. The Crucifix is a 183cm life-size figure of the crucified Christ located above the main altar. In 1914, and repeatedly throughout 1919, the eyes of Christ on the crucifix miraculously came alive, closing and opening repeatedly. Altogether, over 8,000 people saw the apparitions, with 2,500 of these swearing on oath, including priests, doctors, lawyers, professors, university governors, officers, merchants, workmen, country folk, unbelievers and even atheists.

661. Miscellaneous miracles in the history of the Catholic Church have been countless. For our purposes we will relate just a handful. In 1291, a house built of limestone, mortar and cedar, materials native to the Holy Land, suddenly appeared in a field in Dalmatia. At the same time, it was discovered that the house of the Holy Family in Nazareth had disappeared. The same house eventually appeared on the east coast of Italy near the hamlet of Loreto. Pope Boniface VIII declared the tradition worthy of belief and 10 December was appointed as the feast day of the Translation of the House of Loreto.

662. On 13 October, 1917, 70,000 people gathered in Fatima, Portugal, saw the sun spin in the sky and change color successively, before falling to the earth in a terrifying manner. After twelve minutes, the sun resumed its normal place to great cries of relief. Everyone present was left completely dry despite the heavy rains that had drenched the area for hours beforehand. This miracle was witnessed by many skeptics, atheists, socialists, freemasons and the news reporter from 'O Seculo', Avelino de Almeida.

663. On 6 August, 1945, the first atomic bomb was dropped on Hiroshima, Japan, killing 80,000 people instantly. In the midst of the carnage was a community of eight Jesuit Fathers living in a parish presbytery, less than 1.5km away from the detonation point. Their presbytery remained standing, while all the surrounding buildings were destroyed. Examinations conducted by American army doctors confirmed that they had suffered no ill-effects from the bomb. One of the Jesuits, Fr Schiffer, stated that "we survived because we were living the message of Fatima."

664. Nouhad Chami had hemiplegia affecting her left leg, arm and mouth, due to almost total obstruction of the left and right neck arteries. On the night of 22 January, 1993, St Charbel Makhlouf and St Maron appeared and began operating on her neck without anaesthesia. When Nouhad awoke she had a 12cm cut on each side of her neck. She could now use her left arm and walk. To this day, on the 22nd of each month, Nouhad visits the monastery of St Maron at Annaya, Lebanon, where countless pilgrims witness blood appearing from her two open neck wounds on that one day in the month.

Chapter 8
Great Saints!

Preliminary

The Church is currently passing through very difficult times. There is a crisis of holiness, or as Pope St John Paul II once said, a "drought of saints." At the same time we witness almost daily reports of corruption and abuse in the Church, particularly sexual abuse of minors, which are shocking and inexcusable. These scandals cause many to turn their backs on the Church, perhaps never to be part of her life again. This is not surprising, as "sins and disorders ... prevent the radiation of (the Church's) sanctity" (Pope Paul VI, *Credo of the People of God*, para. 12).

Where, then, are the saints? Well, there are many. There are tens of thousands of individuals who have been publicly recognized for their sanctity over the past 2,000 years, including in modern times; there are countless millions more known only to God. Known or unknown, all these saints were faithful to God's graces in the Catholic Church and now enjoy their reward in Heaven with God. This chapter will look at some of the more well known of the recognized saints.

Among the recognized saints we find all sorts of individuals: men and women; young and old; kings and queens; wealthy and poor; lay and religious; priests and bishops; theologians and philosophers; martyrs; virgins; missionaries; founders of religious orders; soldiers and crusaders. Different people with different callings, all who generously responded to God's grace and fulfilled their vocations to the point of 'heroic sanctity.'

The Catholic Church is at its finest in her saints. No greater people have ever lived than the saints of the Catholic Church. This is why we should know the saints, for it is their holiness which best radiates the Church "without spot or wrinkle" (Eph. 5:27). Even if we cannot imitate we can at least admire and let their examples enthuse us to do more for God in a world critically in need of inspirational followers of Christ.

The timely reminder for each of us is that with God's grace sanctity in the modern world is possible. Sanctity is not something that belongs to the past. Sanctity is not just for the few. We are all called to holiness. We only need to will it.

Reasons

665. The Catholic Church recognizes that holiness is the calling of all Christians, without exception.

666. Nevertheless, following Matthew 13:8 the Catholic Church recognizes that not all Christians achieve holiness to the same degree and that there is a category of exceptional saints who follow Christ to an heroic degree: *"Other seeds fell on good soil and brought forth grain, some a hundredfold, some sixty, some thirty. He who has ears, let him hear"* (Matt. 13:8).

667. The process by which someone is officially recognized as a 'saint' is a long and exhausting one. The candidate for canonization is required to pass through three formal stages, namely, 'venerable', 'blessed' and 'saint.' The examination looks at all aspects of their life and calls for unquestionable proof of miracles wrought through the candidate's intercession, leaving no doubt as to their heroic sanctity and place in Heaven.

668. The official canon of heroic Catholic saints includes people from all walks of life: male and female, married and unmarried, young and old, black and white, rich and poor, fishermen and farmers, soldiers and scholars, kings and queens, priests and Popes.

669. Catholics can enjoy the support and prayers of 'patron saints' appointed through the Church's power to "bind and loose" (Matt. 16 & 18). Patron saints are insinuated in Matthew 25, where Christ promises his *"good and faithful servant(s)"* that they will be *"set ... over much"* as a reward for their fidelity (vv. 21 & 23).

670. The greatest of all saints, Mary the Mother of God, was given to us to be our spiritual mother by Christ himself while on the Cross: *"Behold, your mother!"* (John 19:27).

671. Catholics recognize Mary as the *"woman"* whose seed shall *"bruise"* the *"head"* of the serpent (Gen. 3:15).

672. Catholics recognize Mary as the *"woman clothed with the sun, with the moon*

under her feet, and on her head a crown of twelve stars" whose *"male child"* shall *"rule all the nations with a rod of iron"* (Rev. 12:1-5).

673. Catholics recognize Mary as the *"woman"* whose *"offspring ... keep the commandments of God and bear testimony to Jesus"* (Rev. 12:17).

674. Catholics call Mary "blessed" in fulfilment of her own prophecy that *"all generations will call me blessed"* (Luke 1:48).

675. There are thirty-five saints recognized by the Catholic Church who, because of their great scholarship and contribution to teaching Christian doctrine, are recognized as 'Doctors of the Church.' Some of these 'doctors' include St Augustine of Hippo, St John Chrysostom, St Thomas Aquinas, St Teresa of Avila and St Therese of the Child Jesus.

676. St Ignatius of Antioch (+110) was the third bishop of Antioch (after St Peter and St Evodius) and suffered martyrdom in the Roman Colosseum. On the way to Rome he authored seven epistles in which he spoke about the glory of martyrdom, the evil of heresy, the hierarchical nature of the Church and the Eucharist. Of the heretics contesting the Eucharist St Ignatius said: "They abstain from the Eucharist and from prayer, because they do not confess that the Eucharist is the Flesh of our Savior Jesus Christ, Flesh which suffered for our sins and which the Father, in his goodness, raised up again. They who deny the gift of God are perishing in their disputes" (*Letter to the Smyrnaeans* 7:1, c. 110).

677. St Justin Martyr (+165) was a pagan philosopher who came to see that Christianity was the "highest and most perfect philosophy." For over thirty years, St Justin defended Christianity with both word and pen, producing the most significant apologetical works of the 2nd century. Of the Eucharist he wrote: "For not as common bread nor common drink do we receive these; but since Jesus Christ our Savior was made incarnate by the word of God and had both flesh and blood for our salvation, so too, as we have been taught, the food which has been made into the Eucharist by the Eucharistic prayer set down by him, and by the change of which our blood and flesh is nourished is both the flesh and the blood of that incarnated Jesus" (*1 Apol.* 66, c. 155).

678. St Cyprian of Carthage (+258) led the local church in Carthage through the persecutions of the Emperors Decius (249-251) and Valerian (c. 258) before being arrested and martyred on 14 September, 258. Of the authority of the Bishop of Rome St Cyprian said: "... they dare even to set sail and carry letters from schismatics and blasphemers to the chair of Peter and to the principal Church, in which sacerdotal unity has its source; nor did they take thought that these are Romans, whose faith was praised by the preaching Apostle, and among whom it is not possible for perfidy to have entrance" (*Letter to Cornelius of Rome* 59 (55):14, c. 252).

679. St Tarcisius was a young acolyte who, during the Valerian persecution (250s), was entrusted to take the Eucharist to imprisoned Christians. He was stopped by a group of pagan friends who wanted to know what he was carrying. Angry at his refusal to reveal the 'Mysteries', the boys mobbed Tarcisius. A Christian friend drove off the attackers and carried Tarcisius back to the Catacombs, where he died of his injuries.

680. The 'Forty Martyrs of Sebaste' were a group of soldiers belonging to the Twelfth 'Fulminata' (Thundering) Legion of the Roman army. They all refused to obey the decree of the Eastern Emperor Licinius issued in 323 to renounce Christianity and preferred to be stripped and left out to freeze to death on the ice of a frozen pond. Those who had not died by the next morning were summarily executed.

681. St Anthony of Egypt (+356) lived for one hundred and five years, seventy-five of these as a hermit in the desert of Egypt. Though alone in the wilderness, many sought out his advice, including the Emperor Constantine. His influence was enormous, inspiring many others to become hermits or monks. As a consequence, he is considered the founder of the monastic way of life.

682. St Athanasius of Alexandria (295-373) was the great opponent of the Arian heresy and defender of the divinity of Christ. Due to his staunch defense of the Nicene teaching he was exiled five times from his see (335, 340, 356, 362, 365), incurring the wrath of Emperors Constantine, Constantius, Julian the Apostate and Valens in the process. It was largely due to his efforts that Arianism was eventually defeated.

683. St Monica (331-387) was the mother of the great St Augustine of Hippo and model of motherhood and virtue. For sixteen years she persevered in prayer for her son's conversion. On one occasion while speaking to a bishop about the fears she had for her son's salvation the bishop replied, "It is impossible that the son of these tears should perish." In April, 387, in the presence of his mother St Augustine received baptism at the hands of St Ambrose. A few months later, St Monica died after sharing with her converted son the famous ecstasy of Ostia.

684. St Ambrose of Milan (333-397) was made bishop of Milan during the height of the Catholic and Arian struggles (374). His greatness was due to his unending devotion to his flock, his dignified character and lofty views. He always catechized his people in a way that was positive and practical. The conversion of the great St Augustine was directly due to his manner, preaching and teaching. Publicly, St Ambrose is remembered for his opposition to the restoration of the Goddess of Victory statue to the senate chambers and his humiliation of the Emperor Theodosius for the massacre of 7,000 people at Thessalonica in 390.

685. St John Chrysostom (354-407) was the greatest of the Eastern Church Fathers. He acquired the name "Chrysostom" (golden-mouth) for the eloquence of his preaching. As Metropolitan of Constantinople, St John combated corruption and worldliness in court, monastic and city life. For this, he earned the wrath of the Empress Eudoxia, who had him exiled in June, 404, and again in September, 407. It was while on route to his new place of exile that St John died on 14 September, 407.

686. St Jerome (342-420) was the greatest biblical scholar of the ancient Church who translated the Old and New Testaments from Hebrew and Greek to the vernacular language of his time, Latin. The importance of the Scriptures in the mind of St Jerome is evidenced from the following words of his: "Ignorance of the Scriptures is ignorance of Christ." St Jerome also wrote in defense of Mary's perpetual virginity.

687. St Augustine of Hippo (354-430), after converting and being baptized by the great St Ambrose of Milan at the age of thirty-three, became Bishop of Hippo in North Africa and the foremost theologian-philosopher-apologist

of the first millennium of the Church's history. Today, St Augustine is honored as a Saint, Father and Doctor of the Church. Over four hundred of his works are extant and continue to be highly influential in the life of the Church, including his *City of God Against the Pagans*, wherein he formulated the ideal of a Christian state.

688. St Patrick (389-461) was born in Roman Britain and sold into slavery at the age of sixteen by Irish raiders. During his enslavement he underwent a profound religious conversion. Six years later he escaped Ireland and made his way to Gaul, where he joined a monastic community and studied theology. He eventually became a bishop and returned to Ireland as a missionary, spending the next twenty-nine years spreading Christianity among the natives. He was the first Bishop of Armagh and later patron saint of Ireland.

689. St Benedict of Nursia (480-547) founded the Benedictine Order which planted monasticism in the West and went on to preserve the remnants of civilization after the fall of the Roman Empire. His monastic rule was significant in helping to build a new civilization, namely Christendom.

690. St Augustine of Canterbury (+604) was a Benedictine monk who was sent in 595 by Pope St Gregory the Great to Christianize King Æthelberht and his Kingdom of Kent. St Augustine successfully converted King Æthelberht who then allowed missionaries to preach freely. Many conversions followed, including thousands during a mass baptism on Christmas Day in 597. In the same year, St Augustine became the first Archbishop of Canterbury. He is considered the 'Apostle to the English' and a founder of the English Church.

691. St Bede the Venerable (c. 673-735) was a Benedictine monk who wrote numerous works on grammar, history and commentaries on the Scriptures. St Bede's most famous work is the *History of the English Church and People*, for which he is known as the 'Father of English History.'

692. St Boniface (680-754) was an English Benedictine monk who evangelized Germany and much of northern Europe. He directly challenged pagan institutions, most notably his cutting down of the 'Oak of Thor' at

Geismar. His missionary success in Germany led to his appointment by the Carolingian Empire to reform the Frankish clergy. Success in this endeavor resulted in his elevation as Archbishop of Mainz. However, after only a few years he resigned this office and returned to missionary work in Frisia. There he was martyred on Pentecost Sunday in 754.

693. St Anselm of Canterbury (1033-1109) was a Benedictine monk who became Archbishop of Canterbury in 1093 under William II. He was exiled by Henry I from 1097 to 1100 and again from 1105 to 1107 for opposing his interference in the appointment of bishops. St Anselm's significant contributions to theology include his ontological argument for the existence of God and the satisfaction theory of atonement. St Anselm was proclaimed a Doctor of the Church by Pope Clement XI in 1720.

694. St Bernard of Clairvaux (1090-1153) was the greatest saint of the 12th century. He reformed the Cistercian Order, founded one hundred and sixty-nine monasteries, was an outstanding preacher, prolific writer, Marian devotee, and miracle worker. He influenced Kings and Popes, attacked church corruption, and opposed the persecution of Jews. He also preached against the Albigensians and promoted the Second Crusade. The rule of the crusading order of Knights Templar was authored by him.

695. St Thomas à Becket (1118-1170) was Archbishop of Canterbury from 1162 until his murder in 1170. He fell into conflict with Henry II of England over the independence of the Church and was murdered by followers of the king in Canterbury Cathedral. When news of this was brought to the King, he shut himself up and fasted for forty days. He later was compelled to perform public penance. Within three years of his death, St Thomas was canonized as a martyr and his tomb recognized as a site of pilgrimage and miracles.

696. St Dominic Guzman (1170-1221) was ordained a priest in 1199. In 1203, he travelled to French Languedoc to preach against the Albigensian heresy. For seven years Dominic also supported the army of Simon of Montfort in its crusade against the Albigensians. In 1214, he founded the Order of Preachers devoted to the conversion of heretics and the preaching of the Rosary. Dominic travelled across Western Europe

preaching and establishing new houses. The new order was phenomenally successful as it harmonized the intellectual life with popular needs.

697. St Francis of Assisi (1182-1226) most exemplified Christ's exhortation to *"sell what you possess and give to the poor ... and come, follow me"* (Matt. 19:21). He founded the Order of Friars Minor (Franciscans) in 1209 dedicated to preaching, service and evangelical poverty. St Francis is unique in his poverty, simplicity, holy joy and popular appeal.

698. St Clare of Assisi (1194-1253) was a close friend and associate of St Francis. Inspired by St Francis' preaching, St Clare renounced everything and founded the 'Poor Clares', a religious order of nuns devoted to strict penance, living off alms and rejoicing in God's gifts.

699. St Anthony of Padua (1195-1231) was a renowned preacher and wonder-worker and first theologian of the Franciscan Order. Many of his miracles have become legendary, including his carrying of the Infant Jesus and his preaching to the fishes against the Cathars. As a testimony to his great preaching, St Anthony's tongue remains incorrupt. Today he is honored as a Doctor of the Church and is popularly invoked for finding lost items.

700. St Elizabeth of Hungary (1207-1231) was a princess of the Kingdom of Hungary. She married at the young age of fourteen, and was widowed at twenty. After her husband's death, St Elizabeth made solemn vows similar to those of a nun. Using money from her re-gained dowry, St Elizabeth built a hospital at Marburg for the poor and the sick, where she and her friends cared for them. For the rest of her brief life she ministered to the sick and continued to give money to the poor.

701. St Louis IX (1214-1270) was King of France and one of the greatest kings of the Middle Ages. His motto was, "Christ is Victorious, Christ Reigns, Christ Governs." He always remembered his mother's words, "I would rather see you dead at my feet than guilty of a mortal sin." Every day he spent hours in prayer, fed over one hundred poor, and travelled throughout France administering justice, founding hospitals and ministering to lepers. St Louis also led the seventh and eighth crusades in 1247-50 and 1267-70, dying of plague during the latter adventure.

702.St Bonaventure (1221-1274) received his name from St Francis of Assisi, who, foreseeing the future greatness of the child, cried out "O Buona ventura" — "O good fortune!" At the age of twenty-two he entered the Franciscan Order and later as General restored calm where peace had been disturbed by internal dissensions. He became the close friend of the great St Thomas Aquinas. Pope Gregory X obliged him to take the office of Cardinal and Bishop of Albano, one of the six suffragan Sees of Rome. For his lofty writings, St Bonaventure is known as the *"Seraphic Doctor."*

703.St Thomas Aquinas (1225-1274) was an Italian Dominican friar and scholastic philosopher and theologian. His influence on Western thought is profound, particularly in the areas of ethics, natural law, metaphysics, and political theory. His best known works are the *Summa Theologica* and the *Summa Contra Gentiles.* St Thomas is further distinguished for his commentaries on sacred Scripture and on Aristotle, as well as for his Eucharistic hymns. St Thomas is considered the Church's greatest theologian and philosopher and is recognized as the *"Doctor Angelicus."*

704.St Albert the Great (1193-1280) was a great preacher, teacher and leader of medieval scholasticism who authored numerous books on theology, philosophy, logic, ethics and metaphysics, including commentaries on the Scriptures, Aristotle and the *Sentences* of Peter Lombard. St Albert's works are credited for their accessibility, intelligibility and for advancing the unity of faith and reason. St Albert greatly influenced St Thomas Aquinas and is honored as *"Doctor Universalis."*

705.St Catherine of Siena (1347-1380), the great mystic and Doctor of the Church, was primarily responsible for convincing Pope Gregory XI to leave Avignon in France and return to Rome (1377), thus ending seventy years of exile known as the 'Babylonian Captivity of the Church.' She also received visions of Christ and the stigmata. For the last twenty-five years of her life she lived only on the Eucharist received once a day.

706.St John Nepomucene (1345-1393) was a great preacher and confessor in the court of Wenceslaus IV of Bohemia. In 1393, the king twice demanded to know what his queen had said in confession. Fr John refused to obey the king on both occasions, enduring imprisonment and torture. The king then ordered Fr John to be thrown into a river and drowned. Later, a mysterious brightness appeared upon the river. Fr John is now revered as the "martyr of the confessional."

707. St Vincent Ferrer (1357-1419) was a member of the Dominican Order and the most famous missionary of the 14th and 15th centuries. He evangelized most of Spain, and preached in France, Italy, Germany, Flanders, England, Scotland, and Ireland. Numerous conversions followed his preaching, which was accompanied by many miracles. Though it was the time of the Great Schism, St Vincent was welcomed in the regions of both rival Papal claimants. He was even invited to Islamic Granada, where he preached the gospel with much success.

708. St Joan of Arc (1412-1431), at the instigation of St Michael, St Catherine and St Margaret, took leadership of the armies of France and won a spectacular victory against the English at Orleans on 8 May, 1429. She then enjoyed a series of four further military successes, during which Charles VII was able to enter the city of Rheims and be crowned King of France. She was burned at the stake on 30 May, 1431, after an unjust trial conducted by the pro-English Bishop of Beauvais, Pierre Cauchon.

709. St John Capistrano (1386-1456) was an observant Franciscan friar and great popular preacher who, among other things, preached a crusade against the advancing Ottoman Turks. Together with General Hunyadi, St John raised an army of over 10,000 men to raise the Ottoman siege of the city of Belgrade. This famous victory preserved Hungary from any further Ottoman advances for another sixty years.

710. St Rita of Cascia (1381-1457) was married at the age of twelve to a man of violent temperament. It was an unhappy marriage that produced two sons. St Rita would sadly see her repentant husband murdered and her two sons die. She turned to prayer, fasting and charitable works. Later, St Rita joined the Augustinian sisters and devoted herself to the passion of Christ, mystically receiving a wound in her forehead to allow her to share in his passion. After her death, St Rita's incorrupt body diffused a strong perfume and many miracles were reported at her sarcophagus.

711. St John Fisher (1469-1535) was an English Cardinal-Bishop and theologian. He was associated with the intellectuals and political leaders of his day and eventually became Chancellor of Cambridge University. St John was beheaded by order of King Henry VIII for refusing to accept his new title of "Supreme Head of the Church of England" and for upholding the doctrine of Papal primacy.

712. St Thomas More (1478-1535) was Chancellor of England during the reign of King Henry VIII. Following his Catholic conscience, St Thomas courageously opposed the King's new title of "Head of the Church in England." While many others in positions of power and authority acceded to Henry's usurped title, St Thomas preferred the executor's axe and martyrdom.

713. St John of God (1495-1550) as a young man led a dissolute life. After a profound conversion in his early forties, St John employed himself in ministering to the sick, the poor and the homeless. On one occasion he heard the voice of Christ saying, "John, to me you do all that you do to the poor in my name." The local bishop became a supporter of St John's work and gave him the name of 'John of God.' St John died of an illness he contracted after saving a drowning man. After his death, his many followers formed a religious community called the 'Brothers Hospitallers.'

714. St Ignatius Loyola (1491-1556) founded the Society of Jesus (Jesuits) with the motto, "To the Greater Glory of God." With their obedience to the Pope the Jesuits rose to become the 'shock troops of the Counter-Reformation.' They became distinguished for their devotion to the Sacred Heart, scholarship, education and missionary zeal.

715. St Francis Xavier SJ (1506-1552), another of the early Jesuits and dear friend of St Ignatius, single-handedly introduced the Catholic faith to India, Indonesia and Japan, enduring incredible hardships from hostile locals, language barriers, disease and poor climates. Only a premature death prevented him entering the mysterious land of China.

716. Bl. Ignatius Azevedo (1528-1570), together with thirty-nine other Jesuits, were returning by ship to Brazil when they were intercepted by a Dutch

pirate. All were offered their lives and freedom if they apostatized to Calvinism. All of them, to the youngest novice, refused and were subsequently butchered. As he fell, mortally wounded, Bl. Ignatius declared, "Angels and men are witness that I die on behalf of the holy Church, Roman, Catholic, and Apostolic."

717. St Edmund Campion (1540-1581) was an Anglican deacon who in 1569 returned to Catholicism. In Europe he joined the Jesuits and returned to England in 1580 to conduct a secret underground mission to the beleaguered Catholic community. St Edmund's activities incited an intense manhunt that eventually led to his capture and imprisonment in the Tower of London. After refusing to apostatize despite rich inducements, he was tortured and then hanged, drawn, and quartered at Tyburn on 1 December, 1581, on the charge of treason.

718. St Teresa of Avila (1515-1582) reformed the Carmelite Order by founding seventeen houses of 'Discalced' (shoeless) Carmelites. During her work for reform, St Teresa received numerous visions of Christ and wrote a number of works on prayer that are now classics of Catholic spirituality, including *The Interior Castle* and *The Way of Perfection*.

719. St John of the Cross (1542-1591) was greatly influenced by St Teresa of Avila to work for reform within the male Carmelite Order. He overcame imprisonment and torture to see the male Discalced Carmelites eventually recognized. Much of St John's spiritual poetry and his *Ascent of Mount Carmel* continue to be read as spiritual masterpieces.

720. St Margaret Clitherow (1556-1586) was a convert to the Catholic faith who preferred repeated imprisonment to attendance at Anglican services. During the height of the Elizabethan persecution, St Margaret allowed Masses to be said in her home and clandestinely harbored priests, both actions then punishable by death. In 1586, she was arrested and put on trial for her life. St Margaret did not resist the charges and the court condemned her to be crushed under a huge weight. This penalty was executed even though she was possibly pregnant at the time. St Margaret was canonized in 1970 by Pope Paul VI.

721.St Aloysius Gonzaga (1568-1591) at age seventeen renounced his status and inheritance to join the Jesuits. As a novice he was outstanding in virtue and self-sacrifice, assisting the stricken during an outbreak of the plague in Rome. It was while carting plague victims that he himself fell ill, dying at the age of twenty-three. St Aloysius is now honored as the patron saint of youth.

722.St Philip Neri (1515-1595) abandoned the world of business to pursue a life of prayer and solitude. While praying in the Catacombs he felt a globe of light enter his mouth and descend into his heart. As a priest, St Philip loved to hear confessions and founded the Congregation of the Oratory to provide specialized spiritual formation and direction. He was spontaneous and unpredictable, charming and humorous and cultivated different ways to bring people to God. However, St Philip always remained serious about prayer and when asked how to pray he answered, "Be humble and obedient and the Holy Spirit will teach you."

723.St Peter Canisius SJ (1521-1597) was a great apologist and missionary of Germany where, for fifty years, he labored through preaching and writing for the salvation of souls. His catechism, a masterpiece of brevity and clarity, was translated into every European language.

724.St Robert Bellarmine SJ (1542-1621) was a great theologian and Doctor of the Church whose apologetical works against Protestantism were unchallenged in his day. In the field of church-state relations, he took a novel position based on principles now regarded as democratic — authority originates with God, but is vested in the people, who entrust it to appropriate rulers. St Robert was the spiritual father of St Aloysius Gonzaga, assisted St Francis de Sales to obtain formal approval of the Visitation Order, and opposed severe action against Galileo.

725.St Paul Miki was a Japanese Jesuit priest who, together with twenty-five priests, religious and lay companions, was put to death on the 'Holy Mountain' overlooking Nagasaki in 1597. They were executed by a form of crucifixion whereby they were raised on crosses and then pierced with spears. St Paul's last words were, "I forgive my persecutors. I do not hate them. I ask God to have pity on all, and I hope my blood will fall on my fellow men as a fruitful rain."

726. St Camillus de Lellis (1550-1614) was a penniless soldier addicted to gambling when he underwent a profound conversion. He devoted himself to the care of the sick and later obtained permission from his confessor to found a congregation (the 'Camillians') to further his work. This Congregation was approved by Pope Gregory XIV in 1591 and sent members to minister to wounded troops in Hungary and Croatia, the first field medical units. Seriously ill for years, St Camillus resigned as the Order's superior in 1614 and died in Rome that same year on 14 July.

727. St Frances de Sales (1567-1622) was the great apologist and missionary to the Calvinists in the Swiss province of Chablais. Through great patience and kindness, and travelling for three years on foot from town to town preaching and teaching, St Francis managed to convert the whole population of over 40,000 back to Catholicism. When people refused to listen to him, he simply handed out leaflets and pinned them up on town notice boards. He later became Bishop of Annecy, France, and wrote a number of spiritual classics, including *An Introduction to the Devout Life*.

728. Saints Roch Gonzalez, Alphonsus Rodriguez and John de Castillo, were Jesuit priests responsible for the founding of the first 'Reductions' (settlements) in Paraguay and Brazil where natives could be catechized in self-sufficient communities free from exploitation and enslavement. In total, they founded eight Reductions and were intent on founding others in more remote regions but were martyred in November 1628 at the instigation of native medicine men who resented their missionary work.

729. St Lawrence Ruiz was a Filipino laymen who in 1636 travelled to Japan with three Dominican priests to bring the sacraments to the beleaguered Catholic community. They were shipwrecked on the island of Okinawa and later arrested and sent to Nagasaki. There, they endured horrific tortures until they were strung upside down to die of blood loss and suffocation. St Lawrence's last words were, "I am a Catholic and wholeheartedly do accept death for the Lord. If I had a thousand lives, all these I shall offer to him."

730.The Martyrs of Ireland (1579-1654) were 17 victims of the English persecution of Catholics who refused to renounce the authority of the Pope. The highest ranking of these martyrs was the Archbishop of Cashel, Dermot O'Hurley (d. 1584), who soon after his arrival in Ireland was arrested, tortured and hanged. The other martyrs included Patrick O'Healy OFM, Conn O'Rourke OFM, Matthew Lambert, Robert Meyler, Edward Cheevers, Patrick Cavanagh, Margaret Ball, Maurice McKenraghty, Dominic Collins SJ, Conor O'Devany OFM, Patrick O'Loughbrain, Francis Taylor, Peter Higgins OP, Terence Albert OP, John Kearney OFM and William Tirry OSA.

731.St Peter Claver (1581-1654) was a Jesuit missionary sent from Spain to carry out missionary work in the Americas. In his attitude towards Negro slaves St Peter was centuries ahead of his time, being horrified at the treatment meted out to them by their Spanish masters. St Peter viewed the Negros as fellow human beings, encouraging others to do the same. During his forty years of missionary activity he catechized and baptized over 300,000 slaves, advocating also for their Christian and civil rights. St Peter also preached city and country missions to Spaniards, English Protestants and Moslems. During these missions, St Peter insisted always on lodging in the slave quarters.

732.St Vincent de Paul (1581-1660) was ordained a priest in 1600 and after escaping the captivity of African pirates returned to France and began preaching missions. In 1625, he founded the Congregation of the Mission and later the Sisters of Charity, both dedicated to providing charitable assistance to all classes of persons. Despite numerous distractions and public honors, St Vincent remained always intimately united with God and deeply rooted in charity and humility.

733.St Joseph of Cupertino (1603-1663) began to experience ecstatic visions as a child, which attracted ridicule. After several failed attempts to enter religious life, he was accepted by the Conventual friars near Cupertino. However, St Joseph's frequent ecstasies and publicly witnessed levitations were deemed disruptive by his religious superiors and he was denounced to the Inquisition. From 1639, he was kept under supervision during which he practised a severe asceticism, usually eating solid food only twice a week. He lived the last six years of his life undisturbed in the Conventual community in Osimo.

734. St Kateri Tekakwitha (1656-1680) was a native Indian known as the 'Lily of the Mohawks' for her extraordinary mystical and contemplative spirituality. As a child she survived smallpox which left her with scars on her face and body. Her conversion to Catholicism estranged her from her people and she felt obliged to escape for her life. While in the mission of Sault Sainte Marie near Montreal she received her First Communion, took a private vow of chastity and lived the life of an heroic penitent. After her death, St Kateri's faced glowed and all her scars disappeared.

735. St Oliver Plunkett (1629-1681) was Archbishop of Armagh and Primate of Ireland. In 1679, he was arrested and falsely charged with treason. He was brought to London and was put on trial, and due to the evidence of perjured witnesses, was sentenced to be hanged, drawn and quartered at Tyburn. Resigned to his fate, he calmly rebutted the charge of treason and refused to save himself by supplying false testimony against his fellow bishops. Before his execution on 1 July, 1681, St Oliver publicly forgave all those who conspired for his death.

736. St Claude de la Colombiere SJ (1641-1682) was a Jesuit priest and in his early years served as tutor to the son of the powerful French minister Colbert. He acquired a reputation as a distinguished preacher and as superior of Paray-le-Monial became spiritual director to the great St Margaret Mary Alacoque. In that capacity he became one of the leaders in the spread of devotion to the Sacred Heart. While chaplain to the Duchess of York, St Claude was falsely accused of involvement in the Titus Oates Plot, enduring imprisonment and banishment from England.

737. St. Junipero Serra (1713-1784) was a Franciscan missionary who, despite a debilitating injury to his leg caused by a snake bite, became the founder and father of the Californian missions. He personally founded nine individual missions between 1769 and 1782, suffering many trials and severe physical pain during these years. He died on 28 August, 1784, exhausted and ill from his ceaseless missionary endeavors.

738.St Alphonsus de Liguori (1696-1787) founded the Congregation of the Most Holy Redeemer in 1732. For many years he and his congregation fed the poor, instructed families, re-organized seminary and religious houses, preached missions, taught theology, and wrote numerous books, especially on Moral Theology and his *'Glories of Mary.'* St Alphonsus' austerities were rigorous, and he suffered from rheumatism that deformed his body. He also experienced visions, performed miracles, and made prophecies. Deposed and excluded from his own congregation in later life, St Alphonsus suffered great anguish. However, he died peacefully and was declared a Doctor of the Church by Bl. Pius IX in 1871.

739.The eighteen Carmelite Martyrs of Compiegne were outstanding examples of faithfulness in the face of hostile persecution from the French revolutionary government. Rather than accept dispersion or swear allegiance to the new constitution, they preferred public execution. After enduring brutalities and indignities and renewing their baptismal and religious vows, they each individually went to their deaths under the blade of the guillotine on 17 July, 1792.

740.The Christian Brothers Martyrs of the French Revolution included Br Solomon Leclerq, Br Léon Mopinot, Br Roger Faverge, and Br Uldaric Guillaume. All four refused to sign the Civil Constitution of the Clergy and were forced out of their teaching positions as a consequence. They individually suffered vicious and agonizing deaths at the hands of revolutionaries determined to eliminate the Catholic faith from the land. They were together beatified by Pope St John Paul II on 1 October, 1995.

741.The Martyrs of La Rochelle (d. 1794) included John Souzy, Gabriel Pergaud and sixty-two other French priests who resisted the anti-religious edicts of the French Revolution. They were all arrested and imprisoned in slave ships wherein they were subjected to constant darkness, unbreathable air, brutalities and mockery, all without food and water. All signs of prayer and faith were forbidden. They were together beatified by Pope St John Paul II on 1 October, 1995.

742.St John Vianney (1786-1859) was the parish priest of the remote French village of Ars who gained a world-wide reputation as a confessor and director of souls. He heard confessions up to sixteen hours a day and could convert hardened sinners at his word. Though beleaguered by legions of penitents, and attacked by the devil, St John displayed imperturbable patience and retained a childlike simplicity. He practised extreme mortification and constantly engaged in works of charity and love as one constantly after the heart of Christ.

743. St Eugene de Mazenod (1782-1861) was born of a noble family and eventually became Archbishop of Marseilles in southern France. He founded the Missionary Oblates of Mary Immaculate in 1816 to instruct the faithful in rural areas left destitute by the French Revolution. He was a staunch defender of the rights of the Church and the Papacy against renewed secular attacks against the Church. He was also an example of grace, respect and charity to his opponents without compromising principles or the faith.

744. St Andrew Kim Tae-gon (1821-1846) was the first Korean to be ordained to the Catholic priesthood. Secretly returning to Korea from Macau, Fr Kim catechized the faithful in and around his home town. While trying to introduce French missionaries into the country with the aid of Chinese fishermen, Fr Kim was arrested and imprisoned in Seoul, where he was charged as the ringleader of a foreign sect and traitor. He was sentenced to death and beheaded on 16 September, 1846.

745. The twenty-five Dominican Martyrs of Vietnam were led by Bishops Joseph Diaz Sanjuro and Jerome Hermosillo. They number among one hundred and seventeen Vietnamese martyrs who endured torture, strangulation or other abuse due to their refusal to abjure the Catholic faith during the wholesale persecution of King Tu-Duc between 1856 and 1862.

746. The Martyrs of Podlasie were thirteen Polish laymen led by Vincent Lewoniuk who refused an order of Czar Alexander II of Russia in 1874 to convert their parish to the Orthodox faith. As they publicly knelt together singing hymns and repeating, "It is sweet to die for the faith", they were shot dead by soldiers before their families and friends. They were buried by the Russians who forbad any sign of public honor. Vincent and his

companions were beatified by Pope St John Paul II on 6 October, 1996.

747. St Damien de Veuster (1840-1889) joined the Sacred Heart Fathers in 1860. In 1864, he began missionary work on the Big Island, Hawaii. In 1873, he volunteered to work at the leper colony on Molokai. There, Fr Damien cared for lepers one by one, especially the children, and worked tirelessly building hospitals, houses, churches, and some six hundred coffins. In 1885, he announced he was a leper but remained totally committed to those under his care until his death on 15 April, 1889.

748. St John Bosco (1815-1888) founded the Salesian Order in Turin, Italy, to care for and educate neglected boys. From the age of nine, St John was favored with visionary dreams and mystical phenomena, so much so that "the supernatural became the natural and the extraordinary ordinary." Despite this, St John always maintained a joyful, warm and loving attitude to all. St John's advice to his students was, "Enjoy yourself as much as you like, if only you keep from sin."

749. St Therese of the Child Jesus (1873-1897) was a Carmelite nun and mystic. Through her 'little way' spirituality, she showed the world that true sanctity is found in simplicity, humility and charity. Her autobiography, *The Story of a Soul,* made St Therese one of the most popular saints of the 20th century. In 1997, Pope St John Paul II declared her a Doctor of the Church.

750. Bl. Salvatore Lilli (1853-1895) was an Italian Franciscan missionary arriving in Mujuk-Deresa, Armenia, in 1894. In 1895, the area was occupied by Islamic Turks who captured Salvatore and fellow Franciscans Baldji Ohannes, David David, Dimbalac Wartavar, Geremia Boghos, Khodianin Kadir, Kouradji Tzeroum, and Toros David. All eight were ordered to convert to Islam or die. They suffered cruel tortures and were martyred on 22 November, 1895.

751. St Maria Goretti (1890-1902) was a martyr for purity, having repeatedly resisted the sexual advances of a neighbor, Alessandro Serenelli, who in frustration eventually attacked her. Maria desperately tried to fight off her attacker saying, "No! It is a sin! God does not want it!" Alessandro first

attempted to choke Maria and then stabbed her fourteen times. Before she died in hospital, Maria forgave her attacker. A converted Alessandro attended Maria's beatification in 1947.

752. St Mary MacKillop of the Cross (1842-1909), together with Fr Julian Tenison-Woods, founded the religious order of the Sisters of St Joseph of the Sacred Heart in 1866 to provide education and welfare services to the poor throughout the remote rural regions of Australia and New Zealand.

753. Bl. Isidore Bakanja (1887?-1909) was a devout Congolese convert and catechist who in early February, 1909, was ordered by his work supervisor to stop sharing the Gospel and remove his brown scapular. Isidore refused and was savagely beaten and left lying in a pool of blood. Isidore's wounds became infected and his condition deteriorated so rapidly that death was imminent. Missionaries in the area attended Isidore and urged him to forgive the supervisor. He said that he already had, declaring "When I am in Heaven, I shall pray for him very much."

754. St Joseph Moscati (1880-1927) was a medical professor and practitioner who worked to bring Christ to the world of medicine and was distinguished for his amiable piety and sanctification of the ordinary. Besides his work among young doctors, Dr Moscati worked each morning to bring medical care to the poor living among the slums of Naples, especially the young children. Among these poor Dr Moscati labored until his death in April, 1927.

755. St Maximillian Kolbe (1894-1941) was a Franciscan friar who founded monasteries and employed the latest technology to propagate the Catholic faith. After the outbreak of World War II he secretly worked to shelter thousands of Poles and Jews from the Nazis. He also continued to print an underground anti-Nazi newspaper. In May, 1941, St Maximillian was arrested and shipped off to Auschwitz concentration camp. After the escape of a prisoner, ten others were selected to be executed. St Maximillian volunteered to take the place of one of these ten, who were then herded together in a starvation bunker. In the ensuing two weeks St Maximillian encouraged the other prisoners with prayer before being killed with an injection of carbolic acid on 14 August, 1941.

756. Bl. Pier Giorgio Frassati (1901-1925) was the pious son of not-so-devout wealthy and politically powerful Italian parents. Bl. Pier grew up to be a daily communicant and developed a great devotion to the Virgin Mary. Though an outgoing and charming personality, Bl. Pier secretly served thousands of the poor through the work of the St Vincent de Paul Society. It was while serving these poor that he suddenly contracted polio and died in agony on 4 July, 1925. Many of those served by Bl. Pier came to his funeral unannounced, to the surprise of his grief-stricken parents.

757. St Rodrigo Aguilar Alemán (1875-1927) practised his ministry in secret during the height of the Mexican persecution. On 28 October, 1927, he was arrested and taken to the main square of Ejutla to be hanged from a mango tree. A soldier gave him the chance to save himself if he answered the question "Who lives?" with "Long live the supreme government!" But Fr Rodrigo replied, "Christ the King and Our Lady of Guadalupe!" After giving the same answer two more times, the noose was raised and tightened, snapping Fr Rodrigo's neck.

758. Bl. Miguel Augustine Pro (1891-1927) was a Mexican Jesuit priest who secretly labored to administer the sacraments and teach catechetics at a time of intense religious hatred and persecution. On 18 November, 1927, Fr Pro was arrested on trumped up charges of trying to assassinate the country's President. Fr Pro was executed by firing squad on 23 November, his last words being "Long live Christ the King!" Thousands of the faithful defied the government to march in procession behind his coffin.

759. The Martyrs of Guadalajara were three cloistered Carmelite nuns, Sr Maria Pilar, Sr Maria of the Angels, and Sr Teresa of the Child Jesus, who, while fleeing their convent in the face of communist militia groups, were confronted and gunned down on 24 July, 1936. They each preferred to surrender themselves in death rather than deny Christ and the Carmel.

760. St Edith Stein (1891-1942) was a brilliant philosopher who during her search for truth moved from Judaism to atheism and then to Catholicism. She converted to Catholicism in 1922 after reading the autobiography of St Teresa of Avila. She entered the Carmelite Order in 1934 but fled Germany for the Netherlands in 1938 due to Nazi oppression. Together

with her sister Rosa, St Edith was arrested in 1942 and sent to Auschwitz concentration camp where on 10 August she was gassed to death.

761. Bl. Peter To Rot (1912-1945) was a catechist and lay parish leader in his native village in New Britain, near Papua New Guinea. When the invading Japanese occupied New Britain they interned missionaries and harassed their supporters, including Bl. Peter. To win over the locals, the Japanese legalized polygamy. This was openly opposed by Bl. Peter, who was then arrested and sentenced to two months imprisonment. However, while in prison Bl. Peter was beaten and given a lethal injection. He died just one month before the final Japanese surrender.

762. Bl. Karl Leisner (1915-1945) was a German deacon who was arrested by the Gestapo on 9 November, 1939, for criticizing Adolf Hitler while in an infirmary recovering from tuberculosis. Eventually, Bl. Karl was transferred to Dachau concentration camp where he endured three years of cold weather, poor rations and repeated beatings. In 1944, he was secretly ordained a priest and managed to celebrate only one Mass before his camp was liberated by the Allies. Bl. Karl died on 12 August, 1945, from tuberculosis aggravated by his imprisonment and treatment.

763. St Joanna Gianna Beretta Molla (1922-1962) was a doctor and surgeon pregnant with her fourth child when she was diagnosed with a fibrous tumor in her ovary. Rather than abort the pregnancy or undergo any surgery that would harm her unborn baby, St Joanna chose only to have her fibroma removed. The baby was born safely on 21 April, 1962, though St Joanna died of septic peritonitis seven days later. Throughout her sufferings, St Joanna praised God and serenely resigned herself to his will.

764. Bl. Mother Teresa of Calcutta founded the Missionaries of Charity in 1950 to provide "wholehearted and free service to the poorest of the poor." The Missionaries of Charity now number over 4,500 sisters working in one hundred and thirty-three countries running orphanages, schools, soup kitchens, hospitals and homes for abandoned children, the homeless, and those with chronic diseases such as AIDs, leprosy and tuberculosis, etc.

Chapter 9
Great Beauty!

Preliminary

The Catholic Church has always been a great promoter of goodness, truth and beauty. As regards beauty, the Catholic Church has been responsible for inspiring the production of the most renowned and beautiful works known to humanity. Whether they are believers or not, tens of millions of people every year travel to Europe alone just to marvel at countless items of beauty produced by the Church since the days of the Roman Empire. There are also innumerable Catholic treasures scattered throughout every other continent in the world.

There is no limit to the types of beauty inspired by the Catholic Church. For children and families there are the delights of Christmas cribs, wreaths and trees. For the learned and scholars there are beautiful books and illuminated manuscripts. In music, there is Gregorian chant, polyphonies, carols and a myriad of hymns in all different languages. Inside churches we marvel at beautiful floors, stunning mosaics and glorious stained glass windows. Dazzling frescoes and paintings capture our gaze and a limitless variety of statues leave us in awe and wonder. In recesses and corners we behold beautiful candles, whether large or small, glimmering in the dark, or hear the sound of gigantic bells peeling away. On the public stage, Advent and Passion plays capture our attention and deepen our faith. Scattered throughout the world are the great Romanesque and Gothic churches and monasteries whose spires point toward Heaven and speak of strength and beauty. The world's museums are filled with Catholic treasures produced by the greatest artists of all time, including Giotto, Fra Angelico, da Vinci, Michelangelo and Caravaggio, just to name a few.

No single book or chapter on Catholic beauty can ever do justice to the Church's indisputable contribution in this area. This chapter aims only to provide a brief outline of what is finest and most beautiful and give thanks to God for such. In an age when modern society glorifies the ugly and the meaningless, humanity owes a great debt to the Catholic Church for its legacy of beauty.

Reasons

765.The Catholic Church, as a sanctuary, or holy place set apart for God, surrounds its worship with glorious acoustic, artistic and architectural beauty.

766.The Latin language is the official language of the Roman Rite of the Catholic Church. It usefulness lies in its unchanging preciseness, beauty and historical value. The use of Latin reminds Catholics of the Church's ancient origins during the time of the Roman Empire. Though in decline in recent decades, Latin is still used for all official Church documents, in the singing of Gregorian Chant, and in the celebration of the Extraordinary Form of the Roman Liturgy.

767.The 'Chi-Rho' is an ancient symbol of Christ having its origins in the 2nd century. It is comprised of the first two letters of the word 'Christ' in Greek (XP) overlapping each other to form a monogram. The Emperor Constantine employed the symbol on his military standards and it soon after became associated with Christian triumph. The symbol remains in use today, usually depicted on liturgical vestments or in churches, etc.

768.Christmas cribs highlight the truth of the incarnation (the Word becoming flesh) and are a delight for children and families as the Church prepares to celebrate the coming of Christ each December.

769.The Christmas tree is a beautiful medieval tradition that reminds us of the star of Bethlehem, the family tree of Christ going back to King David's father (Jesse) and all the Old Testament prophets who prophesied the coming of the Messiah.

770.Christmas carols are an enchanting centuries-old custom engaging the faithful in songs of joy and praise in celebration of the birth of Christ. There are numerous Christ-centred carols, the most famous being *Silent Night, O Come all Ye Faithful, Away in the Manger*, etc.

771.Advent Wreaths originated in Germany and comprise of a circle of evergreen foliage with four candles (three purple, one pink) lit successively over the four weeks of the season of Advent. They are meant to symbolize the coming of Christ, the "Light of the World" born in Bethlehem.

772. 'Advent Plays' are popular re-enactments of the Nativity story. They vary in form between different countries but have the common purpose of evangelization or catechesis. In Germany they are called *Herbersuchen* ("Search for the Inn") and in Latin countries *Las Posadas* ("The Inns"). In some countries they take the form of a novena, being enacted over nine consecutive nights and concluding with a fiesta.

773. 'Passion Plays' are dignified re-enactments of the Passion of Christ, having their origin in the ritual of the Church during the Middle Ages. They are characterized by their dramatic artistic, costume, music and stage effects. The most famous Passion Play is that of Oberammergau, south-west Germany, conducted every ten years by the people of that village in fulfilment of a vow of thanksgiving made in 1634 after being delivered from the Black Death plague.

774. Easter eggs remind Catholics of the tomb of Christ. Breaking open and eating the same reminds us of how Christ emerged from the enclosed tomb, conquering, death, sin and Hell.

775. The 'Paschal Candle' is a large ornate candle that resides in the sanctuary of each Catholic Church. On the front are the Greek letters Alpha and Omega representing Christ as the beginning and the end, a Cross figure representing Christ's crucifixion, and the calendar year. Also encased in the candle are five grains of incense representing the five wounds of Christ. Every year on Holy Saturday a new Paschal Candle is blessed and lit, symbolizing Christ as the Risen Savior and Light of the World.

776. The 'Baptismal Candle' is a candle lit and used at baptism to signify that each newly baptized, like Christ, has become a light to the world (John 8:12). In some cultures, the Baptismal Candle is kept as a treasured memento and relit on special days (birthdays, name days, First Holy Communion) as a reminder of one's baptism.

777. Bells have been used in the Catholic Church since the 6th century to call people to prayer, to Mass, to public gatherings, or to announce the imminent death of one of the faithful. Over time, bells became the object of reverence in many Catholic countries, being erected in large towers, or the recipients of blessing. The ringing of bells is also associated with the elevation of the consecrated Host during Mass and the recitation of the *Angelus* prayer.

778. Illuminated manuscripts are elaborately decorated pages covered with ornamented initials, borders, margins and page paintings. Originating in eastern monasteries, this form of art spread to Armenia, the Balkans and later to Ireland. Irish missionaries brought this art form to England and the Continent, where it flourished during the Middle Ages.

779. The *Rabbula Gospels* is a 6th century illuminated Syriac manuscript and one of the finest early Byzantine Christian works. It is distinguished for its large miniatures, bright colors, movement, drama, and expressionism. Coming from a period from which little art survives, the manuscript has a significant place in art history. The text is framed with elaborate floral and architectural motifs while the miniatures of the Crucifixion, Ascension and Pentecost are framed with zigzags, curves, and rainbows. The Crucifixion scene is the oldest known in an illuminated work.

780. The *Book of Kells* is a beautiful illuminated Latin manuscript of the four Gospels produced by the Irish monks of Iona sometime during the 8th century. Written in black, red, purple and yellow ink, it is said by some to be the most outstanding of all illuminated manuscripts, a work worthy of the angels.

781. The *Book of Armagh* dates somewhere from the 8-9th centuries and consists of two lives of St Patrick, a life of St Martin of Tours and a non-Vulgate Latin text of the New Testament. It was revered in Ireland for centuries and used for giving testimony and administering oaths. It now sits in Trinity College in Dublin.

782. The ancient tombs of the Apostles Peter and Paul lie beneath the respective Basilicas of St Peter's and St Paul's Outside-the-Walls. Therein

are also found the skeletal relics of both saints, confirmed to be such after rigorous scientific examinations concluding in 1968 and 2009. Pilgrims have the privilege of visiting both magnificent sites and praying nearby each tomb.

783. The Catacombs beneath Rome and elsewhere contain the first examples of Christian art, depicting Christ, Mary, the Apostles, scenes from the Old and New Testaments, the celebration of the Eucharist, etc. They also contain numerous inscriptions and graffiti written as memorials to, and prayers for, the martyrs and other buried Christians.

784. The *Castel Sant'Angelo* in Rome was originally built in the 2nd century as a mausoleum for Emperor Hadrian's family. In the 5th century, the Popes transformed it into a fortress against threats and invasions from barbarians. It is now topped by a statue of St Michael the Archangel in memory of his appearance there in 590 to announce the end of a plague devastating Rome. Rooms within the building are now decorated with stunning artworks sponsored by the Popes, while the bridge in front of the structure is adorned with ten large statues of angels.

785. The Basilica of the Annunciation in Nazareth is built over the original house of St Joseph and the Virgin Mary. On the lower level is 'Mary's cave', where Mary received the annunciation from the Archangel Gabriel. The current building was completed in 1969 and is one of the largest churches in the Middle East. It reaches 59.5m in height and features colorful mosaics and pictures of the Holy Family throughout. Each of these art works was made by a different national community and reflects the national character of the donor country.

786. The Church of the Nativity in Bethlehem is built over the birth place of Christ. A silver star in the grotto's floor has the inscription, "Here of the Virgin Mary Jesus Christ was born." Thirty of the nave's 4th century columns carry faded Crusader paintings of saints and the Virgin with Child. Fragments of wall mosaics dating from the 1160s decorate both sides of the nave, depicting the ancestors of Christ, the decrees of provincial and ecumenical councils, and a series of angels. The main altar is surrounded by gilded angels, icons, chandeliers and lamps.

787. The Church of the Shepherd's Fields is a Franciscan Chapel designed by the famous Holy Land architect Antonio Barluzzi. The sanctuary has a dodecagonal shape (12 sides) with five apses having an inclined plane, recalling the structure of field tents used by shepherds at that time of Christ's birth. The light that penetrates the dome, illuminating the interior, is meant to recall the divine light that appeared to the shepherds.

788. The Church of the Visitation in Ein Karem, Israel, marks the spot where the Virgin Mary visited St Elizabeth (John the Baptist's mother) and recited her song of praise, the *Magnificat* (Luke 1:39-56). The interior of the church contains frescoes depicting the Visitation, Elizabeth holding John the Baptist, and Zechariah. The upper hall is dedicated to Mary and its walls are decorated with paintings in her honor. Verses from the *Magnificat* are engraved on the columns of the church and on the wall opposite are tablets bearing the *Magnificat* in forty-two languages. The church's façade has a striking mosaic commemorating the Visitation.

789. On the northern shore of the Sea of Galilee is the church of St Peter's House perched on eight sturdy pillars and hovering protectively over an excavation site. In one room of this house is scratched graffiti in Greek letters referring to Jesus as Lord and Christ. It is believed to have been the site of St Peter's house, where Christ lodged while staying in Capernaum.

790. The Church of the Beatitudes on the shore of the Sea of Galilee is built near the site where Christ is believed to have delivered his 'sermon on the mount.' The church is Byzantine in style with an octagonal floor plan, the eight sides representing the eight Beatitudes, with a marble veneer covering the lower walls and gold mosaic in the dome. On the pavement in front of the church are mosaic symbols representing the moral virtues of Justice, Prudence, Fortitude, Temperance, and the theological virtues of Faith, Hope, and Charity.

791. The Church of the Transfiguration is located on Mount Tabor in Israel, the site traditionally believed to be where the transfiguration of Christ occurred (Matt. 17:1-9). The church contains three grottoes dating from the Crusader period representing the three huts which St Peter desired to build for Christ, Moses and Elijah. The two chapels at the western end of

the church are dedicated to Moses and Elijah. In the upper part of the church is a golden mosaic representing the Transfiguration. On 6 August each year (the Feast of the Transfiguration), the sun reflects off a glass plate in the floor briefly illuminating the golden mosaic.

792. The Basilica of the Agony is located on the Mount of Olives in Jerusalem, next to the Garden of Gethsemane. Inside is a section of bedrock where Christ is said to have prayed before his arrest (Mark 14:32-42). The church was built from funds donated from many different countries, their respective coat-of-arms embedded in the ceiling. These multi-national donations give the church its other title of "All Nations." Violet-colored glass throughout the church evokes a somber mood reflective of Christ's agony, while the ceiling is painted deep blue to simulate the night sky.

793. The Church of the Flagellation is located in the Old City of Jerusalem and according to tradition enshrines the spot where Christ was flogged by Roman soldiers before his journey to Calvary. The interior of the current church is notable for its three stained glass windows, the first depicting Pontius Pilate washing his hands (Matt. 27:24), the second the flagellation (Mark 15:15), and the third the choice of Barabbas (Matt. 27:26). The mosaic of the dome is designed as a crown of thorns.

794. On Mount Zion in Jerusalem is the Church of the Dormition. The present church is a luminous circular building with several niches containing altars. Above the main altar is a mosaic of the Virgin Mary and the child Jesus with a Latin inscription from Is. 7:14: *"Behold, a virgin shall conceive, and bear a son, and he shall be called Immanuel."* In the center of the crypt, the site ascribed to the Dormition of the Virgin Mary, is a simple bier on which rests a life-size statue of Mary, fallen asleep in death. The dome above the statue is adorned with mosaics of six 'types' of Mary from the Old Testament: Eve, Miriam, Jael, Judith, Ruth and Esther.

795. The Church of the Holy Sepulcher is within the Christian Quarter of the Old City of Jerusalem and for many Christians is the most important pilgrimage destination in the world. Within its confines one finds Calvary, the site of Christ's crucifixion, the Stone of Anointing, which tradition claims to be the spot where Christ's body was prepared for

burial, and the Aedicule, which contains the Holy Sepulcher itself wherein Christ was buried and rose from the dead.

796. The 'House of the Virgin Mary' is a Catholic shrine located on Mount Koressos near Ephesus, Turkey. Pilgrims visit the house based on the belief that the Virgin Mary lived there with St John the Apostle until her Assumption. It is a modest stone chapel dating from the Apostolic age. Inside, there is one large room with an altar and a large statue of the Virgin Mary. A second smaller room on the right side is believed to be the actual room where the Virgin Mary slept. Visiting pilgrims often comment on the great sense of peace felt when inside the chapel.

797. Stained glass was a slowly developed form of decorative art having its beginnings in the 9th and 10th century Carolingian empire. Besides its eloquent beauty, it also possessed an educative role for the illiterate masses, depicting scenes from the Old and New Testaments as well as the lives of martyrs and saints. Stained glass reached its peak during the era of the Gothic cathedral, the most beautiful examples, among others, being found in Notre Dame and Chartres cathedrals in France.

798. Romanesque ("from the Roman") was the predominant form of church architecture in Western Europe from the 11-13th centuries. It is characterized by thick walls, large towers, cruciform ground plans and semi-circular arches, combining together to give the overwhelming impression of massive solidity and strength. The most famous example of this style of architecture is the monastery of Cluny in central France.

799. St Mary and St Stephen Cathedral in Speyer, Germany, is one of the most important architectural monuments of its time and is the world's largest Romanesque church. The mighty main building, consisting of the nave and transept with four towers in a symmetrical design, inspired many other important churches. Another attraction is the fully preserved crypt, which is the largest Romanesque columned hall in Europe and the burial site for Salian, Hohenstaufen and Habsburg rulers. The cathedral represents the ultimate symbol of medieval imperial power.

800. The Cathedral of Our Lady in Tournai, Belgium, is built of local blue-gray stone and combines the work of three design periods with striking effect, Romanesque, Transitional, and the fully developed Gothic. The transept is the most distinctive part of the building, with its cluster of five bell towers and semicircular ends. The square towers that flank the transept arms reach a height of 83m. The rood screen is a Renaissance masterpiece from the 16th century, while the large rose window and organ both date from the 19th century.

801. Santiago de Compostela in Spain is a Romanesque cathedral with later Gothic and Baroque additions. Its most notable features include: the magnificent Pórtico de la Gloria; the adjoining cloisters (the largest in Spain); the spectacular granite Baroque façade; the two huge bell towers; the magnificent quadruple flight of steps; the statues of David and Solomon; the Purgatory and the Last Judgment arches; the sacred relics of St James the Great under the high altar; and the Chapel of the Reliquary with its 9th century gold crucifix containing a piece of the True Cross.

802. Gothic cathedrals built during and after the High Middle Ages represent the zenith of architecture in the Catholic Church. These cathedrals are characterized by pointed arches, ribbed vaulted ceilings, flying buttresses and magnificent stained glass windows. One example of this style of architecture is Notre Dame Cathedral in Paris. With its magnificent façade, stained glass rose window, sculptures, gargoyles, organ, and elegant central spire, it is one of the glories of French architecture.

803. Mont-St-Michel, a Benedictine monastery-fortress situated on the Normandy coast in northern France, is one of the most magnificent Gothic buildings ever constructed. Begun in the mid 9th century, it was not completed until the 13th. The monastic inhabitants survived the Hundred Years' War but not the French Revolution, being ejected to enable the monastery's conversion into a prison. It once again became a place of worship in 1922.

804. Chartres Cathedral, south-west of Paris, is characterized by its two contrasting spires, massive flying buttresses, original intact stained glass windows dating back to the 12th and 13th centuries (especially the *Belle*

Verrière and the north transcept rose window), three great façades featuring hundreds of sculpted figures, and the monumental screen around the choir stalls.

805. Our Lady of Reims Cathedral is built on the site where the first Christian king of France, Clovis, was baptized in 496. The façade is one of the great masterpieces of the Middle Ages. The three portals are laden with statues and statuettes, the central dedicated to the Virgin Mary. The 'gallery of the kings' depicts the baptism of Clovis in the center flanked by statues of his successors. The rose window over the main portal is of rare magnificence. The cathedral possesses fine tapestries, the most important being a series from the 16th century representing the life of the Virgin.

806. Bourges Cathedral in central France is distinguished by its grand west façade with five portals stretching across its whole width. The central portal carries sculpted scenes related to the Last Judgment. Also featured is an extended Genesis cycle telling the story of Creation. Bourges Cathedral retains most of its 13th century stained glass which depicts, *inter alia*, the story of the Patriarch Joseph, several hagiographic cycles, the Good Samaritan, the Prodigal Son, the story of Dives and Lazarus, the Passion of Christ, the Apocalypse and the Last Judgment.

807. The Basilica of St Cecilia in Albi, France, possesses a military exterior built of brick with buttresses almost entirely submerged in the mass of the church. The bell-tower is another notable architectural feature rising 78m. The central choir bay is surrounded by a roodscreen with detailed stone work and polychrome statues. Below the organ is a fresco of the *Last Judgment*, painted by unknown Flemish painters, which originally covered nearly 200m². The frescoes on the enormous ceiling comprise the largest and oldest collection of Italian Renaissance painting in France.

808. Santa María de León Cathedral in north-western Spain is a masterpiece of Gothic from the mid-13th century. It is otherwise known as 'The House of Light' due to its almost 1,800m² of stained glass windows. The great majority of these date from the 13th to 15th centuries and are among the world's finest. Particularly outstanding is the image of the 'Virgin Blanca.' The Cathedral Museum houses almost 1,500 pieces of sacred art, fifty

Romanesque sculptures of the Virgin, a triptych of the School of Antwerp, a Mozarabic Bible and numerous ancient codices.

809.The Cathedral of Saint Mary, Seville, Spain, is the largest Gothic cathedral in the world. Inside, the most noticeable features are the lavishly gilded central nave, the great boxlike choir loft and the vast Gothic altarpiece of carved scenes from the life of Christ. The 105m 'Giralda' is the former minaret of the mosque, now the Cathedral's bell tower. Seville Cathedral has fifteen doors on its four façades depicting scenes from the life of Christ, saints and important persons from Spanish history. The Cathedral is also the burial site of Christopher Columbus.

810.Chur Cathedral in Switzerland was founded in 1151 and bears a mixture of Romanesque and Gothic architectural styles. Built in grey stone, it shelters wall paintings and altars from differing eras, among them Switzerland's most richly ornamented Late Gothic Altarpiece. The intricate depiction of the crucifixion, with Christ stumbling under the weight of the cross, rises from the floor to just below the ceiling. Below the choir, the crypt contains four carved figures of the Apostles dating from around 1200 which seem to grow directly out of the stone.

811.The Cathedral Abbey of St Gall in Switzerland is a monumental Baroque building with a white interior adorned with green wedding cake ornamentation, rose marble altars and a gilded altar screen. Ceiling frescoes depict biblical characters, throngs of cherubs and various saints. A reliquary holds the grave of St Gallus as well as the tombs of St Otmar and several abbots and bishops. The complex contains one of the richest medieval libraries in the world, with over 170,000 books of which 2,100 are handwritten; four hundred of these are over one thousand years old.

812.St Vitus Cathedral in Prague contains the tombs of many Bohemian kings and Holy Roman Emperors. The striking external features include the main tower which is 96.5m high, the front towers each 82m, and the golden mosaic of the Last Judgment. Inside, the main highlight is the Chapel of St Wenceslas, where the relics of the saint are kept. The walls are decorated with over 1,300 semi-precious stones and paintings about the Passion of Christ and the life of St Wenceslas. This Rose Window above the portal depicts scenes from the biblical story of Creation.

813. The Cathedral of St Stephen in Vienna, Austria, is one of the city's most recognizable symbols. Built of limestone, the cathedral is 136m tall at its highest point. The main entrance to the church is named the Giant's Door, over which is depicted Christ Pantocrator flanked by two winged angels. The roof is unique for its 230,000 glazed tiles which form a mosaic of the double-headed eagle that symbolized the Habsburg dynasty, as well as the coats of arms of the city of Vienna and of the Republic of Austria. The main altar is composed of panels which when opened show gilded wooden figures depicting events in the life of the Virgin Mary.

814. Salzburg Cathedral is a Baroque cathedral most noted for its richly decorated façade. The portals are flanked by large sculpted figures representing Sts Rupert, Virgilius, Peter and Paul. The central section of the façade contains statues of Sts Matthew, Mark, Luke, and John and represent the salvation offered through their preaching. On the pediment is represented the Transfiguration on Mount Tabor, showing Christ as *Salvator Mundi* (Savior of the World), Moses, and the prophet Elijah. The three bronze gates represent the three virtues of faith, hope, and love.

815. The High Cathedral of St Peter in Cologne, Germany, is the largest Gothic cathedral in northern Europe, possessing the largest façade of any church in the world. Its many treasures include the black marble high altar, the reliquary Shrine of the Three Kings, the 10th century 'Bishop Gero' crucifix, the 13th century 'Milan Madonna' statue, the five stained glass windows donated by Ludwig I of Bavaria, and the twenty-four ton 'Bell of St Peter', which is the largest free-swinging bell in the world.

816. The Cathedral of Our Lady in Antwerp, Belgium, is the largest Gothic church in the Low Countries. The church's one finished spire is 123m high. The largest of its forty-nine bells requires sixteen bell ringers. There are several small chapels dedicated to ancient guilds and famous families. The west portal features various statues, including one of the 7th century missionary St Willibrord. Most notable of all are the three works by the Baroque painter Peter Paul Rubens, *The Raising of the Cross, Assumption of the Virgin Mary,* and *The Descent from the Cross.*

817. Westminster Cathedral in London is dedicated to the Most Precious Blood of Jesus and is built in the Neo-Byzantine style. Its outstanding features include the Blessed Sacrament Chapel and its mosaics depicting Eucharistic themes, the chapel dedicated to St Gregory the Great and St Augustine of Canterbury with its vibrant mosaics, the ceiling mosaics of the Lady Chapel, the baldacchino over the high altar, and the large Byzantine style crucifix suspended from the sanctuary arch.

818. The Basilica of the Sacred Heart (Sacré-Cœur) is located on Montmartre, the highest point in Paris. It is unique for its blend of Romano-Byzantine features and its travertine stone, which remains clear white despite weathering and pollution. The mosaic in the apse depicting Christ in majesty is one of the largest in the world. The basilica grounds feature a garden for meditation, with a fountain. The portico is adorned by two equestrian statues of King St Louis IX and St Joan of Arc.

819. The Cathedral of St Patrick in New York is a Neo-Gothic style cathedral and a prominent landmark of New York City. It is distinguished by its 100m spires, stained glass rose window, Stations of the Cross, the chancel and grand gallery organs, the 'Saint Elizabeth altar', and various side altars. The *Pietà* is three times larger than Michelangelo's famous *Pietà*.

820. The Basilica of the National Shrine of the Immaculate Conception in Washington DC is the largest Catholic church in the United States, built in Byzantine-Romanesque style. Its notable features include the seventy chapels and oratories honoring Mary and the peoples, cultures and traditions that make up the fabric of the Catholic faith in America, and the numerous domes decorated in mosaics, including the Redemption, Incarnation and Trinity Domes.

821. In the Doge's Palace in Venice is Jacopo and Domenico Tintoretto's *Paradise*, one of the largest oil paintings on canvas ever realized. In the center at the top is Christ crowning the Virgin Mary, while over five hundred angels, prophets, saints, evangelists and common people surround the occasion. The picture is full of Tintoretto's distinctive mystical light.

822. St Mark's Basilica in Venice, Italy, is known as the 'Chiesa d'Oro' (Church of gold) for its opulent design and brilliant gold ground mosaics of Old and New Testament figures and significant saints. The basilica's upper ceilings are completely covered with mosaics dating from the 11th century and total in area about 8000m². The vast majority of these mosaics are of gold glass tesserae which creates a shimmering effect.

823. The Basilica of St Anthony of Padua contains the Chapel of St Anthony, the interior decoration being attributed to Tullio Lombardo, depicting the miracles of St Anthony (*Miracle of the Stingy Man's Heart, Miracle of the Repentant Man*). The Basilica also contains several important images of the Virgin Mary, including the *Madonna Mora* by Rainaldino di Puy-l'Evéque, the *Madonna del Pilastro* by Stefano da Ferrara, and the bronze *Madonna with Child* and six statues of *Saints* by Donatello.

824. The Cathedral of Santa Maria Nascente in Milan is the fifth largest cathedral in the world and the largest in Italy. Its magnificent façade lends it the nick-name of the 'wedding cake.' At forty-five meters, the nave is the world's highest Gothic vault. The roof of the cathedral is a forest of pinnacles and spires, with the baroque gilded bronze statue of the "Madonnina" atop the main spire. The interior of the cathedral includes the famous statue of San Bartolomeo Flayed by Marco d'Agrate, the three altars by Pellegrino Pellegrini, and the huge stained glass apsidal windows.

825. St Mary of the Assumption Cathedral in Pisa, Italy, is a Romanesque cathedral dating from the 11th century. The façade of grey marble and white stone has four rows of statues depicting *Madonna with Child* and the *Four Evangelists*. The interior has a gilded ceiling and a frescoed dome showing *Christ in Majesty*, flanked by the *Blessed Virgin and St John the Evangelist*. The elaborately carved pulpit is one the masterworks of medieval sculpture. The upper section contains carvings in white marble of the Annunciation, Massacre of the Innocents, Nativity, Adoration of the Magi, Flight into Egypt, the Crucifixion, and the Last Judgment.

826. The Basilica of Saint Mary of the Flower is the main church of Florence, Italy. Of Gothic style, it was completed in 1436. The dome engineered by Brunelleschi was in its day the largest in the world and remains the largest

brick dome ever constructed. The neo-Gothic façade in white, green and red marble forms a harmonious entity with the cathedral and is dedicated to the Mother of Christ. The cathedral complex also includes the massive Baptistery of St John and Giotto's magnificent *Campanile* (Bell Tower).

827. The Baptistry of Saint John in Florence was structurally completed in 1128 in the Florentine Romanesque style. The Baptistry is famous for its three sets of bronze doors featuring relief sculptures. The south doors were completed by Andrea Pisano and the north and east doors by Lorenzo Ghiberti. The east doors comprise of ten panels depicting scenes from the Old Testament and were called by Michelangelo the "Gates of Paradise." Vasari described them as "undeniably perfect in every way and must rank as the finest masterpiece ever created."

828. The Basilica of the Holy Cross in Florence, Italy, is the largest Franciscan church in the world. Its most notable features are its sixteen chapels, many of them decorated with frescoes by Giotto and his pupils, as well as its tombs and cenotaphs. It is the burial place of some of the most illustrious Italians of history, such as Dante, Michelangelo, Galileo, Machiavelli, Gentile and Rossini, thus it is known also as the 'Temple of the Italian Glories.'

829. The Basilica of San Domenico, also known as Basilica Cateriniana, was the church wherein St Catherine of Siena prayed and had her earliest mystical experiences. In the center of the church is the St Catherine Chapel, with an altar housing the relics of the saint's head and thumb. These are surrounded by magnificent artworks depicting scenes from the life of St Catherine, including the *Fainting and Ecstasy of St Catherine* by Il Sodoma and *St Catherine's Exorcism* by Francesco Vanni.

830. The west façade of the Cathedral of the Assumption of Siena is one of the most fascinating in all of Italy and combines elements of French Gothic, Tuscan Romanesque, and Classical architecture. The areas around and above the doors, as well as the columns between the portals, are richly decorated with acanthus scrolls, allegorical figures and biblical scenes. Most of the sculpture decorating the lower level of the lavish façade depict prophets, philosophers and apostles, while the statuary

adorning the upper portion include half-length statues of the patriarchs.

831. The inlaid marble mosaic floor of Siena Cathedral is one of the most ornate of its kind in the world, consisting of fifty-six panels in different sizes. They represent the sibyls, allegories, virtues and scenes from the Old and New Testaments, including the *Sacrifice of Isaac, Moses on Mount Sinai, Moses Striking Water from the Rock, Victory of Joshua, Victory of Samson over the Philistines, Story of King David, Scenes from the Life of Elijah, The Slaughter of the Innocents* and *Expulsion of Herod*.

832. Siena Cathedral's valuable pieces of art and sculpture include *The Feast of Herod* by Donatello, and works by Bernini and the young Michelangelo. Michelangelo created the four sculptures of St Peter, St Paul, St Gregory and St Pius in the lower niches of the Piccolomini altar between 1501 and 1504. On top of the altar is the *Madonna and Child*, a sculpture by Jacopo della Quercia. These and many other works of art make Siena Cathedral an extraordinary museum of Italian sculpture.

833. Adjoining Siena Cathedral is the Piccolomini Library, containing stunning frescoes painted by the Umbrian artist Bernardino di Betto. The ten frescoes tell the story of Cardinal Piccolomini, who eventually became Pope Pius II. The ceiling is covered with glorious painted panels of mythological subjects. Beneath the frescoes, the psalters of the cathedral's sacristy are displayed. These exquisite illuminations were initially created between 1466 and 1478 by Liberale da Verona and Girolamo da Cremona and later completed by other Sienese illuminators.

834. The Basilica of St Francis of Assisi is the mother church of the Franciscan Order. It comprises two churches commonly known as the Upper Church and the Lower Church, and a crypt where the remains of the St Francis are interred. The Upper and Lower Churches are decorated with frescoes by Cimabue, Giotto, Simone Martini, Pietro Lorenzetti and Pietro Cavallini. The most famous are the twenty-eight frescoes by Giotto in the upper Church depicting the major events in the life of St Francis.

835. The Basilica of St Clare of Assisi contains precious frescos dating from the 12th to the 14th centuries, including a panel with the "Life of St

Clare" by Maestro di Santa Chiara, as well as frescoes depicting St Clare and biblical scenes by Maestro Espressionista di Santa Chiara. In the nave of St Clare of Assisi is the crucifix which spoke to St Francis and invited him to "rebuild my Church." In the crypt are displayed some important Franciscan relics, including tunics worn by Sts Francis and Clare, a shirt St Clare embroidered, and some locks of St Clare's hair cut by St Francis.

836. The Portiuncula is a small church located within the Basilica of St Mary of the Angels in Assisi. Some of its stones were put in place by St Francis himself while repairing this church. Its most outstanding feature is the six-part fresco in the apse, painted by Ilario da Viterbo, which includes *The Annunciation, St Francis Throws Himself into the Thorny Brambles, St Francis Accompanied by Two Angels, Apparition of Christ and the Virgin, St Francis Imploring Pope Honorius III to Confirm the Indulgence, St Francis Promulgates the Indulgence Accompanied by the Bishops of Umbria.*

837. The Basilica of St Mary of the Angels in Assisi also houses a number of other treasures, including the Chapel of the Transito, the cell in which St Francis died, and the side chapels of St Anne decorated by Antonio Circignani, the Chapels of St Anthony and St Peter in Chains decorated by Francesco Appiani, and the Chapel of the Removal of the Lord decorated by Ventura Salimbeni.

838. The Gothic façade of the Cathedral of Orvieto is one of the great masterpieces of the late Middle Ages. The bas-reliefs depict biblical stories from the Old and New Testaments and are considered among the most famous pieces of 14th-century sculpture. The glittering mosaics mostly represent scenes from the life of the Virgin Mary, from her nativity to her coronation. The rose window is surrounded with mosaics representing the four Doctors of the Church while the three bronze doors at the entrance of the cathedral depict mercies from the life of Christ.

839. Inside the Cathedral of Orvieto are two creations of Ippolito Scalza, the cathedral's large organ, containing 5,585 pipes and the large Pietà of four figures sculpted in 1579. The *Cappella del Corporale* was built in the 1350's to house the stained corporal of the Eucharistic miracle of Bolsena. This chapel is decorated with frescoes depicting the history of the miracle

painted between 1357 and 1363 by Ugolino di Prete Ilario, Domenico di Meo and Giovanni di Buccio Leonardelli.

840. Within the Chapel of the Madonna di San Brizio in the Cathedral of Orvieto are a number of astonishing art works, including *Christ in Judgment* and *Angels and Prophets* by Fra Angelico and Benozzo on the chapel's vault and *The Preaching of the Antichrist* by Luca Signorelli. Among the crowd listening to the Antichrist, Signorelli painted a number of famous figures: Raphael, Dante, Columbus, Boccaccio, Petrarch, Cesare Borgia, Fra Angelico in habit, and himself dressed in noble garments.

841. The Basilica Santa Maria Maggiore in Rome resembles a 2nd century Roman imperial basilica, with a tall and wide nave, an aisle on each side, and a semicircular apse at the end of the nave. The key aspect of the Basilica's interior beauty is the apse mosaic, the Coronation of the Virgin, signed by the Franciscan friar, Jacopo Torriti. The forty Athenian marble columns supporting the nave either come from an earlier basilica, or from another antique Roman building; thirty-six are marble and four granite. The basilica's 16th-century coffered ceiling is covered with gold.

842. The mosaics in Santa Maria Maggiore are some of the oldest representations of the Virgin Mary in Christian Late Antiquity. They were created in part to celebrate the affirmation of Mary as "Theotokos" by the Council of Ephesus in 431. They have ever since been the model for future representations of the Virgin Mary. Other mosaics in the nave and triumphal arch aim to articulate the relationship between the Old and New Testaments and how the former is fulfilled in the latter.

843. In the Borghese Chapel of Santa Maria Maggiore is the famous icon of the Virgin Mary known as *Salus Populi Romani*, or *Salvation of the Roman People*. This icon is at least a thousand years old, and according to a tradition was painted by St Luke the Evangelist using the wooden table of the Holy Family in Nazareth. The *Salus Populi Romani* has been a favorite of several Popes, including Pius XII, Paul VI, St John Paul II, Benedict XVI, and Pope Francis.

844. The Basilica of St John Lateran in Rome dates from the time of the Roman Empire and retains its original Constantinian figuration: a large rectangular hall with imposing nave, flanked by double aisles and terminating in an apse. The central bronze doors date from the 2nd century, originating from the Curia, or Senate in the Roman Forum. In the atrium, an imposing 4th century statue of Constantine is a reminder of his gift of the Basilica to Pope Miltiades. Centuries of embellishment has not diminished the impression of an early Christian temple.

845. The apse mosaic of St John Lateran features a bust of Christ the Savior surrounded by angels, figures of the Virgin Mary and saints, a brilliant jeweled cross, and pleasurable scenes of animals and children frolicking in the Jordan River, as well as miniature portraits of the medieval friar mosaicists, Jacopo Torriti and Jacopo da Camerino, crouched between depictions of the Apostles.

846. Beneath the triumphal arch in the middle of the transept of St John Lateran is the beautiful Gothic Papal altar, which contains a wooden altar on which the earliest Popes celebrated Mass, and silver busts containing relics of the heads of St Peter and St Paul. The Tabernacle was designed by Giovanni di Stefano in 1367 and is surmounted by beautiful frescoes painted by Barna da Siena in 1369. On the second pilaster, between the main nave and far right aisle, is the fragment of a fresco by Giotto of Pope Boniface VIII proclaiming the first Holy Year in 1300.

847. The massive statues of the Twelve Apostles which line the main nave of St John Lateran in marble-columned niches are the works of various Roman Rococo sculptors commissioned to create appearances of exuberance and power. Above these figures are doves (the family insignia of Pope Innocent X) topped by reliefs by Alessandro Algardi of Old and New Testament scenes, and painted medallions with prophets.

848. The cloister of St John Lateran dates from 1215-1230 and is the work of Pietro Vasselletto and his son. It contains jewel-like mosaics, animal and floral motifs, and delicate arches with paired spiral and smooth columns. The latter are of a transitional style between Romanesque proper and Gothic.

849. The Basilica of St Paul's Outside-the-Walls is a reconstruction of the ancient Basilica destroyed by fire in 1823. All that remains of the original Basilica are the interior portion of the apse with the triumphal arch. At 131.66m long, 65m wide, and 29.70m high it is the second largest church in Rome. The nave's most impressive features are its imposing eighty columns, its stucco-decorated ceiling, and its interior walls decorated with scenes from the life of St Paul.

850. The external area of St Paul's Basilica is dominated by the imposing *quadriportico*, 70m long and comprising of one hundred and fifty columns. This was completed in 1928. In the center of the atrium is a dramatic statue of St Paul sculpted by Giuseppe Obici. In the Basilica's center is the monumental green bronze door made by Antonio Maraini in 1931 with scenes from the Old and New Testaments. To its right is the new Holy Door, made of golden bronze, created by the sculptor Enrico Manfrini and erected for the Jubilee year 2000.

851. The façade of St Paul's Basilica is decorated with magnificent mosaics which were completed between 1854 and 1874. They depict the Prophets Isaiah, Jeremiah, Ezekiel and Daniel in the lower section and the mystical Lamb surrounded by twelve lambs representing the twelve Apostles and four rivers symbolizing the four Gospels in the central section. In the upper section, Christ sits enthroned between Sts Peter and Paul.

852. The triumphal arch of St Paul's Basilica dates from the 5th century and portrays the Apocalypse of John, with the bust of Christ in the center flanked by twenty-four doctors of the Church, surmounted by flying symbols of the four Evangelists. Sts Peter and Paul are portrayed at the bottom right and left of the arch, the latter pointing downwards (perhaps to his tomb).

853. In the 5th century under the Pontificate of St Leo the Great, St Paul's Basilica became the home of a long series of large medallions depicting every Pope throughout Church history. These were destroyed in the 1823 fire, but were replaced in the 19th century with a new collection of mosaic portraits forming a high frieze around the transept and nave. Pope Francis' medallion was added in December, 2013.

854. Another highlight of St Paul's Basilica is the Venetian mosaic in the apse. It was created in 1226 for Pope Honorius III, and though severely damaged by the 1823 fire, was carefully restored in 1836. It features Christ enthroned in glory, flanked by Sts Peter and Andrew on one side, and Sts Paul and Luke on the other.

855. St Peter's Basilica in Rome is the most renowned work of Renaissance architecture and remains the largest church in the world. Designed principally by Bramante, Michelangelo, Maderno and Bernini, it is cruciform in shape, with an elongated nave in the Latin cross form, and topped by the largest dome in the world. The entire interior is lavishly decorated with marble, reliefs, architectural sculpture and gilding. The many tombs of Popes and other notable people are themselves considered outstanding artworks.

856. The dome of St Peter's Basilica at 136.57m in height is the tallest in the world. Designed and built by Michelangelo, it has the shape of a parabola rather than a hemisphere. It is possible to climb up to the dome and walk around the cupola, and from there continue to the roof, where one can step outside and enjoy views of St Peter's Square and Vatican City. Above, the dome rises to Fontana's two-stage lantern, capped with a spire.

857. The grand façade of St Peter's Basilica is 116m wide and 53m high. Built between 1608 and 1614, it was designed by Modeno and features twelve giant Corinthian columns. The central balcony is called the Loggia of the Blessings, and is used for the announcement of each new Pope and his *Urbi et Orbi* (for the City and the Globe) blessing. The relief under the balcony depicts Christ giving the keys to St Peter. The façade is topped by thirteen statues representing Christ, John the Baptist, and all the Apostles except St Peter, whose statue is inside.

858. Beneath St Peter's dome stands Bernini's baldacchino, which at 30m is the largest bronze structure in the world. Each of the four massive columns is twisted and decorated with laurel leaves, bees and portrait heads in gold leaf. The whole structure stands as a vast free-standing object above the main altar and creates the effect of linking the dome above with the congregation at floor level.

859. St Peter's Square is outlined by the monumental colonnade of three hundred Doric columns by Bernini, with its open arms symbolically welcoming the world into the Catholic Church. Across the top of the colonnade are one hundred and forty statues of saints, crafted between 1662 and 1703, representing, *inter alia*, St Benedict, St Bernard, St Dominic, St Francis, and St Ignatius Loyola. The Colonnade simultaneously serves as a dramatic frame for the church, an enclosure for crowds of the faithful, and a stage for public audiences, processions and other sacred spectacles such as canonizations, etc.

860. The *Sistine Chapel* is named after Pope Sixtus IV and was completed and consecrated in honor of the Assumption of the Virgin Mary in 1483. Its dimensions mirror Solomon's Jerusalem Temple. The mosaic floor is original and frescos by Botticelli, Ghirlandaio, Rosselli, Signorelli, Perugino and Pinturicchio depicting the lives of Moses and Christ, offset by Papal portraits, feature along the walls. Under Pope Julius II, Michelangelo painted the *Sistine Chapel Ceiling*, a masterpiece without precedent, and *The Last Judgment* for Popes Clement VII and Paul III.

861. The *Pinacoteca*, completed in 1931, was commissioned by Pope Pius XI (1922-1939) to house the Papal art collection in chronological order in eighteen rooms. The collection contains works from the Middle Ages to 1800 by Lorenzetti, Martini, Giotto, Fra Angelico, Emilia, Melozzo, de Roberti, Perugino, Santi, Raphael, Leonardo da Vinci, Bellini, Caliari, Vasari, Carracci, d'Arpino, Barocci, Caravaggio, Domenichino, Reni, Poussin, Van Dyck, Cortona, and Wenzel Peter.

862. In the *Vatican Rooms* (*Segnatura, Heliodorus, Borgo, Constantine*) are found some of Raphael's greatest paintings, including the *Expulsion of Heliodorus, School of Athens, Liberation of Saint Peter, Baptism of Constantine, Vision of the Cross, Battle at Milvian Bridge, Donation of Constantine, Coronation of Charlemagne, Battle of Ostia, Fire in the Borgo,* and the *Disputation of the Holy Sacrament*. The ceiling painted by Tommaso Laureti in 1585 shows the *Triumph of Christianity* over paganism.

863. The *Pio-Cristiano Museum* was founded by Bl. Pius IX in 1854 and contains Christian antiquities — statues, sarcophagi, inscriptions and

archaeological findings – from the 6th century onwards. Noteworthy is the statue of the Good Shepherd as a beardless young man wearing a sleeveless tunic and carrying a bag. This was restored in the 18th century.

864. The *Gallery of the Tapestries* in the Vatican is a 75m long gallery displaying tapestries belonging to two different periods and manufactures: tapestries woven in Rome by the Barberini workshop commemorating important moments in the life of Pope Urban VIII; tapestries woven in the 16th century by the workshop of Pieter van Aelst based on drawings by students of Raphael and depicting episodes from the life of Christ, including the *Adoration of the Magi*, the *Massacre of the Innocents* and the *Resurrection of Christ*.

865. The *Gallery of Maps* takes its name from the forty maps frescoed on the walls depicting the Italian regions and Papal properties at the time of Pope Gregory XIII (1572-1585). They were created between 1580 and 1585 from drawings by Ignazio Danti, a renowned geographer of the time. Taking the Apennines as the dividing line, on one side the regions surrounded by the Ligure and Tyrrhenian Seas are represented; on the other, the regions surrounded by the Adriatic Sea. A map of the principal city accompanies each regional map.

866. The *Sobieski Room* is so named after the large painting by the Polish painter Matejko (1838-1893) depicting the Polish King's victory over the Turks at Vienna in 1683. The other paintings in the same room also date from the 19th century, as well as those in the Room of the Immaculate Conception. The latter contains a large showcase, containing books gifted to Bl. Pius Pius IX (1846-1878) by kings, bishops, cities and dioceses at the time of the dogmatic definition of the Immaculate Conception.

867. The *Apartment of St Pius V* comprises a gallery, two small rooms and a chapel. It was built for Pope St Pius V (1566-1572) and frescoed by Giorgio Vasari and Federico Zuccari. It contains Flemish tapestries from the 15th and 16th centuries, a collection of rich Medieval and Renaissance ceramics, and a collection of minute mosaics made in Rome in the 18th and 19th centuries.

868. The *Scala Sancta* ('Holy Stairs') are twenty-eight white marble steps walked on by Christ now located in a building near the Basilica of St John Lateran. They lead to the 'Holy of Holies', the first private Papal chapel. The stairwell walls and the walls, ceilings, and cupola of the upper floor (Papal and St Lawrence chapels) are covered with numerous frescoes created by artists of the Cavallini School.

869. The Abbey of Monte Cassino rests on the site of the monastery built by St Benedict of Nursia in 529. Inside the main basilica are remarkable frescoes and mosaics. The Chapel of Relics contains reliquaries of several saints. The crypt is filled with stunning mosaics. Inside the museum are mosaics, marble, gold and coins from the early medieval period. Literary displays include fresco sketches, prints, and drawings related to the monastery, as well as book bindings, codices, books, and manuscripts dating from the 6th century.

870. The neo-classical Basilica of Our Lady of the Rosary of Pompeii is outstanding for its frescoed, marble splendor, rivalling any church in Rome for beauty. Built entirely from donations of the faithful, it houses the miraculous image of Our Lady of Pompeii. The numerous frescos, marble ornaments, mosaics, paintings and votives that cover the walls of the church form an impressive testimonial of the miracles granted by the Virgin Mary since the church was consecrated in 1891.

871. The Shrine of St Anthony's Chapel in Pittsburg, USA, was built by Fr Mollinger in the late 19th century. It contains numerous beautiful shelves holding over seven hundred relics of saints and martyrs from all eras of the Church's history, including eighty canonized Popes. There is also some soil from Gethsemane, a fragment of the True Cross and a sliver of the Crown of Thorns. The Shrine is also adorned with many beautiful statues, stained glass windows, and a life-size Stations of the Cross.

872. The works of Giotto di Bondone (1266-1337), the Italian painter and architect from Florence, are considered to be the first of the great works of the Italian Renaissance. His figures and their postures are noted for their accurate portrayal of life and nature. Giotto's masterwork is the cycle of frescoes decorating the Scrovegni Chapel in Padua, which depict

the life of Christ and the Virgin Mary. Giotto's outstanding architectural work is his design of the *Campanile* (Bell Tower) of the Florence Cathedral.

873. Fra Angelico (1395-1455) according to the great Vasari possessed "a rare and perfect talent" and painted his works "with such facility and piety." Among his most outstanding works include his *Annunciation*, the frescoes of the life of Christ decorating the Chapter House and cells of the Dominican friary of St Mark in Florence, the Altarpiece of St Marco's, Florence, the ceiling of the Cappella Nuova in Orvieto, and the Evangelists and saints of the Niccoline Chapel in the Vatican. His works will be forever admired for their brilliance of color and gold and their preoccupation with humanity, humility and piety.

874. *The Last Supper* is a mural painting by Leonardo da Vinci (+1519) in the refectory of the Convent of Santa Maria delle Grazie, Milan. Completed in 1498, it is one of the world's most famous paintings and represents the moment of consternation among the disciples when Christ announced that one of them would betray him (John 13:21). Leonardo's other great religious paintings include: *Annunciation*; *Baptism of Christ*; *St John the Baptist*; *Madonna of the Rocks*; *Virgin and Child with St Anne*; and *St Jerome*.

875. The *Pieta* by Michelangelo is a marble masterpiece completed in 1498 depicting the body of Christ in the arms and lap of the Virgin Mary after his crucifixion. It is one of Michelangelo's most refined works, inspiring replicas that have spread throughout the world. Another of his great sculptures is his *Moses*, which took three years to complete. Michelangelo's Sistine Chapel paintings, *Creation of Adam* and *The Last Judgment*, remain his immortal contributions to Church art.

876. The paintings of Michelangelo de Caravaggio (+1610) are characterized by their shifts from light to dark. His technique is recognized as contributing greatly to the newly emerging baroque style of the late 16th century. His greatest religious works include: *Judith Beheading Holofernes*; *Calling of St Matthew*; *Denial of St Peter*; *Taking of Christ*; *Entombment of Christ*; *Supper at Emmaus*; *Conversion of St Paul*; and *Crucifixion of St Peter*. Caravaggio's epitaph reads, "in painting not equal to a painter, but to Nature itself."

877. In the Basilica of St Denis in Paris is found a tunic traditionally believed to be that worn by Christ before his crucifixion. It is a brown woollen garment with traces of human blood that has been kept under lock and key for the last twelve centuries. Every fifty years the relic is taken from its reliquary for public veneration, usually during Holy Week. Tests have verified that the fabric is of a type used during the time of Christ and that the tunic contains pollens of plants indigenous to Palestine.

878. High up in the Andes mountains (3,832m) on the border between Argentina and Chile is a 12m high bronze statue of Christ known as 'Christ of the Andes.' This statue is made from melted cannons of the two nations and was lifted into place by thousands of Argentinean and Chilean soldiers in 1904 to commemorate the peaceful resolution of a border dispute between the two nations.

Chapter 10
Great History!

Preliminary

Being an institution more than 2,000 years old, the Catholic Church naturally has a very long and detailed history. To record all the significant persons, achievements and events would require multiple sets of encyclopaedias. There are many histories that record what is both great and not so great in Catholic history; there are others that are only interested in recording and amplifying the 'black side' of that history.

Those interested in highlighting only the Church's 'black side' usually have an axe to grind against Catholicism, wishing to argue that any institution responsible for so much 'evil fruit' could not possibly be the true church of Christ. The Crusades, inquisitions, religious persecutions, corrupt Popes and the 'Galileo affair' are the standard examples put forward in support of their claims. Among these same writers, however, one usually finds great imbalance, gross exaggerations, no context, and more than a little hypocrisy. The purpose of this chapter is to show forth a few examples of the great side of Catholic history, that side conveniently ignored by the critics.

There is so much to celebrate in Catholic history: the early martyrs; the conversion of the Roman Empire; the rise of monasticism and the preservation of learning; the missionaries converting Europe and the New World; the establishment of schools, universities, hospitals; the great victories against militant Islam in Spain, the Holy Land and eastern Europe; the great contributions to learning and science, especially by the Jesuits; the opposition to slavery; the heroic resistance in the face of the French Revolution, Napoleon, the Kulturkampf, the Boxer Rebellion, the Mexican and Spanish Civil Wars, Nazism and Communism; the covert support for the Jews in WWII; the charitable efforts of so many Church organizations working tirelessly throughout the world; and the heroic work of the pro-life movement, especially in the USA.

Finally, we also outline examples of the many occasions when Divine Providence intervened in human history, especially the significant apparitions known to and approved by the Church over the centuries.

Reasons

879. The Catholic Church recognizes that the *Acts of the Apostles* is the first history book of the Church. At the same time, the Catholic Church can point to a recorded Christian history continuing beyond AD 63, a history that merges seamlessly into Catholic history.

880. For Catholics, Christian history does not end in 313 with Constantine; nor does it restart in 1517 with Martin Luther. The 2,000 year history of Christianity is one and the same as the 2,000 year history of Catholicism.

881. The first Church historian after the writing of the *Acts of the Apostles* was the converted Jew St Hegesippus (110-180), who authored five 'memoirs', parts of which were concerned with the early days of the Church in Jerusalem and in Rome. From St Hegesippus' writings we learn that the 'brothers and sisters' of Christ were children of Mary and Clopas, the latter being the brother of St Joseph, as well as the names of the first thirteen Popes up till the time of St Eleutherius (175-189).

882. The *Acts of the Martyrs* are a large and varied collection of inspirational writings produced during the first centuries of Christianity that record the martyrdom of saints during the official Roman persecutions. The two most famous *Acta* are those of St Polycarp of Smyrna and St Justin of Neapolis, who were both martyred around the mid 2nd century.

883. The Colosseum in Rome is the ancient site where thousands of Christians were martyred for their faith during the persecutions. Since the 17th century, the Church has regarded the Colosseum as a Christian shrine and to this day the Pope conducts the Stations of the Cross within its walls every Good Friday.

884. The first great Christian school of learning was established by St Pantaenus in Alexandria, Egypt, in the second half of the 2nd century. It provided Christian theological and philosophical instruction to the educated until the late 4th century, and included among its heads great figures such as Clement of Alexandria (+215), Origen (+254) and Didymus the Blind (+398).

885. The Catacombs beneath Rome and elsewhere contain many tombs of early Popes, the first examples of Christian art, evidence of prayers for the dead, petitions asking deceased Christians for their prayers, and altars for the celebration of the Eucharistic liturgy – all proofs that the early pre-Constantinian church was in essence Catholic.

886. St Gregory the Illuminator (+331) was responsible for converting his native Armenia to Christianity after baptizing King Tiridates III in 301. Following this, most of the nobility and large numbers of the ordinary people embraced the Christian faith. The same year King Tiridates decreed Christianity as the state religion, making Armenia the first official Christian kingdom.

887. Constantine, before his victory in the battle of Milvian Bridge (28 October, 312), which brought him to power as the first Christian Roman Emperor, saw in the sky a cross with the words *In Hoc Signo Vinces* – "In this sign you shall conquer." Catholics still commemorate this great event that eventually brought freedom of religion to Christians.

888. The relics of the True Cross of Christ were discovered by St Helena (mother of the Emperor Constantine) in the Holy Land in 326. These relics have been in the possession of the Catholic Church and venerated continually ever since.

889. The Catholic Church was instrumental in the official conversion of the Roman Empire to Christianity under Emperor Theodosius I in 381 after centuries of struggle and persecution.

890. The Catholic Church inspired the abolition by Christian Roman emperors of gladiatorial fights and other forms of killing for sport.

891. The Catholic Church established the first houses for the care of the sick, widows and orphans during the 4th century.

892. The first Christian hermits began to appear during the period of imperial Roman persecution, especially in Egypt, Asia Minor and the Middle East. They modelled themselves on the examples of Elijah and John the Baptist

and aimed to seek union with God through prayer and meditation free from the allurements of the world. Eventually, certain individual hermits began to combine with others to form the first monasteries.

893. Catholic monasteries acted as houses for the sick and the first hotels for weary pilgrims.

894. Catholic monasteries preserved the great manuscripts of Antiquity which otherwise would have been permanently forgotten or lost.

895. Catholic monasteries were centers of learning and civilization during the long night of the 'Dark Ages.' The most notable of these is the Benedictine Abbey Church of Cluny founded in 910 in central France.

896. Catholic monks were responsible for preserving the Scriptures through laborious hand-copying for over a thousand years before the invention of the printing press.

897. Catholic religious orders were responsible for founding the first great universities, including Paris, Oxford, Cambridge and Bologna.

898. Chivalry as a lofty ideal owes its origins to Catholic principles. Knights were expected to be men of honor, true to their word, defenders of the weak and innocent, merciful to all, faithful to their oaths, immovable in their faith, and loyal to the Church. Though not always realized in practice, chivalry prevented Christendom sinking back into barbarism.

899. The King of the Franks, Clovis, was baptized by St Remigius, Bishop of Rheims, on Christmas Day 496 together with 3,000 of his warriors. Much of the Frankish nation eventually followed suit.

900. Hundreds of Irish monks during the 6th and 7th centuries left their native land to spread Christianity across Europe. The chief of these were St Aidan, apostle to Northumbria, St Columba, apostle of Scotland, St Columban, who preached the gospel in France, Germany, Switzerland and Italy, and St Gall, disciple of St Columban and apostle to Switzerland.

901. Anglo-Saxon missionaries including Wilfrid, St Willibrord, St Suitbert and St Boniface evangelized the barbarian Frisians, Hessians and Thuringians of Germany with great zeal during the early 8th century, baptizing countless converts and establishing numerous churches and religious houses.

902. The Benedictine monk St Ansgar labored zealously for the conversion of the Danes and Swedes during the first half of the 9th century. His preaching met with great success and numerous churches, hospitals, schools and religious houses were established. Though much of his work was destroyed after his death, St Ansgar is still remembered by Scandinavians as the 'Apostle of the North.'

903. The brothers Sts Cyril and Methodius labored during the second half of the 9th century to bring Christianity to the Ukraine and then later, with the permission of Pope Nicolas I, to the Slavs in Moravia. At the urging of St Methodius, the Pope gave him permission to use Slavonic in the Mass, in Scripture reading, and in the Divine Office. Methodius also translated almost the whole Bible and other works of the Church into the Slavonic language before his death in 884.

904. During the latter half of the 10th century, St Adalbert of Prague contended against the paganism, polygamy and slave trading of the Czechs. After resigning his bishopric, he travelled to Hungary baptizing Géza of Hungary and his son Stephen, effectively converting that nation to Christianity. Continuing to Prussia, St Adalbert challenged the worship of the 'sacred oaks', before being martyred in 997.

905. The adventurer, marauder, king and convert Olaf Tryggvason (+1000), by his zeal and force of character, was responsible for converting much of Norway, Iceland and Greenland to Christianity, the latter through the conversion and baptism of Leif Ericsson.

906. Through the combined efforts of Emperor Otto the Great, Duke Miecislaw and his wife Dombrowska, Boleslaus I, King Casimir I and St Stanislaus, over the course of the late 10th and early 11th centuries Poland was eventually transformed into a great Christian nation.

907. Lithuania officially embraced Christianity after its leader Jogaila accepted a Polish proposal to become a Catholic and marry Queen Jadwiga of Poland. Jogaila was duly baptized at the Wawel Cathedral in Kraków on 15 February, 1386, and became king of Poland. The royal baptism was followed by the conversion of most of Jogaila's court and knights, as well as Jogaila's brothers Karigaila, Vygantas, Švitrigaila and cousin Vytautas.

908. Under the leadership of Don Pelayo, the first great victory over the invading Moors was won at Covadonga in northern Spain in 722, beginning the epic seven hundred and seventy year 'reconquista.'

909. The Battle of Tours (732) marked the zenith of Moorish-Islamic conquest in Western Europe. The Christian Franks, under the leadership of Charles Martel, won a decisive victory over the invaders, compelling them to leave France permanently. Charles Martel was afterward accorded the title of 'Savior of Christendom.'

910. Charlemagne ruled the Frankish Empire from 768 to 814 and founded the Holy Roman Empire after being crowned Emperor by Pope Leo III on Christmas Day, 800. Charlemagne consolidated Christian laws throughout his lands, advanced Benedictine monasticism, and was an ardent defender of the Papacy. He was also instrumental in the conversion of the Saxon King Hessi to Christianity and drove the Moors from the Pyrenees. The so-called 'Carolingian Renaissance' thrived during his reign, with painters, goldsmiths, sculptors, and schools all receiving Charlemagne's support. Charlemagne also built many roads, established a just system of courts, and summoned local church councils.

911. Under the dogged leadership of King Alfonso II in the 9th century, the Catholic northern Spanish Kingdom of the Asturias survived numerous attacks from the Emirate of Cordoba. During the same period, Alfonso helped develop a national identity for the Asturias by establishing a new capital at Oviedo and protecting the great pilgrimage shrine of Santiago de Compostela.

912. The legendary Rodrigo del Bivar (El Cid) contributed to the reconquest of Spain by capturing the city of Valencia in 1094. Afterwards, El Cid

inflicted the first major defeat upon the Almoravid Berbers on the plains of Caurte and continued resisting them until his death.

913. The Church, together with secular governments, established the Medieval Inquisition in 1184. Its object was to try charges of heresy and to protect the people of God from error while insisting that the accused be brought back into the grace of God. In 1232, Pope Gregory IX appointed the Dominicans and Franciscans as specialist and permanent inquisitors. These religious were dispassionate, unselfish, highly popular, fearless, beyond corruption, and desired solely to serve the interests of the Church and the salvation of souls. Much good was achieved by this inquisition, however, there were numerous abuses and torture. In hindsight, the Church acknowledges that torture and capital punishment should not have been employed. As the *Catechism of the Catholic Church* says, "Torture which uses physical or moral violence to extract confessions ... frighten opponents, or satisfy hatred is contrary to respect for the person and for human dignity ... In recent times it has become evident that these cruel practices were neither necessary for public order, nor in conformity with the legitimate rights of the human person" (CCC ##2297-8).

914. Likewise, the Spanish Inquisition was guilty of many abuses. Nevertheless, as a judicial system it was more just than its contemporary secular counterparts. Though 3,000 persons were executed in its 340 year history, the Spanish Inquisition preserved Spain's Catholic identity avoiding the religious wars that racked the rest of Europe that resulted in the loss of countless lives. In addition, the witchcraft hysteria that swept through Protestant Germany, England, Scotland and America (which saw tens of thousands of women executed on little or no evidence) was found to be baseless by the Spanish Inquisition, saving many more innocent lives.

915. In September, 1213, Simon de Montfort's small force of approximately 1,000 crusaders and knights, aided by the prayers of St Dominic Guzman, routed an Albigensian coalition totaling 40,000 infantry and cavalry at Muret. This remarkable victory broke the military power of the Albigensians in southern France.

916. During the 13th century, the great St Ferdinand III, king of Castile and Leon, extended the Spanish reconquest by capturing the Moslem cities of Cordoba (1236), Jaén (1246), and Sevilla (1248). In addition, Murcia submitted to his son Alfonso (later Alfonso X) and the Muslim kingdom of Granada became his vassal.

917. Despite various shortcomings, the Crusades for the Holy Land from 1095 to 1291 had many positive aspects. The renewed communication with the East brought about a greater exchange of trade and culture; there was renewed contact with beleaguered Christians such as the Maronites in Lebanon; the West benefited from contact with Muslim mathematicians and philosophers versed in Aristotelian thought; the rise and flourishing of the religious military orders of the Knights Hospitallers and the Knights Templars brought about a renewal of lofty ideals and noble fighting spirit; and, most importantly, the Crusades delayed the Islamic invasion of Eastern Europe for nearly two hundred years.

918. In 1456, the city of Belgrade was besieged by an army of 150,000 led by Turkish Sultan Mohammed II. Commanding a relief army of just 10,000 men in a flotilla of two hundred ships, Prince John Hunyadi and St John Capistrano sailed down the Danube and broke the Turkish blockade. After a five hour battle, the relieving Christians entered the besieged city. The Christian defenders then destroyed the counter-attacking Janissaries with a burning wall of sulphur, pitch and gunpowder. After losing their main battery of siege cannons to a Christian onslaught, the Turks retreated. Hungary was saved for another sixty years.

919. During the mid 15th century (1443-1467), George Castriota (Scanderberg) of Albania destroyed sixteen successive Turkish invasions led by Sultans Murad II and Mohammed II. The Turks invaded with armies of 40,000 in 1443, 160,000 in 1450 and two of 200,000 in 1466 and 1467. While Scanderberg lived the Turks could never capture Albania.

920. Isabella and Ferdinand of Spain launched the final phase of the Spanish 'reconquista' in 1482. They proceeded to take the emirate of Granada piece by piece, conquering Ronda in 1485, Loja in 1486, Malaga in 1487 and Baza in 1489. The siege of Granada city began in early 1491 and on

New Year's Day, 1492, Mohammad XII surrendered. The next day Isabella and Ferdinand entered Granada to accept the keys of the city and the main mosque was converted into a church. Begun in 722, the Spanish 'reconquista' was finally complete.

921. In 1565, a Turkish force of 65,000 under Sultan Suleiman the Magnificent invaded the island of Malta, defended by 7,000 Knights of St John Hospitaller led by Jean la Valette. The Turkish siege of the main three fortresses lasted four months. When all seemed lost for the defenders, Spanish reinforcements of 7,000 finally arrived. Only six hundred of the original defenders survived. Turkish losses during the campaign totalled 30,000. In the face of the fresh reinforcements, the Turks abandoned the siege, never to return.

922. The year 1571 witnessed the great naval battle of Lepanto. Under the auspices of Pope St Pius V, an alliance of Spain, Venice, Genoa, the Papal States and Knights of Malta was arranged in May, 1571. Don Juan of Austria was appointed commander-in-chief of the Christian forces. The battle was joined with the Turkish fleet under Ali Pasha in the Strait of Corinth. Losses totalled 7,500 Christians killed, twelve ships lost, 30,000 Turks killed, 8,000 taken prisoner, 225 Turkish ships sunk or captured, 15,000 Christian galley slaves freed. Ali Pasha was captured and executed. St Pius V was told miraculously of the victory which was confirmed two weeks later by courier. The Pope attributed the victory to Our Lady Help of Christians and added this invocation to the Litany of Loreto and decreed 7 October the Feast of Our Lady of Victory.

923. In 1683, 200,000 Turks under the command of the Grand Mustapha besieged the city of Vienna, which was defended by only 10,000 Christian troops. Mustapha decided to starve out the city. Meanwhile, two armies totaling 45,000 men, one from Poland (under King Sobieski) and one from Lorraine, advanced towards Vienna aiming to raise the siege. On 12 September, 1683, these two armies descended on the surprised Turks. The Catholic armies possessed greater discipline and determination and by the end of the day the Turks had fled. On hearing the news of victory, Bl. Pope Innocent XI declared 12 September the Feast of the Holy Name of Mary in thanksgiving for Our Lady's intercession.

924.In 1697, the Turks reinvaded Transylvania at Zenta. A Catholic army led by Prince Eugene of Savoy met them on 11 September. The battle was engaged and ended with 20,000 Turks killed and only three hundred Christians dead. On 26 January, 1699, the Turks signed the Treaty of Carlowitz restoring Transylvania and most of Hungary to the Holy Roman Empire. It was the first time that the Turks had negotiated with Christian forces. The Turks had made their last attack on Europe.

925.Catholics have contributed enormously to the advancement of knowledge and science over the centuries. For example, St Hildegard of Bingen (1098-1179) composed works on natural history and the medicinal value of plants, which were broadly distributed throughout Europe during the Middle Ages.

926.Roger Bacon (1214-1292) was an outstanding Franciscan philosopher, teacher and scientist of the High Middle Ages whose scientific studies and experiments in astronomy, alchemy, optics, mathematics and languages placed him well ahead of his time. Some inventions attributed to him include an early telescope, a flying contraption, gunpowder and eyeglasses. Bacon's many works and writings earned him the title *"Doctor Mirabilis"* during his lifetime.

927.Fr Benedict Goës SJ (1562-1607) discovered and traversed the overland trade route from India to China (c. 1594).

928.Fr Christopher Clavius SJ (1538-1612) was the most renowned astronomer of his time and assisted in the formulation of the Gregorian calendar.

929.Fr Giovanni Battista Riccioli SJ (1598-1671) was an astronomer who, among other things, experimented with pendulums and falling bodies, worked on mapping the moon, and observed and recorded the phases of Venus.

930.Fr Athanasius Kircher SJ (1602-1680) was considered the "master of a hundred arts" and numbered among his achievements the hypothesis that the plague was spread by infectious micro-organisms.

931.Bl. Bishop Niels Stensen (1638-1686) was a noted anatomist, geologist and palaeontologist who laid the foundations of the modern science of crystallography and contributed much to the early understanding of the human brain.

932.Fr Francesco Lana de Terzi SJ (1631-1687) was the first person to conceive how a 'lighter than air' aircraft might be constructed. Fr Terzi also anticipated by more than a century methods of lip reading and Braille writing and reading for the blind.

933. Fr Claude-Jean Allouez SJ (1622-1689) was the first European to sight the shores of Lake Superior in North America in 1667.

934.Fathers Francesco Grimaldi SJ (1618-1663) and Adam Kochansky SJ (1631-1700) developed supporting arguments for the Copernican system. Their research remotely prepared the way for Pope Benedict XIV to order the Holy Office to grant an imprimatur to the first edition of Galileo's complete works in 1741.

935.Fr Francesco Grimaldi SJ (1618-1663) also discovered and named the phenomenon known today as the "diffraction of light."

936.Fr Bartholomew Gusmao (1685-1724) was the first to demonstrate a lighter than air ship in 1709.

937.Fr Samuel Fritz SJ (1654-1728) published the first map of the Amazon River in 1707.

938.Fr Ruggerio Boscovitch (1711-1787) was a professor in mathematics who among his many achievements determined the sun's equator and the duration of its period of rotation.

939.The French Catholic Antoine Levoisier (1743-1794) isolated both hydrogen and oxygen and is regarded as the founder of modern chemistry.

940.Fr Gregor Mendel (1822-1884) founded the science of genetics.

941. The French Catholic Louis Pasteur (1822-1895) founded the science of micro-biology.

942. The Belgian priest Mons. George Lemaitre (1894-1966) pioneered mathematical computations in the 1920s that laid the foundations for the 'Big Bang Theory.' These computations pointed to an expanding universe and, by inference, to a beginning point, or 'primeval atom.'

943. As a young Catholic doctor Prof. Jerome Lejeune (1926-1994) discovered the link between Down Syndrome and chromosomes.

944. Recognizing the inaccuracies of the old 'Julian Calendar', Pope Gregory XIII (1572-1585) commissioned the formation of a committee of astronomers to work towards creating a new calendar with an in-built mechanism to ensure co-ordination with the rotation of the earth around the sun. The result was the so-called 'Gregorian Calendar' which began in 1582 with 5 October being recognized as 15 October. Leap years were added to ensure the new calendar's perpetual accuracy.

945. On 12 February, 1931, Vatican Radio was established by Guglielmo Marconi and inaugurated by Pope Pius XI. The first signal broadcast in Morse Code was, *"In nomine Domini. Amen"* ("In the name of the Lord. Amen."). Since then, Catholics have been at the forefront of employing modern communications at the service of the Gospel, with the most notable examples in the English-speaking world being Archbishop Fulton Sheen and Mother Mary Angelica.

946. The Jesuits were also renowned for their great missionary work. The work of St Francis Xavier in India during the 16th century was built on by Fathers Barzeus, Mesquita, de Torres and Robert de Nobili. Adopting the dress and manners of the Brahmin, the saintly Fr de Nobili, early in the 1600's, penetrated into this hitherto inaccessible caste and began to convert and baptize them. By the end of the 17th century, the Indian mission numbered 150,000.

947. In 1582, several Jesuits under the leadership of Fr Matteo Ricci entered China to establish the first Christian mission there in centuries. They

learnt the Chinese language and impressed the educated through their knowledge of astronomy, mathematics and demonstrating how clocks work. They slowly converted noble and educated families and gained access to the imperial palace. By the time of Fr Matteo's death in 1610, there were 13,000 Chinese Catholics. By the mid-1660s, the Jesuits were ministering to 237,000 Catholics in one hundred and fifty-nine churches.

948. French Jesuits and saints including Fathers Lejeune, Bressani, Jogues, Lalemant and Brebeuf worked tirelessly spreading the Catholic faith among the Iroquois and Huron tribes in northeast America. Epic heroism was notable in the horrific torture of Fr Bressani and the martyrdom of St Isaac Jogues in the 1640's.

949. Fr James Marquette SJ in the years 1673-1675 single-handedly worked to bring the Catholic faith to the Illinois Indians beginning at the site of what is now the city of Chicago. In the process, he discovered the mouth of the Missouri River in North America. He endured cold and illness while living in a rough cabin along the banks of the Chicago River. After suffering an attack of dysentery he died at age 37 near the modern town of Ludington, Michigan.

950. During the late 16th and early 17th centuries, Fr Emmanuel de Nobrega, Bl. Ignatius Azevedo, and St Joseph Anchieta labored for the conversion of the natives in Brazil. The latter, gifted with the charisms of tongues and miracles, wrote a rule of life for the Reductions, communities of native Indian converts.

951. The Jesuit Reductions (or mission settlements) of South America, especially in Uruguay and Paraguay, which operated between 1607 and 1768, were responsible for the conversion of over 750,000 natives to Christianity. At the same time these Reductions protected the natives from the rapacious and exploitative tendencies of the Spanish colonists. Voltaire, a great enemy of Christianity, said of the Reductions, "they appear to be in some respects the triumph of humanity."

952. Fr Pierre Jean De Smet was a Belgian born Jesuit who worked tirelessly establishing many missions among the Indians of the far west United

States. Over a period of forty-seven years, Fr De Smet travelled more than 200,000 miles and made nineteen trans-Atlantic crossings seeking helpers and funds for his missions. Due to his rapport with the natives, he was called upon several times to assist the U.S. Government in their peace negotiations with them. Most notable of these was the peace treaty negotiated with Chief Sitting Bull and the Sioux tribe in 1868. Fr De Smet also helped to negotiate peace among warring Indian tribes.

953. There are many other notable Catholic historical highlights of the past two hundred years. The Vendee uprising from 1793-1796 by the 'Royal and Catholic Army' led by Henri de la Rochejaquelein resisted the French revolutionary government, its Civil Constitution of the Clergy, and the deposition of King Louis XVI. They adopted the Sacred Heart as their emblem and *Pour Dieu et le Roi* ('For God and King') as their slogan. They were eventually crushed for their resistance, with as many as 200,000 Vendeans dying either in battle, public execution, forced drownings, indiscriminate killings, and a ruthless 'scorched earth policy.'

954. The '30,000 Idiots' was an army of Catholic peasants resisting the Napoleonic occupation of their country in Zaragoza, Spain. From June-August 1808, the French launched repeated attacks but could barely get into the city. Napoleon responded by marching an army himself into Spain. He bombarded Zaragoza, gradually reducing it to rubble. However, the defenders refused to surrender. Every church, monastery and house was a fortress; every man, woman and child a soldier. The last defenders were driven to the monastery of St Francis, their only weapons being tiles from the floor hurled at the attackers. On 21 February, 1809, the Spanish finally surrendered. The French had conquered a graveyard of heroes.

955. The 'Oxford Movement' began in 1833 as a movement of Anglican clergy seeking to return the Church of England to Apostolic Christianity. Led by John Keble, Edward Pusey, John Henry Newman and Richard Froude, it emphasized doctrine, sacramental worship and leadership by bishops as successors to the Apostles. Many members of this movement eventually entered into full communion with the Catholic Church.

956. Gabriel Garcia Moreno was President of Ecuador from 1861 to 1875.

During these years he was responsible for a number of initiatives to restore the Catholic faith in the country, including allowing foreign religious Orders, especially the Jesuits, to return and run schools, protesting the annexation of the Papal States by the newly established Italian state, and initiating an Act of Congress that consecrated the nation to the Sacred Heart of Jesus in 1874. The country also prospered economically through the construction of numerous schools, hospitals, roads and railways. Moreno was assassinated by Masonic hands on 6 August, 1875. The murderer shouted, "Die Jesuit!" Moreno's last words were, "Garcia Moreno dies, but God does not die."

957. The Catholic Church from the time of Pope Clement XII (1730-1740) through to the present day has maintained a hostile attitude towards Freemasonry, condemning its embrace of deism, naturalism, anticlericalism and atheism. Though no longer an automatically excommunicable offense, membership of Freemasonry is still prohibited as "irreconcilable with the Church's doctrine" (Vatican decree of 1983).

958. After the formation of the new German Empire in 1871, Chancellor Bismarck launched the *Kulturkampf* ('cultural struggle') designed to break the influence of the Pope and Catholic Church. The 'May Laws' of 1873 sought to bring the Church and education under state control, however, resistance from Catholics to the enactments and the persecution was consistent and heroic, forcing the government to modify its anti-Church policy by 1887.

959. During the Chinese 'Boxer Rebellion' of 1900, fanatical enemies of Christianity and all things foreign went on a wild rampage, destroying numerous churches, seminaries, convents and chapels. The homes of countless Chinese Catholics were destroyed and bishops and priests, both foreign and native, were murdered. 30,000 Catholics became victims of the slaughter or sold into slavery. Nearly one hundred martyrs of this episode have been beatified or canonized by the Church.

960. During World War I (1914-1918), Pope Benedict XV and the Catholic Emperor of Austria, Charles I, devoted much of their time and energy to minimize the material and spiritual havoc caused by the war. In 1917,

Benedict XV offered his services as a mediator to the belligerent nations, but his pleas for settlement of the conflict went unheeded. Charles' attempts to negotiate peace between the warring nations were likewise largely ignored.

961. During the 'Cristeros War' in Mexico from 1926-1929, Catholics successfully resisted the socialist dictatorship of Plutarco Elias Calles and his plan to expel priests and religious orders and take control of education. At one point during the war, Cristeros fighters controlled 75% of the countryside. By the time of the armistice, approximately 90,000 Mexicans had been killed, including 5,000 Cristeros fighters. To date, a total of thirty-five martyrs have been canonized and fifteen beatified.

962. During the Spanish Civil War from 1936-1939, faithful Catholics resisted the Republicans, comprising mostly of anarchists, socialists, communists and atheists. Over 1,500 martyrs have been beatified or canonized to date by Popes St John Paul II, Benedict XVI and Francis, with an additional 1,500 martyrs under process. All up, thirteen bishops, 4,172 diocesan priests and seminarians, 2,364 monks and friars and 283 nuns were killed during Spain's 'Red Terror.'

963. In 1937, Pope Pius XI issued the encyclical *Mit Brennender Sorge* ('With Burning Anxiety') denouncing Nazism for its anti-Catholic and anti-Christian programs and the Nazi regime's numerous violations of the 1933 Concordat. The encyclical was read from the pulpit of every Catholic church in Germany on 21 March, 1937.

964. Resistance to Nazism by Catholic clergy was consistent and heroic. The Church opposed the regime's closure of Catholic schools, organizations and publications and restrictions on religious observance and provided the earliest and most enduring centers of systematic opposition. Bishops such as Konrad von Preysing, Joseph Frings and August von Galen provided a coherent, systematic critique of many Nazi teachings. A number of Catholic priests spoke of the moral dangers to Germany of Nazism, among them Alfred Delp, Augustin Rösch and Laurentius Siemer. Catholic lay leaders who lost their lives for resisting Nazism included the July Plotters Jakob Kaiser, Bernhard Letterhaus and Claus

von Stauffenberg, Caritas activists Gertrud Luckner and Margarete Sommer, Catholic Action leader Erich Klausener, Catholic Youth leader Adalbert Probst, German Catholics' Peace Association founder Fr Max Josef Metzger, and Provost Bernhard Lichtenberg.

965. The Catholic Church from the time of Bl. Pope Pius IX (1846-1878) through to Pope Pius XII (1939-1958) examined and condemned Communism as utterly antithetical to Christianity. Notable Papal encyclicals containing condemnations included *Quod Apostolici muneris* (1878), *Rerum novarum* (1891), *Quadragesimo anno* (1931) and *Divini Redemptoris* (1937). The inspiration of Pope St John Paul II during his pontificate (1978-2005) undoubtedly contributed to the collapse of European communism and the Soviet Empire from 1980 to 1991.

966. Countless millions of Catholics suffered under the tyranny of communist regimes after the Russian Revolution in 1917. Despite relentless persecution and atheist propaganda, large numbers of Catholics held on to their faith in Eastern Europe, especially Poland, and in the Ukraine in the Soviet Union. On 27 June, 2001, Pope St John Paul II beatified twenty-eight Ukrainian bishops, priests, nuns, and one layman who suffered and died for Christ under the communist scourge.

967. In 1947, Fr Petrus Lavlicek founded the Crusade of Reparation of the Holy Rosary for peace in the world and the liberation of Austria from Soviet occupation. It was characterized by Masses, Rosaries, preaching, confessions and blessings of the sick. Fr Petrus would organize prayer 'sieges' and 'assaults' in local towns lasting up to five days as well as huge processions throughout the country with a statue of Our Lady of Fatima. To the world's surprise, the Soviets peacefully left Austria in April, 1955.

968. With the collapse of the Soviet Union in 1991, the persecuted Catholic Church re-emerged from hiding, especially in the Ukraine and Baltic states. They continue to struggle, however, with the after-effects of Communism and the increasing encroachment of Western materialism and secularism. At the same time, faithful Catholics still worship under duress in China, Vietnam, Cuba and North Korea.

969.Faithful Catholics in China have remained loyal to their Catholic faith and the Pope through their allegiance to the 'Underground Church', rejecting any association with the so-called 'Catholic Patriotic Association' founded in 1957. In July, 1991, Pope St John Paul II stated: "With what prayerful longing and love do I follow the life of the loyal Chinese Catholic communities." The most famous of these many loyal Catholics was the late Ignatius Cardinal Kung Pin-Mei (1901-2000).

970.Throughout the history of Christianity, there have been numerous apparitions of Christ, Mary, angels or saints to individuals or groups of Catholics that have been recognized by the Church. St Paul received two such apparitions, one from Christ (Acts 9:1-31) and one from an unnamed "Macedonian" (Acts 16:9). An angel appeared to St Peter to free him from prison (Acts 12:1-19), while the Virgin Mary appeared to St James in AD 40 encouraging him to continue his preaching in Spain.

971.From 9 to 12 December, 1531, the Virgin Mary appeared five times to a recent Aztec convert named Juan Diego in Guadalupe, Mexico, under the name "Mother of the true God who gives life." Mary left a permanent image of herself on the tilma of Juan Diego that subsequently induced the conversion of 8,000,000 natives during the following seven years. These apparitions were formally approved by Archbishop Alonso de Montúfar in 1555.

972.In 1578, the Virgin Mary appeared as a bright light to a pious woodcutter named Thomas Michalek of Lezajsk, Poland, and asked him to approach the Bishop and have a church built in her honor. Scared, Thomas did nothing until the Virgin appeared to him a second time and asked him to break his silence. Thomas was not believed by the authorities and no chapel was built until the death of the Curate who opposed him. In 1606, Bishop Pstrokonski constructed a larger church on the original site of the visions and in the 1630s Bishop Firlej confirmed the apparitions as supernatural in origin. On 8 September, 1752, Pope Benedict XIV personally crowned the image of Our Lady of Lezajsk.

973.From 2 February, 1594, to 8 December, 1634, the Virgin Mary appeared on four occasions to a nun named Mother Mariana de Jesus Torres at her convent in Quito, Ecuador. Mary requested a statue of her to be made under the invocation of 'Our Lady of Good Success' and warned of moral calamities that would envelop the world and the Church from the mid-20th century onwards, as well as the assassination of a great Catholic leader in the 19th century (viz. Garcia Moreno). Mother Mariana's body remains incorrupt to this day. These apparitions were formally approved by Bishop Salvador de Rober on 2 February, 1611.

974. During the summer of 1608, four children tending their sheep in a field on the outskirts of the Calvinist village of Siluva, Lithuania, beheld a beautiful weeping woman standing on a rock with a baby in her arms. Further apparitions occurred over the next four years, while a blind man had his sight restored. As a result of these apparitions, the entire village converted to Catholicism. These apparitions were approved by Pope Pius VI on 17 August, 1775, under the invocation of Our Lady of Siluva.

975. Over a period of fifty-four years from 1664 to 1718 the Virgin Mary appeared to a poor shepherdess from Laus, France, named Benoite Rencurel, exhorting her to "pray continuously for sinners." This apparition was first investigated in 1665 but final approval of the devotion to 'Our Lady of Laus' was only given by Bishop Jean-Michel di Falco of the Diocese of Gap on 4 May, 2008.

976. In Paray-le-Monial, France, from 27 December, 1673, to 16 June, 1675, Christ appeared on several occasions to a Visitation nun name St Margaret Mary Alacoque revealing his Sacred Heart saying, "Behold the Heart which has so loved men ... and in return, I receive from the greater part only ingratitude ... irreverence and sacrilege ... coldness and contempt." Christ also revealed a great promise for those who receive him in Holy Communion on nine consecutive Fridays and asked for the establishment of a Feast in its honor to be celebrated after *Corpus Christi*. Christ entrusted the spread of devotion to his Sacred Heart to the Visitation Order and to the Jesuits.

977. On 18 July and 27 November, 1830, the Virgin Mary appeared two times to St Catherine Labouré in the chapel of the Daughters of Charity of St Vincent de Paul, Paris, instructing her to create a medal to spread

devotion under the invocation "Mary, conceived without sin", later known as the 'Miraculous Medal.' Mary also foretold coming political calamities that would befall France, including the revolution of 1871. The apparitions were approved in 1836 by Archbishop de Quelen of Paris, while St Catherine's body has remained incorrupt since 1876.

978. On 20 January, 1842, the Virgin Mary appeared to an anti-Catholic Jew named Alphonse Ratisbonne while he was waiting for a friend in the church of Sant Andrea delle Fratte. This friend had given Ratisbonne a Miraculous Medal which he agreed to wear as a simple test. Ratisbonne converted to Catholicism, joined the priesthood, and began a ministry for the conversion of Jews under the invocation of Our Lady of Zion. This apparition was formally approved on 3 June, 1842, by Cardinal Patrizi, the Vicar General of Pope Gregory XVI.

979. On 19 September, 1846, the Virgin Mary appeared to two young children, Maximin Giraud and Melanie Calvat, in the village of La Salette high up in the French Alps. Mary appeared crying and warned of future great calamities and evils soon to afflict the Church and the world. To mitigate these calamities, Mary called for conversion, prayer and penance for sins. This apparition was approved by Bishop Bruillard on 16 November, 1851.

980. From 11 February to 16 July, 1858, the Virgin Mary appeared eighteen times to St Bernadette Soubirous at the Grotto of Massabielle in Lourdes, France. Mary eventually revealed herself as "the Immaculate Conception" and called for prayer and penance for the conversion of sinners. Numerous miracles and conversions have flowed from this event ever since and continue to do so. The apparitions were formally approved on 18 January, 1862, and St Bernadette's body has since remained incorrupt.

981. On 13 January, 1866, the Virgin Mary appeared to a bedridden cripple in Filippsdorf, Czech Republic, named Magdalene Kade and immediately cured her. The same year a diocesan commission recognized the healing as supernatural. Afterwards, other healings occurred at the shrine to Our Lady Help of Christians in the town. A minor basilica was completed and consecrated by Pope Leo XIII under the same title in 1885.

982. On 17 July, 1871, Mary appeared to four students, Eugene Barbadette, Francoise Richer, Jeanne-Marie Lebosse, and Eugene Friteau, in the town of Pontmain, France. Mary's message which appeared under her feet was, "But pray my children. God will hear you in a short time. My Son allows himself to be moved by compassion." Mary was also seen by advancing Prussian soldiers who were in France during the Franco-Prussian War. This apparition was approved by Bishop Laval in February, 1875, under the invocation of 'Our Lady of Hope.'

983. From 27 June to 16 September, 1877, the Virgin Mary appeared nine times to two visionaries, Justyna Szafrynska and Barbara Samulowska, in Gietrzwald, Poland, encouraging a return to prayer. Together with the appearance of a healing spring, the villagers soon enough returned to piety and devotion. The apparitions were approved under the title of 'Our Lady of Gietrzwald' by Bishop Pilip Kremetz in 1878.

984. On 21 August, 1879, during heavy rain, the Virgin Mary, St Joseph, St John the Apostle and a lamb on an altar appeared together over the gable of the village chapel of Knock, Ireland, enveloped in a bright light. None of these persons spoke during the course of the apparition which lasted for two hours. Eighteen people, ranging in age between 5 and 75, witnessed the apparition. Since 1879, over three hundred miraculous cures have been associated with the shrine of 'Our Lady of Knock.' The 'Knock Event' received final approval from the Archbishop of Tuam in 1936.

985. From 13 May to 13 October, 1917, the Virgin Mary appeared on six occasions to three young children of Fatima, Portugal, namely, Lucia dos Santos, Jacinta Marto and Francisco Marto, urging praying of the Rosary to end World War I, penance for the conversion of sinners, and devotion to the Immaculate Heart. The apparitions climaxed on 13 October with the great 'Miracle of the Sun' witnessed by 70,000 people and hundreds of simultaneous healings. The apparitions of 'Our Lady of Fatima' were approved by the Bishop of the Diocese of Leiria-Fatima, Jose Alves Correia da Silva, on 13 October 1930.

986. On 22 February, 1931, Christ appeared to St Faustina Kowalska in Cracow, Poland, dressed in a white robe, with his right hand raised in blessing and with red and white rays emanating from his heart. Christ asked St Faustina to have an image painted reflecting this apparition with the words "Jesus, I trust in You" written underneath. The intention was to promote Christ's merciful love for all those who seek it. St Faustina also received many dire warnings for humanity if it refused to follow God's commandments. Her published conversations with Christ (*Divine Mercy in My Soul*) and the Divine Mercy Chaplet were both eventually approved by the Vatican. St Faustina was canonized in 2000 and Divine Mercy Sunday is now celebrated on the second Sunday of Easter.

987. From 29 November, 1932, to 3 January, 1933, the Virgin Mary appeared as the "the Immaculate Virgin" and "Mother of God, Queen of Heaven" thirty-three times to four children of Beauraing, Belgium, namely, Fernande Voisin, Andre Degeimbre, Gilbert Voisin, Gilbert Degeimbre, calling for prayer for the conversion of sinners. The apparitions were accompanied by miraculous cures and the appearance of a fire-ball and received approval from the Bishop of Namur on 2 July, 1949.

988. From 15 January to 2 March, 1933, the Virgin Mary appeared on eight occasions to a young girl living in Banneux, Belguim, named Mariette Beco, promising to intercede for the sick, the suffering and the poor. These apparitions resulted in many conversions and over fifty documented miracles and were approved on 19 March, 1942, by Bishop Kerkhofs of Liege under the invocation of 'The Virgin of the Poor.'

989. From 25 March, 1945, to 31 May, 1959, the Virgin Mary appeared on fifty-six occasions to Ida Peederman in Amsterdam, Netherlands, emphasizing the importance of the Eucharist and outlining the events preceding the triumph of the Immaculate Heart of Mary, including the promulgation of the dogma of Mary as Coredemptrix, Mediatrix, and Advocate. Mary also made numerous prophecies relating to political events and Popes which were all fulfilled. The apparitions of 'Our Lady of All Nations' were approved by Bishop Jozef Marianus Punt of Haarlem on 31 May, 2002.

990. From 6 July to 13 October, 1973, the Virgin Mary spoke on three occasions to Sr Agnes Sasagawa in Akita, Japan, warning of terrible chastisements to afflict the world due to sin and calling for prayer and penance. Mary's messages were spoken through a wooden statue of Our Lady of All Nations. This same statue also wept tears and blood on one hundred and one occasions from 1973 to 1981. Sr Agnes as well received four visitations from her guardian angel. The apparitions of 'Our Lady of Akita' were approved by Bishop John Ito of Niigata on 22 April, 1984.

991. From 25 March, 1976, to 5 January, 1990, the Virgin Mary appeared on thirty-one occasions to Maria Esperanza in Betania, Venezuela, warning of future wars and suffering. Many other phenomena were associated with the apparitions, including cures, a miraculous bleeding Host and stigmata. The apparitions of Mary 'Reconciler of People and Nations' were approved by Bishop Pio Bello Ricardo on 21 November, 1987.

992. Between 28 November, 1981, and 28 November, 1989, the Virgin Mary appeared on many occasions to three young women in Kibeho, Rwanda, namely, Alphonsine Mumureke, Nathalie Mukamazimpaka, and Marie Claire Mukangango, calling for prayer of the Rosary, fasting and penance. Mary also revealed a gruesome vision of future genocide in the country, which later took place in 1994. The apparitions were approved under the title of 'Mother of the Word' by Bishop Augustin Misago of Gikongoro on 29 June, 2001.

993. The Catholic Church has countless world-wide associations dedicated to the charitable service of humanity, too many to enumerate. One of the most famous is the Society of St Vincent de Paul, founded in 1833 by Bl. Frederic Ozanam. It currently numbers over 1.3 million members in some one hundred and forty-eight countries and provides assistance to countless millions of poor and needy on a daily basis. Forms of assistance include home visitations, housing assistance, disaster relief, job training and placement, food parcels, dining halls, clothing, transportation and utility costs, and medical care for the sick and elderly.

994. The Knights of Malta (founded originally in 1113 as the 'Knights Hospitaller' of Jerusalem) is the oldest surviving order of chivalry in the

world and today numbers 13,000 members, 80,000 permanent volunteers, and 20,000 medical personnel working in over one hundred and twenty countries. They provide assistance to the elderly, handicapped, refugees, homeless, and terminally ill in all parts of the world, as well as aid to victims of natural disasters, epidemics and armed conflicts. In several countries the Order is an important provider of first aid training, first aid services and emergency medical services.

995. The Knights of Columbus was founded in the United States in 1882 by Rev. Michael J. McGivney as a fraternal organization of Catholic men dedicated to Catholic action through a variety of religious, educational and social activities. In 2012, the Knights gave nearly $170 million to charity and performed over 70 million hours of voluntary service. It now exists in fourteen countries with a total membership of 1.8 million.

996. Caritas International was founded originally in Germany in 1897. Since then, it has spread to one hundred and sixty countries across the world. It aims to create a 'civilization of love' through the core Catholic values of dignity, solidarity and stewardship. In their own words, they "serve all poor people, of all faiths, all over the world."

997. The Legion of Mary was founded in 1921 in Dublin, Ireland, by Frank Duff as a voluntary lay organization of practising Catholics dedicated to serving God under the banner of Mary. It specifically aims to encourage its members to practise the spiritual works of mercy, especially prayer. With over 3,000,000 members worldwide, the Legion is now the largest lay organization in the Catholic Church.

998. Throughout the world, the Catholic Church continues to run and maintain tens of thousands of schools, hospitals, and orphanages, looking after the education, health and welfare of tens of millions of people around the world each day of every year. The figures in Africa alone are staggering, with 1,137 hospitals, 1,285 orphanages, 93,315 primary schools, and 42,234 secondary schools run by the Catholic Church.

999.The 'pro-life' movement is one of the 'jewels' of Catholic social action. Every year since the infamous U.S. Supreme Court decision *Roe v. Wade* in 1973, around 100,000 Catholics and other pro-lifers gather on 23 January in Washington D.C. to march in protest against the legalization of abortion and the slaughter of the innocent unborn. This annual event continues to this day and increasingly attracts more and more young people to its ranks. The 'pro-life' movement has also been growing in recent years in Europe through the 'One of Us' campaign.

1000. In the year 2000, the Catholic Church celebrated the 'Great Jubilee', commemorating the 2,000th anniversary of the greatest event in world history, the Incarnation of the Son of God, and the commencement of the third Christian millennium.

1001. See Postscript.

Postscript

Well, what can one say after reading 1,000 reasons why it's great to be Catholic? One reaction might be, "Well, that was great, my faith and confidence in the Catholic Church has been restored, or at least reinforced." Another might be, "Ok, where do I sign up to be Catholic?" Or someone else might say, "I'm still not convinced, I need more information." Any one of these three responses would be a step in the right direction.

In summary, after writing this book I know that I belong to a great Church founded by Christ that will be protected by him until the end of time; that the Catholic Church has been led by many great Popes who were outstanding for their witness, their holiness and their leadership; that great Councils throughout the centuries have promulgated great definitions and dogmas; that the Church's teachings form a great body of beliefs touching on every conceivable matter pertaining to faith and morals; that the Church has a great variety of prayers developed over centuries under the influence of the Holy Spirit; that the sacraments given to us by Christ are a great source of grace from cradle to grave; that innumerable great miracles have and still occur as signs of God's goodness and the truth of Catholicism; that numerous great saints have been raised up by God as shining examples of heroic virtue; that Catholicism has inspired the greatest works of beauty in art, sculpture and architecture; and that the Catholic Church's history is filled with much achievement, glory and greatness. One should never deny the existence of the darkness, but one should never dwell on it, remembering that darkness will always be conquered by light: *"The light shines in the darkness, and the darkness has not overcome it"* (John 1:5).

While writing this book I was often concerned that there would not be enough reasons to mention, that there might be only 500, or at most 700-800 reasons. But as I researched more and more, the problem reversed, and soon enough I realized that there were more reasons than I could ever imagine. And that leads me to my final and 1001st reason why it's great to be Catholic, namely, that there are thousands of more reasons why it's great to be Catholic!

- Robert M. Haddad

About the Author

Robert M. Haddad holds qualifications in law, theology, philosophy and religious education, namely, a LL.B (USyd.), Grad. Cert. in RE (Charles Sturt Uni.), Grad. Dip. Ed. (ACU), Grad. Dip. in Teacher Ed. (College of Teachers, London), AMLP (Oxon.), MA Theo. Studies (UNDA – University Medalist), MRelEd (UNDA) and a M. Phil (ACU). For his M. Phil., Robert researched the apologetical arguments of St Justin Martyr.

In addition to his studies, Robert has also authored various books, including *Lord of History Series* (2 volumes), *The Apostles' Creed, Law and Life, The Family and Human Life, Defend the Faith!, The Case for Christianity – St Justin Martyr's Arguments for Religious Liberty and Judicial Justice,* and *Answering the Anti-Catholic Challenge* (ch. 3).

From 1990-2005, Robert worked full-time at St Charbel's College, Sydney, teaching Religion and History. He held the positions of Year Co-ordinator and Religious Education Co-ordinator concurrently for ten years and was Assistant Principal (Welfare) for six years.

From 2006-2008, Robert worked full-time as the Convener of the Catholic Chaplaincy at the University of Sydney. He was also a lecturer at the Center for Thomistic Studies for eleven years (1996-2008), teaching Apologetics, Church Fathers and Church History, as well as assisting part-time with *Lumen Verum Apologetics* (1996-present) and the Catholic Adult Education Centre (2010-2013).

From 2009-2012, Robert was the Director of the Confraternity of Christian Doctrine (Sydney) and in that capacity was the chief editor of the revised *Christ our Light and Life* (3rd Edition) religious education K-12 curriculum used by Catholic students in state schools as well as the *Gratia Series* sacramental programs for children preparing for Reconciliation, First Holy Communion, and Confirmation in the Archdiocese of Sydney. He has recently also edited a new RCIA resource for use in Catholic schools in the same Archdiocese entitled *Initiate!*

Currently, he is the Head of New Evangelization for the Catholic Education Office (Sydney) and lectures/tutors in Theology at the University of Notre Dame, Sydney. From time to time Robert also appears on the Telepace Television Network and Voice of Charity radio.

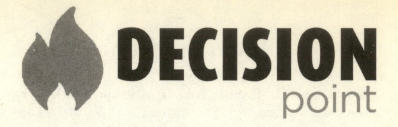
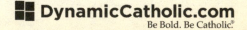

NOTES

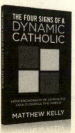

NOTES

NOTES

NOTES

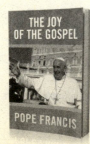

NOTES

NOTES

NOTES

THE
DYNAMIC CATHOLIC
INSTITUTE

[MISSION]

To re-energize the Catholic Church
in America by developing world-class
resources that inspire people to
rediscover the genius of Catholicism.

[VISION]

To be the innovative leader in the
New Evangelization helping Catholics
and their parishes become
the-best-version-of-themselves.

DynamicCatholic.com
Be Bold. Be Catholic.®

The Dynamic Catholic Institute
5081 Olympic Blvd • Erlanger • KY • 41018
Phone: 859-980-7900
info@DynamicCatholic.com